RELE

Ideas of Difference:
Social Spaces and the Labour of Division

A selection of previous *Sociological Review* Monographs

Life and Work History Analyses[†]
ed. Shirley Dex

The Sociology of Monsters[†]
ed. John Law

Sport, Leisure and Social Relations[†]
eds John Horne, David Jary and Alan Tomlinson

Gender and Bureaucracy*
eds Mike Savage and Anne Witz

The Sociology of Death: theory, culture, practice*
ed. David Clark

The Cultures of Computing*
ed. Susan Leigh Star

Theorizing Museums*
ed. Sharon Macdonald and Gordon Fyfe

Consumption Matters*
eds Stephen Edgell, Kevin Hetherington and Alan Warde

[†]Available from The Sociological Review Office, Keele University, Keele, Staffs ST5 5BG.
*Available from Marston Book Services, PO Box 270, Abingdon, Oxon OX14 4YW.

Ideas of Difference

Social Spaces and the Labour of Division

Edited by Kevin Hetherington and Rolland Munro

Blackwell Publishers/The Sociological Review

British Library Cataloguing in Publication Data

A CIP catalogue record for this book is available from the British Library

Library of Congress Cataloging-in-Publication Data applied for

ISBN 0 631 20768 6

Printed in Great Britain by Whitstable Litho Ltd., Whitstable, Kent
This book is printed on acid-free paper.

Contents

Contents

Acknowledgements

Most of the papers in this book arose from a conference on the Labour of Division organized by the Centre for Social Theory and Technology at Keele University in November 1995.

The paper entitled 'The visibility of social systems' by Robert Cooper previously appeared in *Operational Research and the Social Sciences*, N.C. Jackson, T. Keys, S.A. Cropper (eds), Plenum Press, New York, 1989.

The paper entitled 'Gender: division or comparison?' by Marilyn Strathern previously appeared in *Practising Feminism: Identity, Difference, Power*, N. Charles and F. Hughes-Freeland (eds), Routledge, London, 1996.

List of plates

Introduction

Ideas of difference: stability, social spaces and labour of division[1]

Rolland Munro

Introduction

This volume indexes one of the most influential ideas of all, the division of labour. Complicit, for example, in root notions of biology, chemistry and physics, it is also a basic premise that has shaped social thinking profoundly. Yet we're calling it the 'labour of division'. Why?

Over the last thirty years and more, there has been a proliferation of research that challenges the foundations of sociology and social philosophy; foundations made possible by a reliance on categories that divide up the world into capital and labour, hand and brain, nature and culture, society and self, agency and structure; and that go on dividing the world, with labour, for example, being split into bourgeoisie and proletariat, knowledge into art and science, life into work and home, economy into production and consumption, organization into the social and the technical, agency into will and expertise. Across movements as diverse as deconstructionism, feminism and ethnomethodology, all these divisions (and the further sub-divisions that split labour into mental and manual or commercial and creative work) have been placed under scrutiny. The effect has been to call into question the taken-for-granted nature of many of these distinctions. Divisions which looked fixed and fundamental now start to look more precarious and arbitrary.

As the foundations of sociological knowledge begin to look like a heap of abandoned divisions, those concerned with social theory could sympathise with Gesualdo Bufalino's narrator in *The Keeper of Ruins*:

Call it coincidence, call it vocation, but I've done next to nothing all my life but watch over things dead and dying. Now that I'm getting on in years, and can look back from an eminence near the summit, I never cease to be struck, among the random zigzags and paradoxes of my journey, by this persistent thread which gives them, or at least seems to give them, the lie.

But if a distinction dies, it is never an abandonment of truth. For, in the peculiar asymmetry of science pointed to by David Bloor (1976), if a division is abandoned it is only because its true nature has revealed it to have been a lie.

Even after death, difference keeps its value, truth. Perhaps it is for this reason that the idea of foundations never does seem to get emptied out. Indeed, for some considerable time a 'social construction' of reality—despite creating its own problematic dualisms—has informed explanations of a multiplicity in social order. Although divisions are no longer to be thought of as naturally given, they are taken to be fixed by habit, routines, or convention. Thus the critical question: who benefits? Whose interests are being furthered or protected by seeing the world in this way, rather than that? Knowing which set of distinctions is protecting which particular group has become a pressing agenda of sociology.

But this particular twist to foundations cannot be resolved by a new census of interests. For more is at stake. The problem of treating knowledge as a convention is that it opens Pandora's box. Under the idea of 'natural' foundations, it could be held that there are things to see, all manner of things, and we had only to look, whereas the idea of convention suggests instead that there are 'ways of seeing', indeed many ways of seeing. This is the rub. Difference is no longer a resource for settling dispute but becomes a topic in its own right. Its locus shifts from being in the things-in-themselves towards being more a matter of difference in position and perspective. Thus debate centres less on differences *per se*, although these can matter. What seems to be at stake in the new order are *ideas* of difference.

Perhaps this point can be expressed in another way. In any story, it is the divisions that perform as principal artefacts. We see along their 'lines of sight'. Yet once we are wise to this mechanism, it is the *process* of a social construction of reality that begins to capture the focus of our attention. The interest shifts to other questions, such as those about which divisions it is that lengthen, or make more stable, the 'lines of sight'. And for whom? Who gets excluded? In examining any story of a social construction of reality, and there are many, it is the divisions themselves that are in a process of being consumed and reproduced.

The points to make about a labour of division are therefore twofold. First, it can be noted that the labour that 'divisions' demand of people—the way in which we labour for *them*—includes the work of 'seeing' the world from the particular view that each set of divisions afford. Of course. But, under examination, there is also the labour that is demanded in 'holding' to that view. Lest we be caught out as inconsistent, we are expected to hold on, to be committed, to the views we express. This is the relation between the labour of division and identity. The difficulty for those who dodge and podge, and try to see the world only from 'in-between' divisions, is that they can enjoy no membership of it.

Borrowing and belonging

Our phrase, the labour of division, aptly captures what has already been accomplished, not only in social research, but in an imaginative rethinking of the once-upon-a-time hard sciences. In adding process to structure, an emphasis on a labour of division helps place contemporary work alongside Adam Smith and Emile Durkheim; and, dare I say it, Charles Darwin.[2] So it seems timely to re-consider our indebtedness to those who have gone before.

In respect of acknowledging earlier research on the creation and reproduction of social spaces, a seminal line of thought extends from Alfred Schutz's phenomenological emphasis on the 'typification' work of 'insiders', through to Harold Garfinkel's ethnomethodological emphasis on putative members having 'methods' for finding out from each other how to 'do' member. So too, a developing tradition in social anthropology extends the notion of cultural performance from a 'show' of meaning in religious festivals to the more everyday labours of division that eliminate, in Mary Douglas's consumption thesis, 'matter out of place'.

Where all such borrowed divisions add up, it becomes possible to 'see' from a common position. This is the main advantage of consistency, an effacement of difference. Indeed, for those who try to see the world without the aid of these specific divisions, there are two difficulties, commensurate with each of the two forms of labour mentioned above. A first difficulty is an *absence* of vision; they cannot 'see' the point they are supposed to see. But, secondly, in that they do not see the point, they are unlikely also to do the membership work of ensuring that there is no 'matter out of place'. Indeed, in failing to advertise themselves as belonging, it is they who will likely become excluded by others.

But need everything we borrow add up? For example, Victor Turner's emphasis on liminal moments during transition might seem to contrast oddly with Bruno Latour's focus on durable networks. But Turner's (1967) analysis of the rites of passage for neophytes suggests a *multiplicity* to social spaces that could be especially helpful when considered alongside Latour's (1993) stress on the heterogeneity of the social.[3] Similarly, Erving Goffman's insights on an everyday performance of self in encounters can be held alongside Marilyn Strathern's emphasis on extension in the form of partial connections. Although both sets of ideas help decentre the self, Goffman's (1958) focus on hesitancy and embarrassment is suggestive of ways in which we approach the ambiguities of interpretation inherent in encounters, while Strathern's (1991) more radical stance on *undecidability* not only depicts a fluidity in the potential magnification and diminishment of identity, but calls attention to a swiftness in moving between identities: 'cutting' first this figure, then that.

As others, notably Michel Foucault, have emphasised, the equal danger that arises from adopting a hierarchy of divisions is that of being caught in the thrall of a truth regime. Indeed, it has become a commonplace of sociology that a way of 'seeing' is also a way of not seeing. So, against a too-rigid insistence on consistency, might be placed the device of comparison, a juxtaposition of difference. In terms of analysis, there is sometimes more contrast to be gained from moving 'in-between' competing divisions, rather than choosing one over another.

Caution over this theme of deferral is necessary. Keeping 'in-between' divisions is not accomplished so easily as we might suppose. For it is in the nature of being in a truth regime that people cannot also 'see' the divisions that make its vision possible. Nor is there a neutral 'space' from which either to begin a selection or make a deferral. Indeed, we cannot step out of a truth regime, without stepping into another. These restrictions on movement, however, do not mean being completely stuck. Rather it means that all that can be accomplished, at best, is to switch regimes partially—and provisionally—by *withdrawing* from one division by means of stepping—partially and provisionally—into another.

It is precisely to aid this process of transmigration through different spaces that researchers can have 'to hand' divisions that do not add up, even if these divisions are not as 'ready to hand' as other divisions which have been made unproblematic. For in fumbling towards a new position, there is the sensitivity of a 'blindness' that

6

comes from deferral. As David Appelbaum (1995:25) expresses this idea:

> The blind know the stop. They know the stumbling, groping way they walk the earth, they know the effortful experience of uncovering the shape of the world through bodily contact. They know the paramount value of the data of difference.

As he adds, how will they be with the 'unfolding of a reality that leaps with the speed of light across to the other side?' On occasions, surely, the stop, the sensitivity of feeling a way may be preferred to the kind of 'vision', the speed, that is the gift of 'over-looking' distance?

This facility for moving 'in-between' divisions, however slow and contrived, requires, nonetheless, a very different form of labour: a labour of division that helps keep these social spaces apart, preventing them from being 'scrumpled' up (see Hetherington, 1997; Parker, 1997). So rather than valorizing difference, as if it were a good in itself (long live the multiple!), perhaps it is an attempt to understand this work of deferral (not rushing into divisions that flatten the world) which is at the heart of a methodological agreement that brings together most contributors to this volume. Before discussing methodological issues, however, and relating these matters more fully to the labour of division, I want to say something more about ideas of difference.

Ideas of difference

Is difference, as Marilyn Strathern (this volume) suggests, a matter which we approach with division in mind, or comparison? Are parts to be treated in a taken-for-granted way, say as complementary, so that differences can combine—the one including what the other cuts out (Strathern, 1991)? Or is difference seen to be so dichotomous that elements, for example, of femininity would detract from a person being seen as masculine? If so, when does 'more' masculinity fail? Would persons, for example, be more masculine if they had two male parts, rather than one? Why not three? And with genetic engineering in prospect, why stop there?

It is tempting to evade such conundrums by rushing the topic of ideas of difference and approach it with a seemingly fundamental question: how do we *think* difference? But this would be to overlook a key problem in discussing difference, its tendency to appear as both topic and resource. The difficulty in 'viewing' difference occurs because the very conception of thinking, as least for Euro-Americans, may be saturated with the idea of noticing difference.

In this respect, another approach might be to ask: how *should* difference be treated? How are we to stand to difference itself, assuming there is such a thing? For example, in terms of gathering knowledge, are we to see ourselves, in Claude Levi-Strauss's famous division, as 'engineers' or 'bricoleurs'? On the one side are the afore-mentioned foundationalists, those who seek a 'grand dichotomy', an origin, a first dualism from which all other distinctions spring. On the other are the pluralists; those who celebrate a multiplicity in sources of difference. For instance, like many contemporary anthropologists, Jack Goody suggests that the 'grand dichotomy' with its self-righteous certainty should be replaced by many uncertain and unexpected divides (Goody, 1977).

So this is one possible starting point to considering current ideas of difference. Is difference something we think we can, or should efface, alter, or celebrate? What are the moral orders here? These are important questions. But there is another aspect which the topic of difference makes particularly pressing, especially so when difference is also being drawn on as a resource. This is a concern that all this questioning may be just the dull resonance of earlier debates, the far echo of the grand dichotomies. In this respect I want to ask: is the method of difference so much part of analysis, that it is difficult to offer explanation without recourse to further dualisms?

It seems important to steer a course between the one and the many, between the dogma of universal reductionism and the doctrine of 'anything goes'. As a first move here, for instance, it is possible to accept that there is a stability to many divisions (not anything goes), but nevertheless reject the idea that things hold because they are true. Instead, taking the view that things are true *because they hold* (Latour, 1987), it is possible to follow those who stand ready to explain heterogeneity with heterogeneity. Thus Latour (1986:2) while considering their usefulness for teaching and polemics, he argues that these 'great divides' do not provide any explanation. On the contrary, he maintains, it is these very divisions that are the things to be explained.

No doubt. But explain what and to whom? If we are not to end up in yet another backwater, explaining one dichotomy, the 'winners' and 'losers' favoured by Latour, with another, his emphasis on 'long networks' (Latour, 1986:30), it is important to be careful over how to proceed here. As Latour (1986:2) argues:

All such dichotomous distinctions can be convincing only as long as they are enforced by a strong asymmetrical bias that treats the two sides of the divide or border very differently.

Yet this seems to be Latour's own mistake. Brilliant as his analysis is—and it certainly acts as an antidote to more romantic or voluntaristic versions of social constructivism—it is finally too universalizing; and thus too prone to impose its own asymmetry. For, hybridity aside, there is surely more to stability than its being an effect of 'durable', rather than 'non-durable' networks (Munro, 1997).

Good ethnographer of modernity that he is, Latour seems too ready to go native with those who wish to be modern. We can learn to 'see' the long networks when they are long, as he helps us to do, yes; but we need to be careful not to be captured by these in ways that prevent sight of the exact moments when a *dissociation* is being mobilized (see also Strathern, n.d.). As Latour (1991) acknowledges, macro-actors grow because they simplify. If so, it is highly likely that there will also be times when networks dissimulate here; when either they are in 'retreat' in order to recoup the detail, or when they, momentarily, 'diminish' themselves in order to be 'overlooked'. Before considering these possibilities of fluidity further, a closer look at links between the labour of division and the stabilization thesis should prove helpful.

The labour of division

As noted above, modernism is often equated with processes of stabilization. Whenever this is so, the relativism often associated with social constructivism might suggest not only the overthrow of a 'bureaucratization' of thought, but a return to the fluidity of medieval thinking. For example, in a study of 16th-century social life, the historian Lucien Febvre (1982:438) sees people as living in a fluid world:

> . . . where nothing was strictly defined, where entities lost their boundaries and, in the twinkling of an eye, without causing much protest, changed shape, appearance, size . . .

Such contrasts, however, draw on an idea of difference, as I will now discuss.

Developing what he calls a social analysis of the human sensorium, Robert Cooper (reprinted as Chapter 2 in this volume) associates processes of stabilization—including the disciplining processes discussed by Foucault—with a hierarchization of the visual sense over the other senses. He quotes Febvre (1982:437):

> Like their acute hearing and sharp sense of smell, the men of that time doubtless had keen sight. But that was just it. They had not yet set it apart from the other senses.

This fluidity—what Cooper defines as 'interaction'—is contrasted sharply with a putative bureaucratization of thought—what he calls 'hierarchy'.

Adopting these terms for the moment, the question such comparisons raise is whether, in the fall of a foundational approach to knowledge, we have witnessed a collapse in the stabilities produced by 'hierarchy' and are now experiencing a return to the ambiguities of 'interaction'? Certainly, in explicating the earlier transition to modernism, Cooper sees the 'information' of the eye as not yet being in a necessary link with a 'need to know'. As he adds, this 'process of stabilization called for quantification and calculation and this necessarily involved the eye . . . ' (30). For Cooper, the stabilization of the world—the removal of ambiguity and flux (associated with interaction)—required a specialized training of the visual sense as well as its elevation (hierarchization) over the other senses.

It is into this process of stabilization that Cooper first introduces the notion of the 'labour of division'. Noting that it is customary to view the careers of societies in terms of the division of labour, where the emphasis is placed on the specialization of skills and occupations in an hierarchical framework, Cooper (31) suggests an alternative way of viewing this process:

> . . . instead of the 'division of labour', the differentiation of the senses draws attention to the complex processes at work in actively shaping the human agent as a perceiving organism in the social system. This differentiation process we may more accurately call the 'labour of division' since it not only highlights the act of division itself (as opposed to the specific agents of 'labour') but it also suggests that the 'division' in this context is significantly bound up with the act of 'seeing'—that is, vision is an intrinsic component of 'division'.

As Cooper (1993) elsewhere remarks, paraphrasing Heidegger, there is 'no vision without division'. On this analysis, vision is enabled by division. Contrary to a romantic sentiment that, with any division, would have vision cut in two, it is the very possibility of seeing that is created through making these 'cuts'.

Nevertheless, with modernization, there is a twist to all this. Adopting a grand narrative of increasing stabilization, Cooper (this volume: 31) is pointing to what he calls a 'visualization' of perception:

> The conversion of this state of perpetual ambiguity into a more determinate structure necessitated the hierarchical step of raising the status of sight over the 'primitive' senses of touch, taste and smell in favour of a *visualization* of perception.

In respect of the process of stabilization, Cooper (31) develops his argument by tying this labour of division to certain properties of visualization:

> In this way, the general processes of the 'labour of division' enables greater visual control over the social and material world through enhanced clarity, transparency and visual certainty *at a distance*.

The advantages of 'distance' aside, the object of the labour of division is precisely this property of stability, of 'seeing' in a constant, repeatable way—and Cooper deploys Foucault's (1973) discussion of the medical 'gaze' to illustrate this process.

This said, 'seeing' is now no longer quite what it seems. For, drawing on Heidegger's stress on the modern logic of representation as being that which establishes 'knowledge in advance', Cooper (1993:285) spells out the particular way in which we can know beforehand. It is not far-sightedness, in a traditional sense, but precisely a *stabilization* of vision. The gain is not more sight but stable sight. Once vision is subject to a process of representation, the gain of representation becomes one of 'again'—the repeatability of *re*-presentation. Thus it is not vision itself which is the 'gain'; it is the vision that travels before, ready to be seen *again*.[4]

With repeatability, what is to be seen becomes 'visible'. Crucially, it becomes therefore *examinable*. Far from what is to be 'seen' being left ambiguous and undecidable, therefore, 'seeing' becomes a labour that is mechanized in ways that ensure that what is 'shown' is *re*-presentable.

As Cooper goes on to point out, there are three ways in which Foucault (1977) suggests that 'examination' promotes visibility, while at the same time linking the latter to knowledge and power. First, 'the examination transformed the economy of visibility into the exercise of power' (187). It is their presence in fields of visibility (being 'seen'), that activates the previously passive and enables power to be exercised through them. Second, 'the examination . . . introduces individuality into the fields of documentation' (189). Made gradeable, we are now moveable on the grid of a text. Third, 'the examination, surrounded by all its documentary techniques, makes each individual a "case"' (191). As a case, each of us in turn can be made the object of a further process of examination.

Together, in these ways, the labour of division provides a stabilization, a 'grid' of representation within which we are each made visible [or not!]. In Cooper's analysis, therefore, the phrase 'the labour of division' takes on the meaning of a 'general process' (31), a 'look' in which we are 'beheld' by 'eyes that must see without being seen' (37). As Cooper adds:

> Because it cannot be seen, the 'look' cannot be questioned—this is its lethal, invisible power; vision and objectivity are thus mutually defining.

Since it cannot be questioned, this way of seeing can now escape interaction and create, or re-inforce hierarchy. This, at least, is the impression. And it is how Cooper positions the labour of division: as outside interaction and as a process of visualization aiding and abetting hierarchy.

By now we should be clear that Cooper's labour of division—the 'look' or the 'gaze'—is vision on a large scale: the actual eyes, say of a doctor or nurse, do not see. Indeed, we can say they have become blind to what is literally before them and attuned to 'see' that which has been made ready in advance. Enrolled as intermediaries, the eyes might be thought to act more as 'hands' for the divisions of the discipline to provide their vision (see also Latour, 1986).

In what follows, I want to suggest how Cooper's insights over stabilization can be developed by those researchers more concerned with everyday interaction. Instead of treating the labour of division as a determinate way of persons being made 'visible', and thus open only to panoptic forms of surveillance, I will suggest now how the labour of division can become turned on ourselves, displacing rather than eliminating the processes of interaction. Specifically, I suggest how the labour of division can be understood less monolithically and re-distributed in terms of each of us 'seeing' difference in ways—in particular ways, that is, rather than others—that attempt to ensure that each of us leaves no 'matter out of place'.

Hierarchy in interaction

Much of the stabilization thesis not only helps set up a division between 'hierarchy' and 'interaction' but relies upon its very existence. I want now to question the wisdom of making this division prior to analysis. Cooper's reliance on this distinction, however helpful it is in facilitating his own narrative, seems inappropriate in a paper (first published ten years ago) that is also introducing the term 'labour of division'.

First, Cooper's deployment of a division between hierarchy and interaction is unstable on his own analysis, since it mimics the 'confused' relation of subjectivity and objectivity. As Cooper (36, emphasis added) himself notes, Derrida's notion of interaction means 'essentially that *no* division can ever realistically be made between these concepts [subjectivity and objectivity] since they are "confused" with each other'. In particular, his rendering of hierarchy in terms of a 'stabilization' of seeing approximates very closely to post-empiricist definitions of objectivity, such as Karl Popper's definition of objectivity as 'agreement among observers'.

Second, Cooper's analysis of stabilization leaves undecidability *outside* the labour of division. Wittingly or not, ambiguity—defined by Cooper to be the very essence of interaction—is not only excluded from hierarchy, it is implicitly defined as a product of subjectivity. This asymmetry of analysis is all the more unfortunate when a detailed analysis of professional practice (Cooper's exemplar), is considered. For example while the labour of division by nurses or doctors may often be, in Cooper's words, 'to *see more clearly* the difference between "good" and "bad" physical and mental health', sometimes nurses and doctors, as Joanna Latimer (1997) has shown, themselves harness ambiguity to hold two different 'ways of seeing' in place. In this analysis, ambiguity is no longer the haphazard phenomenon of the sixteenth century and has to be reckoned with as integral to professional practice, not as a matter lying outside it.

Third, I take Derrida's point to be axiomatic about divisions in general. All divisions set up a (violent) 'hierarchy', in which one of the terms dominates the other. As Cooper notes, drawing on Derrida (1981:41), 'one of the two terms governs the other (axiologically, logically, etc.) or has the upper hand'. It would seem therefore as appropriate to explore processes of stabilization 'within' interaction, rather than within hierarchy alone. Indeed, in so far as

Cooper's narrative of the triumph of hierarchy over interaction becomes itself 'confused' and unreliable, it would seem that a much more radical understanding of the labour of division is possible and desirable.

Fourth, few terms are deployed today without inversion. Some attention to the agonistics of 'moves' in language games (Lyotard, 1984) should make us watchful, not just for terms which have the 'upper hand', but also for those that are subject to a sleight of hand (see Munro, 1993). It is not so much that there are always a plurality of positions available, for some of these may well appear to be closed off. The potential is also for a semiotic slippage that can help avoid a purely reactional move (a reply coded in his or her capacity of addressee or referent), and help mount a successful 'counter-move' (Lyotard, 1984:16) by upstaging the other (and returning oneself to the position of 'sender'). In the visual metaphor we are currently deploying, this deployment of a move that indexically shifts the language game, is to suggest that, in interaction, we can slip from merely having to 'see', into re-framing the very 'way of seeing'.

Without losing Cooper's insights over visualization, then, it would seem likely that the effect of a repeatability of representation—the gain of again—can be appropriated by social actors more locally. Such an effect could include the use of a 'normalizing judgement' (Cooper, this volume 33) of the form Foucault envisaged. But, as several chapters in this volume depict, in so far as the processes of stabilization are open to other tactics and interests—although not necessarily in ways that people intend—the field which is opened up by an attention to the labour of division is that much wider. A fuller discussion of this point requires some passing attention to the modernism/postmodernism debate.

'Seeing' difference

Considered more as a feature of society, difference might be said to enjoy mixed fortunes. Sometimes, difference is in vogue; it is perceived as a thing to be welcomed and may be referred to wholesomely in such terms as 'diversity'. On other occasions, as seems the case with modernism, it is viewed as something more shadowy, even malevolent, with any difference being treated as deviant. Unless this smoulders like Northern Ireland or explodes into a Bosnia, we could perhaps think of this as a shift in mood, much as we either view a glass as half empty or half full. But why would we think of diversity as good and deviance as bad? Or half-full as good, and half-empty as bad?

Without stretching the point too much, is it possible to suggest that things *are* different today? So that a postmodern 'attitude' perhaps becomes one in which Euro-Americans at least have gotten used to endless inversions and reversals? If so, the elusive postmodern mood might amount to an increasing *accommodation* of the ability to see difference, rather than just an acceptance of difference, a feature more likely to be true of Febvre's sixteenth century. Postmodernism, then, could be understood less in terms of it being a mood of celebrating difference, and much more in terms of being ironic to it. Perhaps. But, equally, this matter of irony, or distance to difference might suggest instead that palettes have become jaded by variety; a kind of anomie which leaves many people stuck 'in-between' positions, reluctant to come off the fence by virtue of being tired of 'seeing' difference?

Where this is so, it is likely that it is no longer just difference that mutates between being celebrated and effaced. It is, as mentioned earlier, perhaps more a matter of each of our very *ideas* of difference coming under scrutiny. Thus the question is never just a matter of this or that (or a matter or here or there, or of then and now), it is to ask instead: how is it possible to see *that*? Or see that *there* and this *now*? For, once the doctrines of social constructivism are abroad, is not the suspicion that any remarked-upon difference will turn out to be an artefact arising out of a difference in the way of looking?

The refusal, if refusal it is, becomes one of *stopping* oneself from just 'seeing' difference as presented by a speaker. This kind of refusal is certainly present in the Anglo-American academy, where French thinkers, without having been read, are typically accused of dressing up old wine in funny new bottles. But more generally, this suspicion of difference—we could even call it a mutual surveillance—is culturally abroad as a repertoire of everyday citizens and organizational participants.[5] For example, the phrase 'I hear what you say' represents more than a deferral of sanctioning, affirmatory or otherwise. Although insisting on the hearer's ability to 'see what you say', it also constitutes a refusal by them to 'see' the action that might flow from this.

A 'withdrawal', a deferral on seeing the other's point of view, need hardly be considered to be a new social phenomenon.[6] Nevertheless, its existence points to possibilities for a rather different type of

15

stabilization than that anticipated by Cooper and illustrates how 'interaction' rather than 'hierarchy' might be given a somewhat closer look, especially if we are to understand more fully what may be entailed by a labour of division. In particular, for example, we should anticipate that the reflexive mood need no longer be engaged solely in moving, say, from figure to ground; or from an initial position to one requested by the other. Instead, reflexivity can be understood in terms of the attempt to see a figure almost simultaneously (figuratively speaking) alongside the ground within which the figure is being performed. It is to ask—sometimes at the same time as 'seeing' a difference—where the speaker is 'coming from'. Precisely. Surveillance shifts from an examination over what is to be 'seen' into examining how the other is 'seeing the world'. What is at stake is identity in terms of a consistency of 'position'.

It is this turn to reflexivity which provides, I suggest, a quite different version of the stabilization thesis, one whose implications are enormous and far-reaching in reworking our understandings of social life. For if a 'view' has been stabilized, it can of course be 'black-boxed' as Latour (1987) suggests. But, more, once a view has been 'boxed-up', it lends itself to a surveillance over its stability— say by asking the other to repeat themselves. It is worth remembering here that Derrida (1982:315) places *iterability*—the possibility of being repeated—at the heart of the very possibility of writing and, *ipso facto*, of communication. This is perhaps the value of a difference made stable and, returning to Cooper's phrase, one way of understanding 'the gain of again'. But it need not, as I have suggested, lead us back to the 'solidarity' of communal determinism, mechanical or organic. Iterability, it should be stressed, is not the mechanical replication discussed by Dale (this volume). For despite the heightened surveillance, there is a multiplicity for self that is opening up: the iterability of a view also offers a 'space' which can be slipped into at any time.[7]

The theme of multiple realities is of course hardly novel, in sociology, but much of the reasoning has relied on 'contexts' being different. For example, in Schutz's analysis, a person moves from being the hard-nosed businessman at the place of work to being the loving father at home. Or in Goffman's later writings, people can be in the same place, but are 'framing' the encounter in different ways. But a repeatability of re-presentation implies also that views can be drawn on—iterated—and thus operated in a different way. For example, if 'views' are themselves, at least partially, context providing, then this, in turn, implies that explorations and explanations of sociality have to conjure with a multiplicity that is much more dynamic. It is not just that people are mobile and can travel quickly through spaces, aided by immutable mobiles. It is social space itself that is iterable; and hence 'motile' to the adoption of different divisions.

Sociological in-difference

This speculation suggests that a further, and perhaps the most exciting, version of the labour of division. In ways that are perhaps akin more to Jean-Francois Lyotard's discussion on a *multiplicity* of language games, mentioned above, people can slip among diverse, folded social spaces in the slide of a division.

In much recent social research, boundaries and divisions are no longer seen as lying outside practices. Instead of treating this material as context or background, divisions are seen as cultural artefacts that are consumed and reproduced continuously. Thus, although we seem ever forgetful about this, it has become a point of contemporary knowledge that all divisions have to be continuously made and re-drawn. The consequence for analysis has been to draw 'knowing' back into the world as part of the very labour that is being analysed. But the immensity of this version of social constructivism need not stupify us into thinking that all the divisions of the world need to be enacted by everybody, or even all at once.

While not falling back on treating it as an immutable commentary on the world, knowledge can be seen as already widely distributed in diverse social practices that are being practised daily in order to create and iterate different 'ways of seeing'. And it is this simultaneous *division of labour* over knowing, which not only necessitates a grounded study of the labour of division but, I think, gives its study particular interest. For it is possible to study practices locally, to see which divisions are being deployed and when.

How then to proceed? Well, as researchers, we need to go on treating divisions as cultural artefacts. But, rather than place what is considered to be key divisions outside analysis, keeping them distinct as part of one's own analytical armoury, all distinctions, great and small, should be given to those who perpetuate them. Thus, rather than co-opt an exclusive range of distinctions, as if these could be kept pure and inviolate as part of the researcher's toolkit, the interest is in finding better ways of tracing their general or specific circulation.

In this way researchers can try to become, as Harold Garfinkel suggested some thirty years ago, sociologically indifferent. As I understand it, the strategy of sociological indifference is a willingness to treat *all* social actors as culturally reflective, not just the researcher. In particular, it is to admit them to be researchers who are *also* trying to find out the knowledge that is necessary for them to be treated as members, or included in the group of social actors. In terms of the present discussion, this strategy would insist on the 'great divides' becoming part of the study. Of course, as pointed to above, if social constructivism is to be taken seriously, there is a sense in which *all* divisions must be restituted in the local. While the researcher needs to be wary of forgetting this potential, the actual work in the field may be helped by an implicit or explicit hierarchisation over ideas of difference. More critically, how do the processes of iteration make some differences present and others absent?

Stated another way, it is unlikely that all members of a group begin by adopting the same set of typifications. Instead, it is to accept that members have 'methods' for finding out how to 'do' member. Thus any mutual surveillance over 'ways of seeing' is likely to circulate around the acceptance of certain key divisions, with differences in the use of other divisions being overlooked or ignored, but with one important reservation. Members do not ever finally know how to do member, they are caught in the endless process of finding out. As researchers, they too face Anthony Cohen's (1987) bar that stops any inference that seeks to adduce any sharing of meanings from a sharing of expressions. Thus any surveillance here is also implicitly, or explicitly, a form of sanctioning each other (see also Munro, 1997) that mediates iterability.

The particular interest for the researcher of group work therefore is with noting one specific form of the labour of division—the asymmetries committed by members of groups. Given the theme of a multiplicity of social spaces addressed above, however, the focus of research should not be restricted to asking what makes them work as groups. This aspect to the labour of division is of course vital, but we should also be interested in the variation and modulation that is necessitated in preserving multiple memberships. For example, the researcher can follow the nurse as she moves from holding the patient's hand at the bedside, to speak with the doctor at the foot of the bed. In Strathern's (n.d.) parlance, the nurse is not only 'cutting' the network anew, she also 'cuts' the figure that is appropriate to the moment.

In this respect, researchers could begin to focus on a competence in making divisions as part of the 'methods' by which membership is accorded or withdrawn—discovering in the process what counts as commonly accepted, taken-for-granted divisions. Thus, rather than think of the labour of division globally, as if created from a distance, it is possible to ask how the local is also being manufactured under people's noses? Nor should we ever think here that there is just one local. In order to see how difference is being created and reproduced, identified and manipulated, researchers need to enter not just one version of the local, but appreciate the difference between iteration and mere repetition—since it is this difference that helps both create, and preserve, a fluidity of identity and a multiplicity of social spaces.

Outline of the book

The current tendency is to reject universalism and, in line with a greater respect for the linguistic integrity of specific practices, go the other way, preferring the emic to the etic, or local distinctions to global abstractions. Indeed, as ethnographers, many of us are committed to exploring what might be better called difference-in-use. So in a negative mode, it is perhaps important to say what this book is not about.

With Strathern, in her treatment of difference as cultural artefact [reprinted in Section I], most of the contributors to this volume seek to study the effects that flow from the presence of difference, rather than to impose a new formula upon difference itself. As Brown's chapter shows, a concept is inseparable from the 'event' in which it is deemed to take place. In his view, against hopes of a 'democracy of concepts', or a 'confusion of difference machines, all labouring noisily', it becomes less obfuscatory to suggest that the labour of division, as a concept, can only have its being in *taking place.*

The implicit suggestion for studying everyday interactions, or mundane encounters that takes place at the hospital or on the factor floor, is that not all the divisions are ever active at once. But it would be a mistake, as I hope to have shown, to discount altogether a story of stabilization, such as is captured by Cooper [also reprinted in Section I]. The point to which I want to give emphasis, is that it is not only stable 'views' to which divisions give rise; and which are then consumed. Alongside the insights which are gained by viewing the divisions as labouring *us*, there is, as has increasingly been acknowledged, a cognitive and emotional labour in *our* making these divisions present. For divisions to take effect, they have to be activated, accomplished as an effect of someone's performance.[8]

In Section II of the book, much of the emphasis is on divisions as labouring. Whether divisions are devices put into place to discipline ways of seeing, as Cooper has suggested, or whether their consequences are more unintended, as Dale in her chapter on identity in the 'culture of dissection' suggests, the 'urge to anatomize' affects our understandings of the body, self and knowledge. In a highly stratified society, including the contemporary organizations that are the focus of Parker's study, it is always important to consider the effects these divisions are also performing (although these never act alone as the locutions 'us over here' and 'them over there' suggest). This is made especially evident when, as Watson's chapter also suggests, people's identity work is complicit in the production and reproduction of these divisions.

In Section III, the theme of divisions as having stable 'effects' is continued but the emphasis is on the spatial hierarchies that, once accepted, facilitate a mobility across social spaces. For example, in their reading of perspective in four paintings, Law and Benschop suggest how, in the switch of divisions, things can be made near or far, or the world turned upside down. But any ease of slippage here should not be mistaken for voluntarism or free will. As Hetherington suggests, social spaces, such as the home, are often well-rehearsed; with a stability of entry greatly aided by durable materials, such as slippers, which are kept ready to hand in ways that *re*-mind us which social space we are trying to occupy. Indeed, as Hinchliffe depicts, mobility is usually highly constricted: certain effects may only be called up by the adoption of particular divisions in particular ways. The availability of cultural repertoires can depend on those divisions which are brought 'near', only with some serendipity, from 'other' networks.

Section IV, in its emphasis on 'motility', offers a more temporal quality to the labour of division. In different ways both it and the previous section can be understood as exploring the question of *presence* over divisions; which divisions are present? However, if the chapters in the previous section attended to those divisions made present by spatial hierarchies—the how question—the chapters in this final section attend to the divisions raised by more temporal hierarchies—the when question. Höpfl's chapter is particularly salutary in its subtle arrest of time, so that we begin to feel, palpably, the overwhelming effects of a proliferation of divisions; and the banality that this surfeit can bring to our lives. Hendriks develops this theme further by exploring how the banal can exist for the autistic, who lack a (our?) sense of difference and cannot 'stop' an activity once started. His finely attuned study depicts how a mundane deployment of materials, such as an egg-timer, helps mediate the agency of two different senses of timing. If Höpfl and Hendriks' chapters raise questions about 'affirmation' and 'the stop', Latimer's final chapter, in its attention to our 'disposal' of older people, opens up this debate in a more general way.

This, then, is the agenda set up by the labour of division. An agenda to rework the problem of social order by rethinking its representations. Which is, when we think about it, our systems of divisions. This is not, of course, a new agenda. As I have already acknowledged, this reframing of our thought is already taking place. So much so, that we *already* stand in a tradition, one more neatly summarized by our epithet, the labour of division.

As with much of the best recent social research, a principal focus of the contributions to this book is on boundaries—the spaces or intervals between divisions. Yet instead of just celebrating and reproducing this tradition, the purpose of the book is to understand it. We want to understand divisions as artefacts that are not only produced in our representations of the social, to ourselves and to each other, but as that which we consume as a continuous labour. And, yes, we want to understand how, when, and for whom, everyday divisions 'speak'. But so, too, do we want to excavate these shaping effects as stemming from a central truth regime in which we now stand immersed.

Using the labour of division, then, as both scalpel and mirror, we want to recognize, if we can, the disciplining powers of our current truth regime. How, for example, a prejudice for the fluid and the marginal has crept in, how biases towards 'cutting' continue. How anything that has a 'stop' on it has been viewed as conservative; and yet how the very lack of a stop might put others in jeopardy. Yes, we want to understand how social spaces are brought into being, by divisions that are not only themselves 'labouring' but are also being made stable *and* multiple by the iterability of our 'own' labour of division. All this, with one addendum. Perhaps it will be only by virtue of a readiness to place a 'stop' on these lines of sight, even to the extent of unsecuring our own memberships, that researchers can start to notice these interweavings of mobility and motility. Or accept how ready we are to slip across divisions in our labour to see?

Notes

1 This is necessarily a partial introduction, in both senses of the word. In first suggesting the theme of the labour of division for the Centre of Social Theory and Technology's first conference, my hope was that a diverse set of understandings of the phrase would appear. The diversity of approaches in this volume speak for themselves. My grateful thanks go to Barry Barnes, Kevin Hetherington, Nick Lee, Paul Smith and Marilyn Strathern for their comments and suggestions on earlier drafts of this chapter.

2 Darwin's theory has many interpretations. In its contemporary account, however, the labour of the environment, selection, is usually kept separate from the differentiation work of the species, with its small, random mutations. While Popper (1981) suggests that Darwin's theory is prototypical of all scientific theories, I suspect that it is more a division in the formulation of labour that is copied.

3 Both deploy the term liminal, but do so in very different ways. I am not proposing therefore that the differences in usage should be overlooked. To the contrary, it would seem of paramount importance that they be preserved. The difference between Turner and Latour's usage lies not only in their roots, a difference between phenomenology and realism, it is their implications that diverge. Briefly, for Turner, the liminal is occasional, momentary and a matter for personal experience; for Latour, the liminal is pressing, imminent and universal.

4 I should add here that, whatever the accuracy of his analysis of modernity, Heidegger would view this mechanization of sight with a degree of horror. Related more to his concept of correctness, this repeatability of re-presentation stands quite other to his own emphasis on *aletheia*, truth being experienced in a momentary 'unrevealing'.

5 Deferral is a commonplace of conversation, often marked by expressions of non-committal, such as an 'uhuh' or 'mm'. Such expressions can serve the function of keeping the listener 'in-between' affirmation and disagreement, particularly in situations where silence might be interpreted as disagreement.

6 This ability to bracket off someone's view might be better characterized as a product of modernism, not postmodernism, since the refusal to understand the so-called irrational has long been held. Indeed, the break with modernism can hardly be considered to be reflexivity itself, as some have suggested, but seems rather to be attributable to the lack of a single account of rationalism within which to dispose of ambivalence.

7 This is not the place to hazard an explanation of these viewing 'boxes', but I want to note that we need not have immediate recourse to 'hierarchy' to explain their stability. Some stability, for example, might arise from their being circulated and developed continuously within interaction. Used in this way, interaction can be deployed as a process of 'testing' the reception to one's untried views. This is not unsimilar to the process discussed by Latour (1987) over simulation. When the first astronaut puts his first foot on the moon, he has been there a hundred times before, each simulation strengthening the last and bringing it (somewhat) closer to the 'final' experience.

8 This aspect should not be thought of in too idealistic terms; it is not as if a withdrawal of this labour by any one actor might cause the whole stratification to collapse. The crux of the matter is more one that has occupied the attention of the sociology of translation—especially in its less actor-network mood—when it

accepts Derrida's theme of iteration and notices that a token is never repeated, but always translated.

Bibliography

Appelbaum, D., (1995) *The Stop*, Albany: New York State University Press.

Boor, D., (1976) *Knowledge and Social Imagery*, Chicago: University of Chicago Press.

Cohen, A.P., (1987) *Whalsay: Symbol, Segment and Boundary in a Shetland Island Community*, Manchester: Manchester University Press.

Cooper, R., (1993) 'Technologies of Representation' in P. Alionen (ed.) *The Semiotic Boundaries of Politics*, Berlin: Mouton de Gruyter.

Derrida, J., (1981) *Positions*, translated by A. Bass, Chicago: University of Chicago Press.

Derrida, J., (1982) *Margins of Philosophy*, translated by A. Bass, Hemel Hempstead: Harvester Press.

Febvre, L., (1982) *The Problem of Unbelief in the Sixteenth Century*, Cambridge: Harvard University Press.

Foucault, M., (1970) *The Order of Things: An Archaeology of the Human Sciences*, London: Tavistock.

Foucault, M., (1973) *The Birth of the Clinic*, translated by A. Sheridan, London: Tavistock.

Foucault, M., (1977) *Discipline and Punish*, translated by A. Sheridan, London: Allen Lane.

Garfinkel, H., (1967) *Studies in Ethnomethodology*, Englewood Cliffs, NJ: Prentice Hall.

Goffman, E., (1958) *The Presentation of Self in Everyday Life*, Edinburgh: University of Edinburgh Social Sciences Research Centre.

Goody, J., (1977) *The Domestication of the Savage Mind*, Cambridge: Cambridge University Press.

Hetherington, K., (1997) 'Museum Topology and the Will to Connect', *Journal of Material Culture* 2:199–218.

Latimer, J., (1997) 'Giving Patients a Future: the constituting of classes in an acute medical unit', *Sociology of Health and Illness*, 19:160–85.

Latour, B., (1986) 'Visualization and Cognition: thinking with eyes and hands' in H. Kuklick and E. Long (eds) *Knowledge and Society: Studies in the Sociology of Culture Past and Present*, Volume 6, Greenwich, Conn.: JAI Press.

Latour, B., (1987) *Science in Action: How to Follow Scientists and Engineers through Society*, Milton Keynes: Open University Press.

Latour, B., (1991) 'Technology is Society Made Durable' in J. Law (ed.) *A Sociology of Monsters: Essays on Power, Technology and Domination*, Sociology Review Monograph 38:103–31, London: Routledge.

Lyotard, J.-F., (1984) *The Postmodern Condition: A Report on Knowledge*, translated by G. Bennington and D. Massumi, Manchester: Manchester University Press.

Munro, R., (1993) 'Just When You Thought It Safe To Enter the Water: accountability, language games and multiple control technologies', *Accounting, Management and Information Technologies*, 3:249–71.

Munro, R., (1997) 'Power, Conduct and Accountability: Re-distributing Discretion

23

Rolland Munro

and the Technologies of Managing', *Proceedings of the 5th Interdisciplinary Perspectives on Accounting*: 4.2.2–4.2.10, Manchester: University of Manchester.

Parker, M., (1997) 'We Have Always Been Scrumpled: a response to Hetherington', *Journal of Material Culture*,

Popper, K., (1981) 'The Rationality of Scientific Revolutions' in I. Hacking (ed.) *Scientific Revolutions*, Oxford: Oxford University Press.

Strathern, M., (n.d.) 'Cutting the Network', mimeograph.

Strathern, M., (1991) *Partial Connections*, Maryland: Rowman & Little.

Turner, V., (1967) *The Forest of Symbols: Aspects of Ndembu Ritual*, Ithaca, NY: Cornell University Press.

Section I
Labouring division

Introduction

The most remarkable and ambitious study of ideas of difference is perhaps Michel Foucault's *The Order of Things*. In Foucault's (1970:340) view, modern thought is no longer one that moves 'towards the never-completed formation of Difference' in what might strike us today as an inventory of monsters. Instead, it moves 'towards the ever-to-be-accomplished unveiling of the Same'. What counts as modern knowledge involved a process in which the monsters are expulsed as aberrant, as deviant.

This 'unveiling' of the Same, however, is not to be considered as taking place merely 'in' knowledge, as if knowledge has its own body and could act as a vast repository for its representations. For modern knowledge, while still representational, no longer attempts to produce itself as an immutable commentary on the world. The vain attempt to provide a pure representation—a picture of the world that did not itself mediate the world—has been abandoned. Indeed, it is precisely the ability of knowledge to mediate the world that becomes its desirable property. For Foucault, the more knowledge takes its positive form, description (it 'is' this way), the more knowledge becomes charged with its normative form of prescription (it *should* be this way). The world is about to be re-made into the form of its picture.

From the moment when Man begins to 're-apprehend himself as a labouring being' (330), knowledge has (re)-entered the world as one of its forces of production. In one way, Robert Cooper's chapter addresses this issue. Through Foucauldian notions such as 'visibility' and the 'gaze', Cooper suggests how social systems 'see' where they are going. Which is to say, as Darwin held, that they cannot. They are blind. But they can labour a *di*-vision. On the one hand, insofar as positive knowledge can produce a 'world picture', social systems can simulate sight, with targets and goals to aim towards. And on the other, in so far as the eyes of men become its 'hands', social systems can change the world, bending it towards these targets and goals.

For this labour of 'di-vision' to work, however, two things seem necessary. First, whatever societies are working towards must be stabilized. This insight is an important contribution of Cooper's chapter: stability is necessary in order that the 'world picture' can simulate the vision of the eyes. Second, the labouring of the 'hands' must be working together. It is in this second sense that Cooper, despite drawing on Foucault, can also be considered to be addressing fruitfully the problem of 'solidarity', the central issue that informed Durkheim's formulations of the division of labour. Thus Cooper's reworking of the division of labour in the form of the 'labour of division' is no mere passing inversion. In a number of subtle and productive ways, Cooper is developing Foucault's ideas of 'visibility' and the 'gaze' in order to rewrite Durkheim's arguments over social order. This said, Cooper's formulation cannot be said to align Foucault's work with Durkheim, so much as it helps to bring them near. His juxtaposition of Foucault's pivotal writings on disciplining with Durkheim's key text on belonging, makes it seem unhelpful to dismiss the work of either, even if Cooper's own picture of power and domination leaves them as yet unreconciled.

But there is another side to the theme of labour *as* di-vision which Cooper overlooks. In one of the more enigmatic passages of *The Order of Things*, Foucault (1970:340) points to the Doubles— the doppelgangers—that haunt the human sciences. The trajectory of modern knowledge, the 'unveiling' of the Same is not accomplished:

> . . . without the simultaneous appearance of the Double, and that hiatus, minuscule and yet invincible, which resides in the 'and' of retreat *and* return, of thought *and* the unthought, or the empirical *and* the transcendental, of what belongs to the order of positivity *and* what belongs to the order of foundations. (340)

Treated as a history of difference, Foucault's analysis depicts how 'difference' mutates from being understood as a property of things-in-themselves, to becoming embedded *within* the human sciences. In the search for the identical, difference retreats to the 'shadows', providing its contrasts both in the margins as deviance *and*, more centrally, in the form of the unseen See-er: the contesting and ever-circulating sets of divisions, such as structure and function, that act as the foundations of the human sciences.

If Foucault's analysis is a history of difference—*his* story—Marilyn Strathern deploys the anthropologist's device of the ethnographic present to confront modernity with its gendered rendering of itself. Picking the 'myth of matriarchy' as a twentieth-century supposition that the 'variety of human forms of organization are bound to provide examples opposed to patriarchy', Strathern examines the 'constructions of a living, and very much contemporary culture', which she calls the Euro-American.

Among other things, gender constructions for the Euro-American entail a supposition about addition: that addition is augmentation. Masculinity or femininity are treated as a matter of degree, to be gauged from a multiplicity of attributes. Thus, if persons display more, or less, masculinity, so too can social organizations be considered as being more, or less, influenced by female principles. Unfortunately for this picture, heterogeneous elements seem contradictory. For example, earlier anthropologists of the Trobriand Islands tried to explain how descent through women (matriliny) could co-exist with women moving to their new husband's village (virilocality).

To appreciate how such long standing local arrangements might seem self-contradictory to earlier anthropologists, Strathern focuses on the role of comparison in Euro-American discourse. Comparison is central to feminist practice but, as Strathern points out, difference is made manifest in comparison: 'divergent attributes become significant in respect of some continuum or quality otherwise held in common'. Thus, although it appears that each sex comes to be judged in respect of the other, this is not so. Already his-story is setting up what is to be held in common. This is how domination enters: the male exercise of (formal) power becomes the common measure by which male and female dominance are compared. So is there a comparison? This is what Strathern sets out to provide, but we have already been warned that this will not be easy to see.

In general parlance, division segments what 'already exists as a whole'. For example, in Melanesia, a principal site of Strathern's fieldwork, many groups gender values, institutions and the acts of persons but, otherwise, it is androgyny that is taken for granted. Thus, at least in terms of gender, people seem to have to 'work to divide themselves off from each other'. A singular (undivided) gender identity is seen to be created only by the active shedding of the 'other' (cross-sex) component. What 'completes' could never be more male or female parts, but rather cross-sex 'complements'. Each orientation complements the other.

What becomes exaggerated in these Melanesian systems is the practice of division: not adding everything together but, instead, repeating and thus duplicating the division of female from male members, maternity from paternity. Difference is made manifest, but instead of being treated as 'matter out of place', it is preserved through *iteration*: the 'same' division (between male and female) is repeated over and again through different phenomena and in different contexts. Similarly, even in so-called patrilineal, virilocal, male-dominated societies found elsewhere in Melanesia, a 'man is not made "more" a man'. Instead, each division 'creates again the separation of a man from female parts of himself, a woman from her male parts'.

These considerations lead Strathern to consider a number of examples in which an entity, such as fatherhood, is *divided* into differently gendered versions of itself, namely 'fatherhood' and 'motherhood'. Which is exactly, Strathern points out, what Euro-Americans would *not* say. Instead, sexes are compared to what is imagined as common between them, eg being 'human'. Distinctiveness is imagined as *deviation* from what is held in common; so much so that it becomes feasible to contemplate *degrees* of distinctiveness: a series that allows one sex to be modelled on the other, providing the 'best' example of this or that attribute.

If what is the case for gender, follows also for the Euro-American 'individual', then we are back of course to a disciplining thesis. With a difference. Against Cooper's normalizing replication of identity, Strathern is stressing *iteration*. And there are two quite different processes of iteration to compare: a division, as in Melanesia, that is essentially preserving of *complementarity*; and a process of comparison, conducted by Euro-Americans, that reduces us to *supplementarity*. What is so confusing in trying to think this comparison is that complementarity is not at all what it seems. Indeed, as long as they keep trying to add up their comparisons, it becomes almost impossible for Euro-Americans to think through this form of complementarity! In their will to seek always more of the same, moderns are for ever stuck in a form of supplementarity.

In presenting these conundrums, Strathern asks us not to be put off by her examples which are 'trivial' in comparison: 'making the data so presented apparently outrun the theoretical effort to comprehend it'. It is in this last respect that Steve Brown's chapter quite deliberately follows suit. However, by the time he asks: 'So what did happen?' the irony intended in this wanting-to-know is already clear.

Brown begins his chapter with an apparent contradiction in post-structuralist writing. The marked hostility of Foucault and Derrida to classical notions of the concept is in sharp contrast to their fascination with the exemplary use of concepts. It is as if they too, for all their protestations, are attracted by the 'dazzling power' of the concept and its ability to hold 'disparate things together'. Brown resolves this difficulty, however, by suggesting that a concept can be explored, not through its logical relations, but as a kind of *machine* for making elements cohere as an 'event'. In respect of this metaphor of machine, he quotes Deleuze and Guattari who see the concept as defined by 'the inseparability of a finite number of heterogeneous components traversed by a point of absolute survey at infinite speed'.

Brown's empirical concerns are with a related group of concepts: stress, hysteria, and dancing mania, all drawn from differing historical milieus. The method he deploys to explore these relations is to stage a series of events by way of each concept. Thus, rather than adopting theoretical devices, such as 'sharpening' a concept prior to its examination of the empirical world (a dissection that is intended to 'see' the world more clearly), Brown is interested in how these concepts 'position' themselves relative to one another. The question is how they 'resonate', rather than cohere or correspond.

Brown's position here is one of a poststructural 'withdrawal' from the use of concepts. But this withdrawal from concepts, as he shows, should not be mistaken for their dismissal. Rather the fascination with exemplary usage might be better seen for what it is: an avoidance of the exercise of power—the speed of sight given by the use of concepts—and marking instead a more reflective attention to the *appearance* of concepts themselves. This version of poststructuralism registers a shift away from a formal attention to concepts towards a study of how the concept both folds up practice and yet itself unfolds in practice. Treating the concept 'as event' is a concern to bring together a study of what concepts are mobilizing in practice with a raised attention to how concepts are themselves mobilized in the process.

The visibility of social systems

Robert Cooper

Introduction

The role of the senses in social life is a neglected theme in social analysis. Despite the philosopher Whitehead's (1938) early call for systematic study of the 'organization of the sensorium' in human communication, it is only recently that this has been taken up as a serious challenge by the human sciences. Much of this work has focused on the dominance of vision, especially in modern social systems subjected to 'bureaucratization' and the processes of formal organization more generally. As Rorty (1980) has reminded us, modern thought has privileged the eye as the sense organ by which we may represent the world to ourselves most effectively. Yet it was not always like this. The historian Lucien Febvre (1982), in a study of 16th-century social life, comments on the underdevelopment of sight in that period:

> Like their acute hearing and sharp sense of smell, the men of that time doubtless had keen sight. But that was just it. They had not yet set it apart from the other senses. They had not yet tied its information in particular in a necessary link with their need to know. (p. 437)

Consequently, they lived in a fluid world 'where nothing was strictly defined, where entities lost their boundaries and, in the twinkling of an eye, without causing much protest, changed shape, appearance, size . . . ' (p. 438). The stabilization of the world required a specialized training of the visual sense and its elevation over the other senses. The process of stabilization called for quantification and calculation and this necessarily involved the eye: 'The passage from the qualitative to the quantitative is essentially linked to advances in the predominance of visual perception' (Rey quoted in Febvre, 1982, p. 432).

It is customary to view the careers of societies in terms of the division of labour where the emphasis is placed on the specialization of skills and occupations in an hierarchical framework. The social analysis of the human sensorium suggests an alternative way of viewing this process: instead of the 'division of labour', the differentiation of the senses draws attention to the complex processes at work in actively shaping the human agent as a perceiving organism in the social system. This differentiation process we may more accurately call the 'labour of division' since it not only highlights the act of division itself (as opposed to the specific agents of 'labour') but it also suggests that the 'division' in this context is significantly bound up with the act of 'seeing'—that is, 'vision' is an intrinsic component of 'division'. We can take this analysis further through the work of the philosopher Jacques Derrida (see, for example, Norris, 1987) who views the logic of 'division' in terms of (1) *hierarchy* and (2) *interaction*. (These are not Derrida's terms—I have retained his ideas but used a more familiar terminology.) In hierarchy, it is recognized that systems, social or otherwise, are structured around binary oppositions (eg, good-bad, male-female) in which one of the terms dominates the other. As Derrida (1981) writes: ' . . . we are not dealing with the peaceful co-existence of a *vis-a-vis*, but rather with a violent hierarchy. One of the two terms governs the other (axiologically, logically, etc.), or has the upper hand' (p. 41). In interaction, as Derrida reminds us, there is a continuous double movement *within* the binary opposition so that the positively-valued term (for example, good) is defined only by contrast to the negatively-valued second term (for example, bad). In fact, the relationship between the apparently opposing terms is really one of mutual definition in which the individual terms actually inhabit each other. In other words, the separate, individual terms give way 'to a process where opposites merge in a constant *undecidable* exchange of attributes' (Norris, 1987, p. 35). Interaction describes precisely the fluid, changing forms of perception characteristic of the human agent in the 16th century, as noted by Febvre (1982). The conversion of this state of perpetual ambiguity into a more determinate structure necessitated the hierarchical step of raising the status of sight over the 'primitive' senses of touch, taste and smell in favour of the *visualization* of perception. In this way, the general process of the 'labour of division' enables greater control over the social and material world through enhanced clarity, transparency and visual certainty *at a distance*.

Visibility and the development of modern social systems

The first widespread attempts to organize and systematize the social world occurred in the 16th century. As Foucault (1979) points out, the 16th century saw the emergence of an increasing concern with the 'art of government' and political economy, that is, with the management of people, territory and raw materials. Perhaps for the first time, people began to be defined in terms of their relationship with 'wealth, resources, means of subsistence, the territory with its specific qualities, climate, irrigation, fertility, etc.' . . . as well as in their relation to 'accidents and misfortunes such as famine, epidemics, death, etc.' (Foucault, 1979, p. 11). In short, the management of social-economic systems began to take shape in men's minds. The creation of visibility, the harnessing of a precise visual bias to the control of people and things, was a necessary component of this development.

In his study of hospitals and medical practice at the end of the 16th century, Foucault (1973) identifies a new phenomenon of organized perception—the 'gaze'—which subjected the individual to the definition of a new social practice, ie, medicine, that assumed the authority of a 'science'. The concept of the gaze as a technique for ensuring the maximum visibility of individuals is further elaborated in Foucault's (1977) study of the prison system in which the gaze finds its special pedigree as a power (here the significance of the French '*pouvoir*', with its inclusion of the verb 'to see', underlines the imbrication of power, knowledge and visibility) that 'must see without being seen' (p. 171). The necessary role of surveillance in the construction and maintenance of visibility is perhaps best exemplified in Jeremy Bentham's architectural concept of the Panopticon, 'the polyvalent apparatus of surveillance, the universal optical machine of human groupings' (Miller, 1987, p. 3). The Panopticon was a circular building with a central tower from which continuous surveillance could be unilaterally exercised on inmates housed in perimeter cells. The Panopticon represented a more general idea—the Panoptic principle—in which Bentham dreamt 'of a transparent society, visible and legible in each of its parts' (Foucault, 1980, p. 152) which would expurgate 'the fear of darkened spaces, of the pall of gloom which prevents the full visibility of things, men and truths' (p. 153) that haunted the second half of the eighteenth century. Hence the need to elaborate that compendious theoretical system of administration which absorbed so much of

Bentham's life in the pursuit of the criteria of visibility: transparent knowledge *at a glance* through surveillance at a distance.

The pursuit of visibility was advanced, as Foucault (1977) notes, through the introduction of the 'examination', a technique which combines the power of an 'observing hierarchy' with that of a 'normalizing judgement'. The examination 'is a normalizing gaze, a surveillance that makes it possible to qualify, to classify and to punish. It establishes over individuals a visibility through which one differentiates them and judges them' (p. 184). In the eighteenth century, the hospital emerged as one of the first modern examples of an 'examining apparatus'. It regularized the form and frequency of the medical inspection and made it 'internal' to the hospital. Formerly a religious hospice, the hospital became subject to medical authority and the physician, hitherto an external element, displaced the religious staff into a subordinate role in the technique of examination. The hospital became a place of training and of the development of a form of knowledge which had as its object the subjection of the patient through techniques of surveillance and the normalizing gaze. The medical examination exemplified the logic of division: it hierarchized individuals into the categories of 'normal' and 'abnormal' and, just as importantly, it served to prevent the 'interaction' or intermixing of these categories. Ultimately, it enabled everyone *to see more clearly* the difference between 'good' and 'bad' physical and mental health.

In the same way, the early schools became a sort of examining apparatus. 'The Brothers of the Christian Schools wanted their pupils to be examined every day of the week: on the first for spelling, on the second for arithmetic, on the third for catechism in the morning and for handwriting in the afternoon, etc.' (Foucault, 1977, p. 186). The school examination made the pupil subject to a 'discipline' of continuous surveillance and visibility: 'it guaranteed the movement of knowledge from the teacher to the pupil, but it extracted from the pupil a knowledge destined and reserved for the teacher' (p. 187).

There are three specific ways, according to Foucault (1977), in which the examination promotes visibility while at the same time linking the latter to knowledge and power. First, '*the examination transformed the economy of visibility into the exercise of power*' (p. 187). In contrast to traditional forms of power whose efficacity rested on the full display of the power holder (eg, king, general) and the passive invisibility of its servitors, the new examination-based disciplinary power reverses this process by imposing a 'compulsory visibility' on its servitors while it itself remains invisible. 'In discipline, it is the subjects who have to be seen. Their visibility assures the hold of the power that is exercised over them. It is the fact of being constantly seen, of being able always to be seen, that maintains the disciplined individual in his subjection' (p. 187). Second, *'the examination . . . introduces individuality into the field of documentation'* (p. 189). The examination not only locates individuals in a 'field of surveillance' but it 'also situates them in a network of writing: it engages them in a whole mass of documents that capture and fix them' (p. 189). Through administrative writing it became possible to describe, identify and record in precise form the visibility of individuals according to the logic of division. Through what Giddens (1985) has called 'textually mediated organization' (p. 179), the examination made it possible to develop a system of accountability for 'normal' and 'abnormal' behaviour: it enabled 'the constitution of the individual as a describable, analyzable object, not in order to reduce him to "specific" features, as did the naturalists in relation to living beings, but in order to maintain him in his individual features, in his particular evolution, in his own aptitudes or abilities, under the gaze of a permanent corpus of knowledge' (Foucault, 1977, p. 190). Third, *'the examination, surrounded by all its documentary techniques, makes each individual a "case"'* (p. 191). Through writing, the examination documented the individual as a 'case', made him visible as an object of 'normalizing' management or, more precisely, 'an object for a branch of knowledge and a hold for a branch of power' (p. 191). The management and control of social systems finds its leverage increasingly at the level of the bio-scopic individual 'case'.

Against this background of the visible insinuated within the lisible, Hoskin and Macve (1986) have traced the history and development of accounting out of the technology of the examination. Accounting is that branch of modern management which has capitalized most on those two characteristic features of writing's visibility—*instantaneity* and *distance*; in other words, writing enabled information to be made available *at a glance* and in a *depersonalized* form (ie, free from the possibility of 'contamination' by social 'interaction', in Derrida's sense). Writing within the general context of Foucault's analysis of 'knowledge-power', Hoskin and Macve argue that 'examination, discipline and accounting are historically bound together as related ways of writing the world (in texts, institutional arrangements, ultimately in persons) into new configurations of power' (p. 107). These new ways of re-writing the social world date conceptually from antiquity but their influence is limited until medieval times when a 'new knowledge elite appears, centred around the nascent universities' (p. 109). The new elite of clerks and masters 'produce a vast new range of pedagogic re-writings of texts, ie, techniques which grid texts both externally and internally in the service of information-retrieval and knowledge-production' (p. 109). Hoskin and Macve note that 'the scholars of the cathedral schools and universities began to use visualist metaphors both to denote reading (eg, *videre, inspicere*) and composition (*scribere* for dictare)' (p. 110). Above all, the gridding of texts—the use of alphabetical order, a visually-oriented layout, systems of reference—and the substitution of read-easy arabic numerals for the more clumsy roman numbers created a new ordering of knowledge and understanding based on visibility. The new techniques were first perfected in the universities, especially those of Paris and Bologna, but later the exponents of these methods took their places as 'professionals' either in the church or at court. They included men like Thomas à Becket, who began his career, after qualifying in Paris, as a clerk-accountant in London in the 1140s. Double-entry book-keeping appeared in the thirteenth century as a particularly sophisticated form of the new examination-based writing. Significantly, as Hoskin and Macve point out, 'double-entry' was based upon the visualist metaphor of the Mirror—it was a mirror-book that reflected the 'equal and opposite signs of debit and credit' (p. 121). This, too, owed its emergence to a university teacher and cleric—Pacioli. Despite its relative sophistication, 'double-entry' was limited to 'financial examinatorial control' and therefore could not make 'human accountability' more visible. Hoskin and Macve argue that the accounting of human behaviour in terms of the debit-credit system had to await the introduction of the examination mark into the educational system in the 19th century (pp. 129–30).

Visibility, knowledge-power and professionalization

The point of Hoskin and Macve's analysis is to reveal the power of accounting to create a specific form of knowledge (knowledge-power) which subjects individuals to a fixed and determinate visibility. As such, it is a specific example of a more general trend in modern society—the development of knowledge-power by means of professionalization. In fact, Hoskin and Macve characterize accountancy as a profession that is squarely founded on the knowledge-power of accounting technology. The implication here is that the professions are those groups in society that are accredited with the task of creating and maintaining the appropriate 'visibility' of social agents through such techniques as the examination. This view of the professions is clearly at odds with the prevailing general and academic understanding of the professional's contribution to society as being both benevolent and selfless. As Goldstein (1984) points out, the sociological definition of a profession rests on four criteria: (1) it is a body of highly specialized knowledge which has to be formally mastered before it can be practised; (2) it is a monopoly, ie, the body of knowledge is recognized as the exclusive competence of those who practise it; (3) it is autonomous, ie, the professionals control their own work and how it should be done, and (4) it embodies a service ideal, ie, 'a commitment of ethical imperative to place the welfare of the public or of the individual client above the self-interest of the practitioner, even though the practitioner is earning a living through the exercise of the profession' (p. 175). This is essentially a 'theory' about certain kinds of occupational groups. When Foucault's ideas about 'disciplines' and knowledge-power are applied to the professions a totally different picture emerges. In fact, as Goldstein argues, the sociologist's professions turn out to be none other than Foucault's 'disciplines'. Like disciplines, the professions are now seen to be not only bodies of esoteric knowledge but also social practices. As social practices, disciplines/professions institute and maintain procedures for 'disciplining' individuals in the sense of subjecting them to the new forms of theoretical knowledge that epitomize the major professions. Human subjects become 'framed' in a 'picture' that is meticulously drawn in the practice of the professional's knowledge-power. Hence they can be made operationally visible.

Another version of this argument has been presented by Frug (1984) who has identified professionalism with bureaucratic legitimation. In an exemplary analysis which uses Derrida's idea of 'interaction', Frug shows that the central problem of bureaucracy (as studied by organization theorists and scholars of corporate and administrative law) is that of reconciling the relationship between *subjectivity* and *objectivity*. Derrida's notion of 'interaction' means essentially that no division can ever realistically be made between these concepts since they are 'confused' within each other. But the visual imperative that orders the social world means that (somehow) they must be kept apart—otherwise they could not be 'seen'.

All the stories of bureaucratic legitimation . . . share a common
structure: they attempt to define, distinguish, and render
mutually compatible the subjective (and objective) aspects of life.
All the defences of bureaucracy have sought to avoid merging
objectivity and subjectivity—uniting the demands of
commonness and community with those of individuality and
personal separateness—because to do so would be self-
contradictory. Moreover, it has never been enough just to
separate subjectivity and objectivity; each must also be
guaranteed a place within the bureaucratic structure

(Frug, 1984, p. 1287). In this case, the process of making bureaucratic structures clear and legible is self-deceiving for while the
'objective' qualities of professionalism are seen 'as something outside the individual to which he must adapt, they are qualities that
the professional himself helps to define' (p. 1331). Such interweav-
ing of objectivity and subjectivity necessarily undermines the 'transparent' or 'obvious' features of bureaucratic logic—the lack of
division or distinctness between the two making it difficult to see
either. The answer to the problem is the creation of a 'fiction' of
objectivity. The suspicion that this 'fiction' may be vision-based is
suggested in a study by Weinstein and Weinstein (1984) of what
they call 'the visual constitution of society'. Briefly, Weinstein and
Weinstein base their study on Sartre's famous analysis of the 'look'
(*le regard*)—essentially, Foucault's gaze—which functions to *objec-
tify* the social world by fixing or freezing individuals in a determinate framework from which they cannot escape since they are held
(and, of course, *beheld*) by 'eyes that must see without being seen'
(Foucault, 1977, p. 171). Because it cannot be seen, the 'look' cannot be questioned—this is its lethal, invisible power; vision and
objectivity are thus mutually-defining. The significance of the 'look'
is not only that it objectifies but also that it is the prototypical form
of visual interaction in formal social systems such as bureaucratic
organizations.

It would be myopic to assume that the visual bias of the 'objectifying gaze' is limited to the examples of the disciplines/profes-
sions—medicine, accountancy, etc.—we have discussed here. The
definitive feature of modern society is not so much the presence of
'disciplined vision' in formally-recognized institutions but its unobtrusive diffusion in the least expected places. For example, Bové
(1986) has recently shown how the institution of modern Anglo-
American literary criticism was 'professionalized' by the famous

39

Cambridge critic, I.A. Richards, beginning in the 1920s. Significantly, Richards was a follower of Jeremy Bentham and Bové shows in some detail how Bentham's Panoptic principle— Foucault's gaze again—shaped Richards' model of literary worth as well as his teaching practice. Literary criticism became less concerned with novels and poetry as an expression of human endeavour and emotions but was turned into a 'project for the production of knowledge, the exercise of power, and the creation of careers' (Bové, 1986, p. 48) on the model of 'the other positive disciplines such as economics, psychology, medicine, and anthropology' (p. 48). Richards' project was concerned with the training (ie, 'disciplining') of teachers and readers as part of a wider programme which would 'manage (the) larger forms of sociocultural and political difference between men and women, various classes, and competing ideologies and nations' (p. 53) . . . 'reducing the complex function of modernist literature to an ahistorical training school for teacher education in cultural management' (p. 55). His purpose was to develop a *way of seeing* the world and its literature according to a 'normalized' and 'transparent' perception. Like the early constructors of the objectifying gaze studied by Foucault in the fields of medicine, prisons, education and the human sciences, Richards succeeded in applying the same normalizing vision to a body of expression traditionally valued for its exploration of precisely those areas of human sensibility which lie beyond the 'gaze of discipline': the spontaneous, the erotic, the uncanny, etc.

The analysis of knowledge-power and the 'labour of division' in social systems has two important critical functions: (1) it reorients analysis away from the static picture of social structures produced by the division-of-labour perspective to reveal 'division' as a central force in the social production of 'visibility', and (2) it underlines the cardinal role of the discipline-professions as social practices which create and maintain 'division' through 'visibilization' techniques.

References

Bové, P.A., (1988) *Intellectuals in Power: a Genealogy of Critical Humanism*, New York: Columbia University Press.

Derrida, J., (1981) *Positions*, Chicago: University of Chicago Press.

Febvre, L., (1982) *The Problem of Unbelief in the Sixteenth Century*, Cambridge: Harvard University Press.

Foucault, M., (1973) *The Birth of the Clinic*, London: Tavistock.

Foucault, M., (1977) *Discipline and Punish*, London: Allen Lane.

Foucault, M., (1979) 'Governmentality', *Ideology and Consciousness*, 6:5.

Foucault, M., (1980) *Power/Knowledge*, Brighton: Harvester.

Frug, G.E., (1984) 'The ideology of bureaucracy in American law', *Harvard Law Review*, 97:1276.

Giddens, A., (1985) *The Nation-State and Violence*, Cambridge: Polity Press.

Goldstein, J., (1984) 'Foucault among the sociologists: the "Disciplines" and the history of the professions', *History and Theory*, 23:170.

Hoskin, K.W. and Macve, R.H., (1986) 'Accounting and the examination: a genealogy of disciplinary power', *Accounting, Organizations and Society*, 11:105.

Miller, J.-A., (1987) 'Jeremy Bentham's panoptic device', *October*, 41:3.

Norris, C., (1987) *Derrida*, London: Fontana/Collins.

Rorty, R., (1980) *Philosophy and the Mirror of Nature*, Oxford: Basil Blackwell.

Weinstein, D. and Weinstein, M. (1984) 'On the visual constitution of society: the contributions of Georg Simmel and Jean-Paul Sartre to a sociology of the senses', *History of European Ideas*, 5:349.

Whitehead, A.N., (1938) *Modes of Thought*, New York: Macmillan.

First published in *Operational Research and the Social Sciences,* N.C. Jackson, T. Keys and S.A. Cropper (eds) 1989, Plenum Publishing. Reprinted with the permission of the publisher.

Gender: division or comparison?

Marilyn Strathern

If one were ever to make a list of anthropological reconstructions of feminist arguments, fairly near the top would have to come debunking the 'myth of matriarchy'. The very idea of matriarchy in 20th-century understandings—the supposition that the variety of human forms of organization are bound to provide examples opposed to patriarchy—itself derived from an older evolutionary anthropology—with its supposition that the invention of paternity changed the bases of human organization. In searching for matriarchy, Euro–Americans have searched for organizational forms shaped instead by maternity, and for systems where women have been dominant and have wielded power. Anthropologists have for a long time now been sceptical about the power and the dominance. Comparisons between the significance of maternity and paternity, on the other hand, continue to be made. I shall dwell not on the mythical nature of the ideas about matriarchy but on certain of the gender constructions on which they are based. These are the constructions of a living and very much contemporary culture.

The culture in question I call Euro–American, to refer to the largely middle-class, North American/Northern European discourse of public and professional life. The gender constructions entail among other things a supposition about addition or augmentation. There is a sense in which masculinity or femininity can be construed as a matter of degree, to be gauged from a multiplicity of attributes. Thus a person can display 'more' or 'less' masculinity, or a type of social organization can be 'more' or 'less' influenced by feminine principles. This may be accompanied by an interpretation of identity that presupposes some kind of unity between elements, so that all the bits will 'add up' to a whole. As a consequence, heterogeneous elements will seem contradictory and have to be explained. Hence early and mid-twentieth-century anthropologists had to explain how a rule of group organization that traced descent through women (matriliny) could co-exist with rules of residence that meant a woman moved to her husband's village at marriage.

A principal anthropological example came from the matrilineal Trobriand Islands in Melanesia. The point was that such a hetero-geneous combination of apparently 'male' and 'female' principles of organization seemed counter-intuitive to the Euro–American anthropologist. It was much easier to understand systems where tracing group ties through men (as in patrilineal descent) matched a local organization based on women joining their husbands at mar-riage (patri- or virilocality) and the exercise of power in male hands. Arrangements augmenting the importance of one sex at the expense of the other—men as ancestors, fathers, leaders and so forth—seemed self-evident. One is a man by doing masculine things and acting in a male way with men's interests at heart. How 'com-pletely' male, or female, this or that person or organization is will depend on how everything adds up. The augmentation or exaggera-tion of gender attributes is no problem in this view; on the contrary it is evidence of an unambiguous identity. What become problem-atic are borrowings between or cross-overs from gendered attrib-utes otherwise conceptualized as distinct. Hence, for some anthropologists, a social system based on matrilineal descent and virilocal marriage seemed to be based on contradictory elements.

I raise the question of the addition or augmentation of identity in order to comment on certain consequences that recent debate over the new reproductive technologies hold out for Euro–American dis-course on gender. Rather than beginning with these concrete and probably now familiar examples, however, I begin in a less familiar place, and in an unfamiliar way. The point is that I wish to set the scene by reference to other cultural materials, and in doing so to pursue the role that *comparison* plays in such Euro–American dis-course. Comparison is central to feminist practice. In offering a critical commentary on some of the ways it is deployed, I wish to render unfamiliar the question of how it is that 'male' and 'female' attributes come to be compared at all.

The Euro–American question of 'how much' masculinity or femi-ninity can be recognized depends in part on the degree of difference between male and female, and difference is made manifest in com-parison. Divergent attributes become significant in respect of some continuum or quality otherwise held in common. The result is that each sex may be judged relative to the other, as in the case of mod-els of matriarchy. Here the male exercise of (formal) power becomes the common measure by which male and female dominance are compared. And I stress comparison rather than division in order to reserve the term *division* for a different mode of conceptualizing gender difference altogether. This introduces into the chapter a certain division of material.

The field of gender relations from which I draw concerns parenthood; the reader will note that I make a division here between two modes of gender differentiation and proceed to compare them. These two modes themselves comprise 'division' and 'comparison'. They are elucidated (compared) through different cultural materials. I would add that the divisions and comparisons I offer are in fact trivial by contrast with the conundrums these materials pose. The presentation thus remains true to a certain brand of empiricism: making the data so presented apparently outrun the theoretical effort to comprehend it.

Division

In general parlance, division segments what already exists as a whole; thus arithmetic division presupposes a number to be partitioned. The 'division of labour' understood as a single manufacturing or production process divided into separately organized components exemplifies such partition. Indeed, 20th-century Euro–Americans have no trouble in recognizing the divisibility of work processes. But gender? There are certain situations where what goes for number can also go for gender. Thus Mimica (1988) describes a Melanesian people whose counting system is based simultaneously on divisions of the human body and the division of an original androgynous cosmos into male and female elements (also see McKinnon, 1991). It is the androgyny that is taken for granted. Indeed for Melanesia in general, I would argue, insofar as people there seem to gender values, institutions and the acts of persons, their discourse suggests the sexes have to work to divide themselves off from each other. They present persons as though they were socially composite, and divisible, entities. A singular (undivided) gender identity is seen to be created only through the active shedding of 'the other' (cross-sex) component. Unitary or singular (same sex) identity is thus in a sense always incomplete. By the same token, this is also an active or generative condition. What, in these formulations, completes a person is not 'more' same-sex attributes but their cross-sex complements.

Consider the Trobriands. Mosko (1995) argues that the way in which matrilineal Trobriand Islanders vest political leadership in men and emphasize residence at the husband's village draws on an explicit metaphor of paternity.[1] Trobriand fathers are nurturers of their children as husbands are of their wives, and village headmen and chiefs are cast into the nurturant role of 'fathers'. The point is that this fatherhood requires a man being able to divide his activities as 'father' from those he performs as a male member of his matrilineage. The stringent avoidance between the Trobriand brother and sister in all matters to do with sex and marriage emphatically separates these facets of a man's activities from those he has vested in his sister. As 'father' he is sexual partner to his wife and fathers her children; this constitutes his paternity. As a male member of his matrilineage he has rights and duties towards his sister's children; in this sense he is a 'male mother' (to use an African idiom) and this we may say constitutes his maternity. If a man thus divides his paternity from his maternity, a woman divides her maternity (as a matrilineage 'mother' and future ancestress, she bears children for her brother) from her paternity (as 'female father', to continue the idiom, towards the children whom her brother fathers). Each orientation complements the other.

What is true of the Trobriand person is also true of the way the lineage group claims a single gender identity through division. It emerges in its most unitary form on the occasion of a death (Weiner, 1976). During the mortuary ceremonies, the deceased's matrilineage finally pays off all the debts that the lineage member accumulated in life. Above all these are debts to the lineage of the person's father and spouse for nurture given. The food and assistance that made 'body' of the deceased is thereby sent back to whence it came. The paternally, and conjugally, derived parts of a person become separated from the maternally derived parts (cf. Battaglia, 1990), and the deceased person is reclaimed as pure matrilineal spirit. In life, however, nurture always takes place across lineages, one feeding another (cf. Foster, 1990; Wagner, 1986), and it is in their role as 'fathers' that men are most active in political and economic activities, conducting exchanges with partners, and engaging in sexual activity. The same is true of women as 'spouses'. Paternal and conjugal activity thus gives body to matrilineal spirit, and the living person is imagined as a composite (androgynous) being. What becomes exaggerated in such a system is the practice of division as such—not adding together everything that makes up a group or a person, but instead repeating, and thus duplicating the division of female from male members, maternity from paternity. Difference is made manifest in division. However, differentiations are not cumulative; rather the 'same' division (between male and female) is repeated over and again through different phenomena and in different contexts.

Such gendering is no less true of those systems in Melanesia that appear to be founded on consistent, homogeneous principles, namely, those patrilineal, patrilocal, male-dominated societies of interior Papua New Guinea where ideologies of power and gender seem by contrast to present a unifying picture. I would argue, following Mosko, that in these systems also each assertion of the male ethos depends on a fresh division of a composite identity into male and female components. Godelier's (1986) account of the patrilineal Baruya (cf. Strathern, 1992: ch. 7, 1991a) is a case in point.

The initiation rituals which preoccupy so much of Baruya male life are predicated on the necessity to partition men from women, sons from mothers, semen from milk, one kind of semen from another kind of semen, and so forth. Men in effect divide themselves off from other parts of themselves so that it is out of a composite that a 'man' momentarily creates a singular gender identity. In the case of semen, what is divided is regarded as a finite stock or reservoir of substance (each transmission of semen to nourish boys or to inseminate wives depletes the Baruya stock and has to be replenished). There is so to speak only 'one' amount of semen, as semen is the only 'one' source from which all persons are made (cf. Gillison, 1987), that source being divided into male (semen) and female (milk) versions. The difference between male and female is thus the outcome of partition. So at initiation boys are separated from their mothers and secluded with their fathers, while girls are separated from their fathers and secluded with their mothers. Repetition does not augment gender so to speak—a man is not made 'more' a man or a woman 'more' a woman thereby. Rather, each division creates again the separation of a man from female parts of himself, a woman from her male parts.

Duplication

Gender through division would seem to be one of the processes entertained in two tales interpreted by Houseman(1988) for Samo and Beti, West African societies 'patrilineal' in kin reckoning. (They are also preoccupied as we shall see with generational difference through division.) Here people are talking out loud, so to speak, about the possibilities of duplication. It is not too fanciful to read both stories as turning on the same question: if a man had two penises would this double his generative power?

In Euro–American we might put the question: would a man with more than the usual number of organs be 'more' of a man? I start with the Beti version. A Beti father cannot transmit his patrilineal identity unless he has sons borne to him (by other men's daughters); however he always has the possibility of persuading the man married to his own daughter to give up 'jural' fatherhood and remain attached to his household simply as a 'physical' father who would provide future generations for his own (the father-in-law's) patriline.[2]

> Once there was a big chief who had lots of wives and riches but no sons, only a single very beautiful daughter, whom he loved very much. Not wanting her to marry, he decreed that he would only give her to a man having two penises. Many suitors arrived— important men, white men—but all in vain: the girls would not give in; the father refused. Then an impoverished young man decided to try his luck. Going to the girl's father he announced: 'Here. I am just made that way. I have two penises.' The chief is astonished and decides to give him to his daughter. Festivities are organized, and that evening, the girl prepares herself for having sexual intercourse with a man for the first time in her life. She is very happy as the other women have told her that it is very good. She draws her future husband into her room and lays down naked beside him. But he just goes to sleep! The girl gets angry. The young man explains: 'My father gave me this recommendation: "Because you have two penises, never ever make love at the girl's home." ' 'All right,' says the girl, 'let's go to your place.' They get up and begin walking in the middle of the night. The girl walks in front. All of a sudden, in the midst of their journey, the young man begins to wail. 'What's the matter?' asks the girl. 'Alas, I've lost one of my penises' he answers. Retracing their steps, they search in the darkness in vain; they cry and wail. [Back at the girl's village] the girl tells this suspicious story to her father. 'Father, did you check?' she asks him. 'Bah!' he answers. 'If he lost it, it's not his fault; he still has one penis left and I am going to marry you [to him] anyway. (Houseman 1988:661)

A man without sons tries to turn his daughter into an heir; in this condition, as Houseman explains, the son-in-law cannot represent his own patriline, and his children would be assimilated to his wife's.[3] Unfortunately, the doubling of the organ on which the father-in-law insists renders the suitor impotent, until, that is, he acts on advice *his* father gave which causes him to 'lose' one of the two. He becomes a father through triple partitioning.

First, the son (the father-to-be) abandons one of the organs in the context of another kind of doubling, between himself and his own father. He cannot be his own father, as the two organs might suggest, and is restored to potent singularity when he acknowledges the distinct existence of his senior parent (the point at which he recalls his father's admonitions). An appropriate duplication of persons (father and son) substitutes for the inappropriate attachment of both organs to one man. Second, the same duplication of persons also substitutes for the inappropriate duplication of another pair of persons. If the Beti hero could not be a father himself till he had divided his potentiality between two persons, the appropriate persons are son and father, not son-in-law and father-in-law.[4] I would suggest that the father-in-law was trying to keep both his maternal and paternal identity—both giving his daughter in marriage and endowing the son-in-law with 'his' own extra organ. Third, then, the Beti son, in separating off the superfluous organ also creates the difference between two types of fathers, the men who will be father's father and mother's father to his children. Only once that separation is done has he the potential to be a father himself. In Houseman's terms this is as a jural and physical father who can transmit property to his sons (he is 'completed' by the cross-generational parent). In terms of the gender constructs I have been discussing, the man's potential to be a father is also realized in his ability to have intercourse with his wife (he is 'completed' by the cross-sex partner).

The Samo story about two organs also gives a man an unlikely double endowment, but does so against the background of women's constitutional doubling. The patrilineal Samo hold that each generation of persons is replenished by an infusion of blood (cf. Héritier-Augé, 1989). Blood is constituted through semen (semen turns into blood inside a woman's body, so much of a child's maternal blood is the husband's semen transformed; a woman's own blood comes from her father). But while the transmission of paternal substance (blood/semen) can be thought of as continuous over the generations, the maternal contribution to procreation creates discontinuities. Indeed, maternity is obliterated at each generation, for a woman passes on only part of her father's blood: she cannot transmit her mother's. The principal blood she transmits is that which she makes from her husband's substance. Women are thus vessels for the transmission of male blood. The importance of shedding the 'female line' is brought out in the Samo story that Houseman (1988:665) quotes:

> One day, a man, who already had a first wife, decided to marry again. . . . While the first and second wives were spinning cotton together, the first said to the second, 'I am very happy that you have come to join us, but I must warn you about one of our husband's peculiarities.' 'What might that be?' asked the second wife. 'He has two penises,' the first wife answered. 'Consequently,' she continues, 'when he comes to make love to you, be sure to grab hold of one of them, for if both enter at the same time, it is very painful.' The second wife listened to what the first wife told her. When, that night, the husband came to make love to the second wife, the latter grabbed hold of his penis. The man jumped back in surprise. He approached her again; the same thing happened. The same thing went on until dawn, at which time the second wife ran away to return to her home. Upon arriving, she learned that her mother had just died. Soon after, her husband arrived looking for her [saying] ' . . . If you do not explain everything to me, it is not only your mother who will be buried today, but you as well, and in the same tomb.' The second wife was afraid, and recounted everything the first wife had told her. When the husband heard this he said, 'I understand,' for the first wife had told him that the second wife was a penis snatcher, the reason for which he jumped away whenever she grabbed his penis.

The woman who imagines that her husband has two penises has a (same-generational) double in a co-wife. But she is only able to consort with him when she realizes that after all he has only one organ for her. That realization occurs, in this story, after her (cross-generational) mother dies.

It is the Samo woman who has to differentiate between her father/husband, for she cannot reproduce via both of them (be both herself and her mother). That differentiation is brought home, I surmise, through the mother's death. With the removal of the mother comes the removal of the person who once worked transformatively on the father's blood; the heroine comes to her husband constituted through blood whose paternal source alone is evident. Over the generations, blood is thus constantly divided, as daughter is divided from mother. In the separation of daughter from mother, the daughter (the 'wife' in the story) in effect partitions herself: her own future pregnancy will allocate the blood within her to its sources in two men (father and husband), and as a 'mother' she will above all transmit (her) husband's paternal blood.

Now the Beti son-in-law shedding his extra organ by invoking (an admonition from) his own father suggests a parallel to the Samo woman discovering her husband's single penis after her mother dies. Houseman dwells on the fact that the former story stresses a connection with the senior parent (father–son continuity), and the latter an opposition (mother–daughter discontinuity). He finds paradoxical the opposition of motherhood to itself, and takes this referencing as evidence of a role that is indeterminate or uncertain (1988:666). Motherhood in Samo, he argues, has to be proved as, for very different reasons, fatherhood does in Beti.[5] Thus the Samo asymmetry between motherhood and fatherhood rests on the indeterminacy of motherhood (it has to be proved through parturition); at the same time, he argues, the need to overcome this indeterminacy formally subordinates the father to the mother. To the degree that motherhood is doubly established, through the reference to the other mothering figure, Houseman takes the Samo mother as the superior figure in a hierarchical relationship. I would add that we can also read the differentiations as division: in that case, what is being duplicated over and again is the need to divide one organ (the Beti penis) from another, one substance (Samo blood) from another and (in both cases) one parent from another.

The gender of persons is an apposite framework for analysis insofar as both stories turn on the proposition that attributes such as the generative power of the male organ or of female substance are in human relationships properly distributed between (divided between) persons. Thus the male organ is only double in its generative capacity when it is attached to a human double, that is, distributed between two different women (Samo) or belongs to the persons of two different fathers (Beti). And in the same way as Samo blood is only procreative when a woman obliterates her mother's contribution, so the Beti father-in-law can only bestow a procreative daughter on a man who has an exclusively (singular) paternal organ: maternity properly comes from the daughter and was quite improperly pre-fixed in the man's second penis. Male and female attributes, then, are duplicated or divided in differences between persons: it is persons who differentiate the effectiveness of particular organs and substances.

Comparison

In all four cases, those considered in the section on division and those considered in the stories of duplication, one kind of parent is being defined by reference to another. For Baruya we may say that semen and breast milk are analogous to each other as male and female versions of the nutritive/generative substance from which human beings are created. At the same time both can appear in a single encompassing manifestation, semen, that also stands for them both, since it is semen that takes either a male or female form (as semen, as milk).[6] Following Houseman's argument for the Beti one could say that semen is thus defined with reference to itself—it appears in a duplicated form like the double Beti father—whereas milk is not. (Milk, maternal semen, is not passed on but shed afresh each generation.) But there are two forms of gender duplication in these constructions. First, 'one' entity may be divided into two same-sex versions of itself, as Beti fathers are divided into senior and junior manifestations of fatherhood; here the same-sex link is also a cross-generational one. Second, in a cross-sex mode one (same-generational) entity is divided into differently gendered versions of itself, as fatherhood is divided into 'fatherhood' and 'motherhood'.

In colloquial English (Euro–American), however, this is exactly what we would *not* say. We would recognize the first gender duplication as a kind of augmentation (fatherhood vindicated by fatherhood). But the second? Here we would have to say that 'parenthood' is divided into motherhood and fatherhood. English-speakers would reconcile the apparently contradictory elements by appeal to a superior class taken to be a different order of phenomenon from the elements it thereby unifies.

To discover the class to which things belong, items that already appear different in kind, as the sexes do, can be compared by virtue of what is common between them, eg, being 'human'. That commonality gives a measure of what they share, whether it is literally imagined as a higher-order class or as the common denominator on which difference is built. What is similar is taken as belonging to the class, and what is different as the distinctive and pre-existing identity of the individual components. I have elaborated elsewhere (1991b) and in another context of Euro–American thought, namely in the relationship between individual and society, the way an overarching entity, as 'society' is imagined, appears to be of a different order from the individuals that Euro–Americans say 'make it up' (so where Melanesian constructs appear to divide persons from persons, Euro–Americans try to see how they can bring individuals together in society). Distinctiveness can thus be imagined as deviation from what is held in common, and it becomes feasible to contemplate *degrees* of distinctiveness. One can in Euro–American ask, by reference to features connoting masculinity or femininity, how 'male' is this man, how 'female' is this woman—that is, how differentiated are they not only from each other but from what they otherwise have in common. This leads to normative possibilities, for instance that 'men' do some things more appropriately, 'women' other things. As a result, one sex may be modelled on the other as providing the 'best example' of this or that attribute.

The abstract possibility of a common measure against which comparison proceeds is part of what makes Euro–Americans imagine equality between the sexes. In the Melanesian and West African cases I have referred to, equality in the Enlightenment sense is simply not an issue. One gender may be taken either as the analogue to the other or else as encompassing it, as a male may appear in female form or female in male form.[7] It is thus as a *father* that a male Trobriand Islander is 'like' a mother; in no way equal, the claims of fathers in mortuary ceremonies are very different from those of mothers, as they make quite distinct contributions in the person's lifetime. It is the claims to distinctiveness that are analogous. By contrast, when Euro–Americans champion equality they often try to submerge difference. So Euro–Americans might argue that a father is like a mother in being *a parent*; in the same way as a woman is like a man in being *human*.[8]

The Euro–American notions of 'parent' or 'human being' provide a common measure across the gender classes, mother/father and man/woman. If within each class the measure is that of divergence (how much of a female, ie, not a male, is this particular woman?), between the classes the measure is what they have in common (who is 'more' a parent than the other, a mother or a father?). I say this on grounds of social practice. It has become accepted in recent years, for instance, that litigants in custody disputes may appeal to evidence about which parent has been 'more' of a parent to the child(ren) than the other. The claims of mothers and fathers are adjudicated on the grounds of comparison. In cases of assisted conception adjudications may turn further on which of two mothers (or fathers) is the 'real' (more of) mother (or father).

Analogies

It is to late-20th-century Euro–American social practices that I now turn. As elsewhere the sexes are opposed and contrasted, their attributes seemingly divided off from one another; however, I wish to pursue the extent to which such differences draw not on the kind of division found in the Melanesian and West African cases but on a form of analogy that I have been calling comparison. Examples derive from the field of recent Euro–American debates over the social implications of new reproductive technology.[9]

First: a piece of speculation. This comes from a columnist (Ellen Goodman, *Albuquerque Journal*, 6 November 1990, paragraphs elided; my emphases) syndicated in the American press.

BOSTON—Not long ago, after a midnight session with a male friend who was considering fatherhood at 50, I decided that middle-aged men suffer from a distinct biological disadvantage. They don't go through menopause. This was a fairly quirky, contrary point of view. . . . It is more often women who resent the biological clock ticking loudly over their leisurely plans. If anything, the female fertility deadline seems positively un-American, unfair. We are, after all, citizens of a country that believes in endless choices and unlimited options. Moreover, this biological destiny seems like a remnant of inequality: *If men can have babies in their seventies, why not women?* Still, it seemed to me that the biological clock was a useful warning system about the life cycle. It was a way of saying that life changes and time runs out . . .

Now it appears that the biological alarm has been turned down. We are reading headlines that would have confounded our grandmothers: 'Menopause Found No Barrier to Pregnancy'. Doctors have discovered a way to beat the clock. . . . The promise is that women can keep their biological door open, at least with the help of a stranger. The problem is that it also prevents closure. . . . When you remove nature from the equation, there is a whole new set of calculations to be made. They bear, not surprisingly, a strong resemblance to the ones that men have faced. . . . The issues become energy, and age gaps, and the real midnight on the biological clock: mortality. One infertility counsellor who heard about this 'breakthrough' asked out loud, 'When do you say, enough is enough?' The female body once said it for us. *Now women, like men,* will have to use much less predictable organs: the heart and the brain.

Here what women can do is compared to what men can do, but with reference to what? The reference point is the potential of the human body as a gender-free category, manifest in the biological clock that both share despite their different experience of it. Now perhaps they will be able to experience it in similar ways! The other idea is that it is possible to add to or supplement natural endowment by new techniques. In this case the extension of a woman's reproductive clock can be taken in one of two ways—it may make her 'more' a woman, that is, augment her capacity to experience motherhood for a longer period in her life; or it may make her 'more' like a man, that is, bring the comparison closer, for men can in any case conceive a child till well into old age.

Second: a commentary in the popular British press (*Sunday Express*, 10 January 1993, paragraphs elided) which sets out the same comparison with further explicitness. The context was the possibility of harvesting ovaries from (aborted) foetuses, which would enable not just otherwise infertile women but women past the menopause to have children. The spokesman is from King's College Hospital, London:

> The female menopause in humans is one of nature's design faults.
> In all other animal species, the menopause occurs very close to
> the time of death. Only in humans do you have the female having
> this relatively premature menopause and spending about a third
> of their lives in a hormone-deficient state.

And to underline the comparison with the rest of the animal kingdom:

> Men are far better designed when it comes to fertility and
> hormones.

The gentleman clearly thinks he is on the side of women, for he adds: 'The menopause is profoundly sexist. It is one colossal bit of biological sabotage on women'.[10] Again, this view simultaneously affirms about women what appears most feminine (*viz.* the capacity to bear children) and offers an unfavourable comparison with men (women do not enjoy men's prolonged fertility).

Third: a comparison that presupposes rights to act on or claims to press. In 1990, a solicitor wrote to the London *Times* in the following vein: 'Parliament appears to be proposing to perpetuate a definition of motherhood which flies in the face of present genetic knowledge' (cited by Morgan and Lee, 1991:154). The Human Fertilisation and Embryology Act going through Parliament that year contained what he claimed was an anomaly with respect to surrogacy arrangements. An amendment (Section 30) had been introduced to bypass the cumbersome procedure of insisting that commissioning parents adopt their child.[11] The solicitor was moved to write on behalf of a client who had been required to fulfil the legal criteria for adoption. Of the two parents, the mother was at a disadvantage in a way the father was not, for already existing conventions concerning illegitimacy recognized the genetic claims of paternity.

> My client, the genetic mother, would appear to have no legal rights whatsoever in her own children. On the contrary, her husband, the genetic father, would have the right to apply under the guardianship legislation to have himself recognized as the father of illegitimate children and no doubt, custody, if he required; a truly anomalous situation in these days of the equality of the sexes. *Surely genetic mothers, at the very least, should be accorded the same rights and privileges as genetic fathers.* (D.B. Forrest, *The Times*, 28 February, 1990, cited in Morgan and Lee, 1991:153–4; my emphasis)

In appealing to equality, he states the common ground: a genetic mother ought to be accorded the same rights as the genetic father. We might note that the law is to be persuaded by an appeal to what is already the case. On the grounds of the pre-existing convention that the genetic father of an illegitimate child can already have his paternity recognized in law it is proposed that the 'same' right should be extended to the mother. An alternative option could be to suspend all genetic claims; were neither to press claims on the grounds of genetic relationship, equality, if little else, would be as well served. Instead, the father's pre-existing claims appear as an exemplar for how to consider the mother's. So what starts out as a comparison by appeal to a common measure—mother and father are equally genetic parents—ends up with a comparison that wishes to bring mothers' rights in line with the kinds of rights that fathers presently claim. The father's position is presented as a norm from which (through social inequality) the mother's deviates. The maleness of the common standard becomes explicit.

Fourth: the gender of gametes. This last example comes from the work of Haimes (1993) on gamete donation. Differences between gametes lead to evaluations, and Haimes makes a direct connection between comparison and gender stereotyping (for an American case, cf. Martin, 1991). As in the previous example, debate is based both on the possibility of equality *and* on striving towards an always incomplete equality by assimilating female claims to male ones.

What began Haimes's investigation was the claim that egg donation is the 'female equivalent' to semen donation. Thus the 1984 Warnock Report:

> It is both logical and consistent that the law should treat egg
> donation in the same way a AID [DI]. (Warnock, 1985:36)

An analogy is thus sustained with regard to the desirability that the law treat both equally. But why should the mother's contribution be modelled on the father's? Here too one might imagine an alternative: to think of the transaction not as a donation but as the rendering of services. However, although women have been known to 'help' one another in such matters, the law at least in recent years (see Smart, 1987:101), never recognized an illegitimate mother (the natural mother was the mother). There was no construction in place as a model for adjudicating claims between different types of mothers. Instead, semen donation provided the model for thinking about egg donation, and the act of 'donation' was thereby created as the common measure between male and female procreative assistance. With this common measure in place, people have a ground for considering all the features that also make the acts different. Comparisons abound.

Since semen donation was already tolerated, there could be no objection to donation as such; however, in her discussions with members of the Warnock Committee, Haimes found that many had disliked the idea of it, both as a sexual practice on the male donor's part and from the point of view of the donor as a third party. The idea of egg donation was more palatable. Indeed, egg donation could be assimilated to presumptions about other aspects of women's mothering roles—altruism, concern for others, passivity, liability to exploitation. As in the discussion of menopausal pregnancy, the comparison between semen and egg donation both affirmed the femininity of women (the female act was compatible with other female acts, and augmented them) and simultaneously offered men's acts as a model for them (the female donation approximated to the male one).

While for the subjects of Haimes's study semen donation had on balance negative (assertive) overtones, egg donation had positive (passive) ones. Arguments in favour of anonymity for semen donors included the desire to protect the recipient couple from 'the invasion of the third party into the family' (Warnock, 1985:25), whereas in the case of egg donors, reference was made to their potential closeness (cf. Price, 1989:46–7); it was conceivable that they might be related (as sisters say). In the eyes of some, the motives of either men or women might be equally suspect; however, their pathology was then differently constructed:

> male concerns in reproduction were presumed to revolve around ideas of virility, genetic continuity and generally being assertive and in control. Female concerns were presumed to revolve around the need to become a mother which led to a form of pathological assertiveness when otherwise the woman's role was characterized by passivity. (Haimes, 1993:87)

The mother's assertiveness is thus compared with the father's.[12] Semen donation evoked a sense of unregulatable excess, fears of men siring too many children. Egg donation was regarded as more benign, an intervention that could be monitored. In that the male act carried resonances of an unregulated 'nature', the female act evoked the kind of potential that technology could domesticate to social ends.

Haimes relates these several differences to a familial ideology concerned to protect the family's boundaries. I would underline the mode of comparison. When a baseline provides a common point of reference, either sex may seem closer to the norm. Divergence is also implied. For instance by comparison with the (natural) process of conception through sexual intercourse, semen donation was formerly regarded as 'unnatural'; the complex arrangements that nowadays attend egg donation have since made semen donation appear as a relatively simple, 'natural' matter. In these discussions, and whether negatively or positively, the already acknowledged donation of semen appears as the principal discursive reference point for thinking about the new and complex processes of ovum extraction as another type of donation.

Duplication or fragmentation?

Between these many examples lie my own divisions and comparisons, including the way I have considered both 'division' and 'comparison'. The exposition is intended to exemplify certain Euro–American approaches to gender difference, both anthropological and feminist. The observer may augment the perception of differentiation, adding up everything that seems to be germane, comparing one arena with another, or may instead shed some differences in an attempt to reduce manifold differentiations to the one that appears analytically potent. These two modes were evident in the old gender arguments about matriarchy to which I referred at the beginning. On the one hand, questions about the power of women could be answered in terms of the numbers of powerful attributes or examples of influence that could be added together; on the other hand, there was an implicit comparison with the kind of authority with which men were traditionally credited, and this served as a common measure for considering degrees of women's power and authority. The same could be said of cultural difference: in this chapter I have both duplicated the cultural materials offered here (Melanesian, West African, Euro–American) and offered a single axis of differentiation (an analytical contrast between division and comparison).

The chapter has dwelt on conceptualizations of persons and their attributes. It has become an issue for the lines along which Euro–American are invited to think about the consequences of new reproductive technology, and is in this respect an issue for feminist practice. It concerns the kinds of identity to be constructed from the way persons are regarded as sharing characteristics with other persons. The sharing may be bodily (sharing genes, sharing blood) or may rest on differences or similarities in endowment or behaviour. Any critical commentary on the gender of male and female attributes needs to reflect the conceptual strategies through which cultures divide the one from the other or, for that matter, compare them.

The way in which the distribution of attributes between persons in the Melanesian/West African cases is imagined as the duplication of 'one' already existing entity (such as an organ or a substance) seems to be echoed in apparent duplications afforded by present Euro–American techniques of assisted conception. But what kind of comparison is this? Are Euro–Americans acting out the partitioning of parenthood for which the Melanesians and West Africans in my examples construct ritual or myth? When Mary Warnock says *apropos* egg donation,

> Egg donation produces for the first time circumstances in which the genetic mother (the woman who donates the egg), is a different person from the woman who gives birth to the child, the carrying mother. The law has never, till now, had to face this

problem. There are inevitably going to be instances where the
stark issue arises of who is the mother . . . (Warnock, 1985:37)

she means that what has to be compared between the two women is
the weight given to their claims of maternity. It looks like duplication. Yet what is at issue is not the doubling of two (single) figures,
but distribution of a single (biological) process between persons.
Moreover, there is no logic to them being 'two', as in a pair; rather,
'two' are only the beginnings of a potentially infinite proliferation.
Proliferation raises questions about which component will establish
the superior claim. A moral philosopher (Wolfram, 1987:200) puts
the issue plainly. English law previously recognized 'two possibilities as to who is the father of the child' whereas there was ever 'only
one possible "real" mother'. Now both motherhood, and fatherhood, as in Wolfram's juxtaposition, must be subject to the kind of
practices of verification for which fatherhood alone once stood.

The explicitness of the comparison across gender classes (mother
modelled on father) offers a measure for parenthood (the role of
gamete supplier) in the context of ambiguities raised by the addition of persons to the procreative process. The proliferation of
'mothers' does not seem to have had the effect of making motherhood a more powerful force. On the contrary, it is interesting that
far from being regarded as an augmentation of motherhood, the
new proliferation may colloquially be described as a 'fragmentation', reducing the claims of each and dispersing the bundle of
attributes that before held together as a potential whole. Writing at
the beginning of the present debates on artificial reproduction,
Snowden, Mitchell and Snowden (1983:32–5) had no compunction
about referring to 'the complete father' and 'the complete
mother'.[13] When, by contrast, all the manifold attributes that add
up to making a mother are instead divided between persons, the
presence of other mothers makes any one mother appear less than
complete. It was the traditional wholeness and hence indissolubility
of the mother–child bond that appears to have been the principal
sticking point in the Warnock Committee's treatment of surrogacy
(after Cannell, 1990:673). While the HFE Act did find itself able to
make a decision on the rights of 'gamete-donors' in the case of a
baby being carried by another woman (Section 30) [see above], it
was all but silent on the practice of surrogacy itself.

The debate surrounding surrogacy at the time of the Act introduced a new measure for comparing mothers with mothers: who
is 'more' of a mother could be settled partly by reference to the

standard expectation that 'real' mothers are 'good' mothers. If the surrogate introduces the idea that there can be two kinds of carrying mothers (the 'natural' and the surrogate), public opinion would add that there can be two kinds of surrogates. Fenella Cannell describes how the press dwelled on the difference between the good and the bad. Surrogates were positively valued in the context of creating a child as an act of love or altruism for childless women; negatively when they were seen as prostituting maternity for money. In fact, the bad surrogate was compared with the unscrupulous semen donor; both exploit innate capacities for personal ends (however obscure), whereas the good surrogate/donor acts out of compassion for others. However, if the good surrogate augments some of the qualities of maternity by her selfless act, on the evidence of public opinion at the time it would seem that the bad surrogate mother is 'worse' than the bad semen donor. She offends against nature where he is simply being irresponsible.

So whereas egg donation is regarded as relatively benign by comparison with some of the apprehensiveness surrounding semen donation, when semen donation becomes the measure for maternal surrogacy the values are reversed. Indeed, in respect to modern European views in general, Giulia Sissa (1989:133) is able to assert that donor insemination 'is considered perfectly acceptable social practice, whereas the notion of a surrogate mother is often found distressing and shocking'. The single male act thus provides a double comparative measure: semen donation affords a reference point for *both* egg donation and maternal surrogacy.

Rather like the duplication of organs and substances in the West African stories, gamete donation and surrogacy arrangements provide limiting cases for the kinds of comparisons through which Euro–Americans think about degrees of motherhood or fatherhood. But the limits depicted in these accounts speak to different cultural practices of differentiation. Although I have confined my observations to what in turn has been a limited, and in some cases rather eccentric, range of material, there will be many other contexts to which they can apply. At any rate, my own argument tries to practice what it preaches. Thus the chapter is as much organized through the division and comparison of materials as it is about such organization. I hope that this might stand for a larger intention of the chapter as a whole. Among the many traditions that feed into feminist practice, de-familiarization is crucial. But one cannot de-familiarize the world all at once; one has to proceed from the side, literally from the eccentric, in order to make the most obvious of questions seem not so obvious after all. Comparing what men and women do, or comparing male and female attributes, seems a completely obvious procedure. By giving a certain weighting to a contrast between comparison and division, I have tried to suggest that already built into the idea of comparison are the very ideas about the construction of divisions, such as that of gender, that lead Euro–Americans back to their familiar questions.

Acknowledgement

I take my cue from the rubric of a Swansea seminar series: 'Gender Divisions: Subordination, Difference and Power', and appreciate the comments of the Swansea Department of Sociology and Anthropology. Andy Holding's (University of Manchester) pursuit of anthropological constructions of similarity and difference have been influential here. Parts of this chapter come from a lecture to the Society for the Anthropology of Europe, Chicago, 1991, and I thank Michael Herzfeld and Jane Schneider for the commentaries at the time. I am also grateful to Jane Schneider for a longer review. A specific inspiration for its argument was Houseman's paper, which is why I dwell on the Samo and Beti cases, although I turn his analysis to my own ends.

Notes

1 See also Mosko (1992), and for elsewhere on the Massim, Damon (1983).
2 Houseman is concerned with a relationship between 'jural' and 'physical' parenthood that I do not address here.
3 The Beti woman's situation is different: she may be regarded as the mother of children whether or not she bears them, for it is through marriage that she becomes mother to her own or (if 'childless') to other women's children. Maternity is created by marriage and does not have to be further proved. However, marriage seems to pose some problems for the ethnographer. It does not seem to him a sufficient basis for parenthood, and Houseman interprets motherhood as part of a larger parenting role evident in the figure of the father. In Houseman's view, Beti fatherhood is defined with reference to prior fatherhood and this renders the father an indeterminate figure *vis-à-vis* the mother (in this interpretation, 'father' cannot stand by himself as a single figure but requires emphasis in order to be effective).
4 Houseman's preference is to analyse this as the invocation of jural status: he argues that the man becomes a father in his own right by virtue of his jural identity as a patriline member.
5 Samo fatherhood is, by contrast, in his argument, unproblematic: a Samo man is virtually a father by the fact of his own birth—provided he is married, children

borne by his wife are credited to his (patri) lineage, and he does not have to prove physical paternity. However, while even a childless man will have someone to perform sacrifice (and thus recognize him) after death, a childless woman in Samo is divested of personhood. She can only be a jural mother through physically giving birth.

6 The Baruya ethnography indicates semen as the substance that is divided over and again into different versions of itself; as milk it does not have the same 'divisibility' (milk is not encompassing in the same manner as semen is).

7 Melanesian representations of androgynous, composite entities invariably cast them into a male or female form (thus the Mountain Ok ancestress Afek is an androgynous mother; the Iqwaye ancestor Omalcye is an androgynous father).

8 'Parent' and 'human' appear to be gender-free terms. It is an established point of feminist critique that the unmarked term, the standard, is likely to be based on specifically 'male' values.

9 Two briefly: the second two, given at more length, have been deployed in another context (Strathern, 1991c).

10 The view is one in the long line already documented by Emily Martin (1987) which sees the postmenopausal body with aversion.

11 The fact that the gametes (egg, sperm) of the commissioning parents had contributed to the child would be sufficient grounds on which they could be treated as its parents in law. The particular case that the solicitor pressed led to a further amendment to allow a retrospective application of this ruling to already existing surrogacy arrangements.

12 Haimes is here referring to reports of commissions in 1948 and 1960 which preceded the Warnock Committee. She also notes that the whole context of sperm donation was, in these two earlier reports, associated with ideas of inappropriate sexuality: adultery, masturbation and illegitimacy. By contrast, the woman's receipt of the donation is regarded as a passive act, essentially asexual in that no activity is required of the woman.

13 In their formulations, the former combines genetic and nurturing roles, the latter genetic, carrying and nurturing roles (1983:34).

References

Battaglia, D., (1990) *On the Bones of the Serpent: Person, Memory and Mortality in Sabarl Island Society*, Chicago: University of Chicago Press.

Cannell, F., (1990) 'Concepts of parenthood: The Warnock Report, the Gillick debate, and modern myths', *American Ethnologist*, 17:667–86.

Damon, F.H., (1983) 'Muyuw kinship and the metamorphosis of gender labour', *Man* (n.s.) 18:305–26.

Foster, R., (1990) 'Nurture and force-feeding: mortuary feasting and the construction of collective individuals in a New Ireland society', *American Ethnologist*, 17:431–48.

Gillison, G., (1987) 'Incest and the atom of kinship: the role of the mother's brother in a New Guinea Highlands society', *Ethos*, 15:166–202.

Godelier, M., (1986) (trans. R. Swyer) (1982) *The making of great men. Male domination and power among the New Guinea Baruya*, Cambridge: Cambridge University Press.

Haimes, Erica, (1993) 'Issues of gender in gamete donation', *Social Science and Medicine*, 36:85–93.

Héritier-Augé, F., (1989) 'Semen and blood: some ancient theories concerning their genesis and relationship' in M. Feher (ed.) *Fragments for a History of the Human Body*, Vol. 3, New York: Zone.

Houseman, M., (1988) 'Towards a complex model of parenthood: two African tales', *American Ethnologist*, 15:658–77.

McKinnon, S., (1991) *From a Shattered Sun: Hierarchy, Gender, and Alliance in the Tanimbar Islands*, Madison: University of Wisconsin Press.

Martin, E., (1987) *The Woman in the Body. A Cultural Analysis of Reproduction*, Boston: Beacon Press.

Martin, E., (1991) 'The egg and the sperm: how science has constructed a romance based on stereotypical male–female roles', *Signs*, 16:485–501.

Mimica, J., (1988) *Intimations of Infinity: The Cultural Meanings of the Iqwaye Counting System and Number*, Oxford: Berg.

Morgan, D. and Lee, R.G., (1991) *Human Fertilisation and Embryology Act 1990: Abortion and Embryo Research, the New Law*, London: Blackstone Press Ltd.

Mosko, M., (1992), 'Motherless sons: "divine kings" and "partible persons" in Melanesia and Polynesia', *Man* (n.s.), 27:697–717.

Mosko, M., (1995) 'Rethinking Trobriand chieftainship'. *J. R. anthrop. Inst. (NS)* 1:763–85.

Price, F., (1989) 'Establishing guidelines: regulation and the clinical management of infertility' in R. Lee and D. Morgan (eds) *Birthrights: Law and Ethics at the Beginnings of Life*, London: Routledge.

Sissa, G., (1989) 'Subtle bodies' in M. Feher (ed., with Ramona Naddaff and Nadia Tazi), *Fragments for a History of the Human Body*, Vol. 3, New York: Zone.

Smart, C., (1987) ' "There is of course the distinction created by nature": law and the problem of paternity' in M. Stanworth (ed.) *Reproductive Technologies*, Cambridge: Polity Press.

Snowden, R., Mitchell, G.D. and Snowden, E., (1983) *Artificial Reproduction: A Social Investigation*, London: George Allen & Unwin.

Strathern, M., (1991a) 'One man and many men' in M. Godelier and M. Strathern (eds) *Big Men and Great Men: Personifications of Power in Melanesia*, Cambridge: Cambridge University Press.

Strathern, M., (1991b) *Partial Connections*, ASAO Special Publication 3, Savage, Maryland: Rowman & Littlefield.

Strathern, M. (1991c) 'Disparities of embodiment: gender models in the context of the new productive technologies', *Cambridge Anthropology*, 15:25–43.

Strathern, M. (1992) *Reproducing the Future: Essays on Anthropology, Kinship and the New Reproductive Technologies*, Manchester: Manchester University Press.

Wagner, R., (1977) 'Analogic kinship: a Daribi example', *American Ethnologist*, 4:623–42.

Wagner, R., (1986) *Asiwinarong: Ethos, Image, and Social Power among the Usen Barok of New Ireland*, Princeton: Princeton University Press.

Warnock, M., (1985) *A Question of Life: The [1984] Warnock Report on Human Fertilisation and Embryology*, Oxford: Basil Blackwell.

Weiner, A., (1976) *Women of Value, Men of Renown: New Perspectives in Trobriand Exchange*, Austin: University of Texas Press.

Wolfram, S., (1987) *In-laws and Outlaws. Kinship and Marriage in England*, London: Croom Helm.

First published in *Practising Feminism: Identity, Difference, Power*, N. Charles and F. Hughes-Freeland (eds) Routledge, London, 1996 Reprinted with the permission of the publisher.

In the wake of disaster: stress, hysteria and the event

Steven D. Brown

Preface

> In truth it is not enough to say, 'Long live the multiple', difficult
> enough as it is to raise that cry. No typological, lexical or even
> syntactical cleverness is enough to make it heard. The multiple
> *must be made.* (Deleuze & Guattari, 1987:6)

> We are on the edge of disaster without being able to situate it in
> the future: it is always already past, and yet we are on the edge or
> under the threat. (Blanchot, 1986:1)

One of the more contentious legacies of French theory is its marked
hostility to classical notions of 'the concept'. Whether it be
Derrida's incessant reiteration that difference is 'neither a word nor
a concept' (1982:7) or Foucault's subordination of concepts as
adjuncts to statements (1972a), poststructuralist writing exercises a
continual vigilance for the slightest hint of idealism. Yet it also displays a fascination toward exemplary uses of concepts. Derrida, for
example, writes with admiration of the 'hyperbolical audacity of
the Cartesian Cogito' (1978:56). What attracts is the force brought
to bear by a concept-in-use, the dazzling power to hold disparate
things together that emerges in its application. Indeed it is possible
to speak of concepts purely in terms of this holding power:

> The concept of a bird is found not in its genus or species but in the
> composition of its postures, colors, and songs . . . The concept is
> an incorporeal, even though it is incarnated or effectuated in
> bodies . . . It has no energy, only intensities . . . The concept
> speaks the event, not the essence or the thing . . . It is like the bird
> as event. The concept is defined by *the inseparability of a finite
> number of heterogeneous components traversed by a point of
> absolute survey at infinite speed.* (Deleuze & Guattari, 1994:20–1)

What emerges is a concern with the machinery of a concept, or rather the processual manner in which a concept enables a number of elements to be ordered in time and space. From this it follows that a concept is explored not through its logical relations or formal standing, but as a kind of machine for making elements cohere as an event.

In this chapter my own concerns are with a related group of concepts, drawn from differing historical milieus: stress, hysteria and dancing mania. I am interested in how these concepts may be positioned relative to one another, how they 'resonate rather than cohere or correspond' (Deleuze & Guattari, 1994:23). The method I use to explore these relations is to stage a series of events by way of each concept, in other words to explore the concepts *as events*, as processes of ordering. What I also hope will emerge from this method is a premonition of what the labour of division might itself mean as a yet further event.

Riverdale

In 1994 six casualty workers at a California hospital collapsed whilst attempting to revive a thirty-one year old woman dying of cervical cancer.[1] The patient was admitted complaining of chest and stomach pains. Shortly after admittance, she vomited in the emergency room. A blood sample was taken. Several staff members in attendance promptly fainted. They later complained of 'ammonia-like' fumes. The patient entered cardiac arrest and thereafter died. Measures were taken to avoid further contamination; the emergency room was sealed with suspicions of poisoning by unknown chemical agent. Surgeons in protective suits laboriously performed an autopsy. No significant source of the contamination could be located. Tests on the recovering staff likewise found no obvious abnormality.

The State Department of Health conducted their own investigation. They concluded that the medical staff had actually not been the victims of poisoning, but had instead suffered from a 'psychological stress reaction' brought about by the 'smell of death'. The reaction occurred on a collective level, engendered by the intensity of the situation, with the severe physical condition of the dying patient acting as final 'trigger' for the mass faintings. This pointed to a psychological, rather than biochemical cause for the incident, thus explaining the failure to find any trace of the mysterious chemical toxin. It also accounted for the puzzle that over thirty other staff present in the emergency room at that time remained unaffected.

This kind of explanation seems to make more sense of the Riverdale event. Psychological factors can reasonably fill in for the lack of any clear organic cause. The overwhelming pressures of emergency room work are well recorded, it is perhaps only to be expected that within the constant stream of exposed and damaged bodies there is some combination of elements that can overwhelm any individual's ability to cope.[2] If such reactions are a human given and the fundamental nature of emergency room work unchangeable, then the organizational response can only be that of 'disaster management' (see Haas & Drabek, 1970). This involves providing personal support for the afflicted and allowing adequate space for de-briefing and emotional disclosure (Taylor & Frazer, 1982). In the absence of lesions of aberrant biochemistry, it is the vicissitudes of individual psychological processes (feelings, needs, self-esteem) that become subject to treatment.

The turn to individual psychology met with resistance. One doctor began legal proceedings, suing for $6 million over what she interpreted as an accusation of 'unstable personality' and 'professional negligence'. Whatever theoretical claims can be made for the general status of vulnerability as a part of human nature, the suggestion is an anathema to the highly socialized culture of medical omnipotence. Even though it implies no personal culpability, in the medical context the psychological proves an unacceptable source for personal disaster because a 'professional' worker already practices self-examination for signs of stress, no less rigorous than those applied to detect bacterial infection. There must be, it was argued by lawyers for the doctors, something else involved:

> This report may be based on politics or ignorance, but it's not based on science. These are professional emergency room workers. They don't become hysterical because of heart attacks. (cited in Rosch, 1995:73)

A further laboratory based investigation was launched, focusing on two factors—an 'oily sheen' observed on the patient's body by eyewitnesses and mysterious crystals noted in the blood sample drawn prior to the faintings. A hypothesis was offered that the patient might have self-treated with DMSO, an industrial solvent normally used on animals but also in use as a local home remedy, applied externally to human soft-tissue injuries. Under specific combinations of oxygen and heat, a reaction could have occurred between DMSO and blood chemicals to form dimethyl sulphate, a nerve gas. Small amounts of this agent would be enough to produce the symptoms suffered by the hospital staff.

This revised poisoning hypothesis clearly differs from the stress explanation in terms of what is involved and the nature of the effects. By suggesting a causal chain of substances, resulting in an identifiable agent of the fainting, the explanation claims foundation in empirical hard evidence. Most importantly, there is the ability to make visible the missing 'something else' in the laboratory. The latter process is not, though, unique to the poisoning explanation. A mass of relevant data exists from research programmes in the 1950s which engineered the disintegration of organized behaviour under 'stressful' laboratory conditions (eg, Pronko & Leith, 1956; Funkenstein *et al.*, 1957). All of the elements involved in the stress explanation, from the distressing situation and subsequent attempts to cope, up to the sudden fainting, can be operationalized for empirical study. Indeed, it is the similarities between the two explanations that is most striking. Both posit the existence of a series of interlinked, specifiable reactions (psychological/biochemical) which may, under particular circumstances, combine in a supervenient mediating 'presence' (stress-induced fainting/nerve gas), where a previously absent 'something else' is produced at the critical moment.

What fascinates about the Riverdale event is the initial absence of direct causal agent. In this respect the two explanations heighten rather than satisfy the fixation. The chain of proximate causes worked out in each draw an outline round a plausible identity for the agent. The laboratory simulation acts more as a piece of theatre, where a particular telling of the Riverdale event is staged, culminating in the partial unmasking of the hitherto obscured protagonist. Such theatre plays upon the lure of mystery: there is a gap or puncturing in knowledge arising from the event, the narrative tells of the gradual, painstaking recovery of knowledge through the careful suturing of the gap. What compels is the dialectic whereby pure presence as the 'bubbling source of life itself, life in an uncaptured state' (Foucault, 1972a:76) tears into knowledge, only to be recovered and subjected to synthesis within a greater advance of human understanding.

Yet this is patently not what is achieved by dint of either explanation, nor in their combination. Instead of 'life itself', what is revealed is a similarity in the composition of explanations, marking a shared form of limiting discourse. There is a generalized method of appropriating the mysterious. Hence the double appearance of a multivariate causal model in either a psychological or a biochemical approach.

It is not then at the supposed heart of the event, with the fainting, that the dynamic is to be found, but rather at its edge, in the production of further discursive objects as the fainting is worked into different explanatory series. Rather than getting close to the desired moment, the effect is to carry it farther afield:

> One could say that . . . depth having been spread out became width. 'Depth' is no longer a complement . . . Events are like crystals, they become and grow only out of the edges, or on the edge. (Deleuze, 1990:9)

In a sense it is no longer causes (which elements or pathway) that are at issue, but the order of effects in which the fainting becomes enveloped (the moral standing of the medical staff, the administration of health care). The addition of explanatory series opens the event onto different judicial and managerial processes. It acts as part of the 'material dispersion' of the event,[3] including operations such as the long term treatment programme for the recovered doctors and the burial procedure of the deceased patient.[4]

Effects are subject to two general conditions. There is a question of 'divergence'. The selection of the stress or poisoning explanation will depend on how they unfold within the ensuing legal battles, or else on the degree to which they allow the incident to be comfortably located in the ongoing moral universe of the emergency room.[5] Each series is then read in terms of the way it passes across the interstice of local medical and legal practice.

There is also a question of 'conjunction'. Riverdale is enmeshed within two series. It might be asked how many others could be added, that is, what further effects can be worked out of the event. One direction might be to push even further with a psychological approach, perhaps to emphasize unconscious identifications, object relations or defensive mechanisms in play. A new series composed of dreams, fantasies and associations could appear. Alternatively, the nature of medical ritual might be examined. The fainting could be located within the context of ritual medical examination, and the further ceremony of 'decontamination'. A series drawing on the symbolic register of medical technology, the elimination of infection and the gaze of the doctor (see Atkinson, 1995).

The addition of effects, whilst not changing the fainting as an event, does act upon its cause or, rather, in making visible new proximate causes there is a shift in the ordering of bodies composing the event. If 'dreaming', 'identifying' and 'examining' bodies or 'reading' technological displays are at issue, then dreams, symbols and touches, as well as numbers and measures are entered into relation with the collapsing medical staff. By the working of small, discrete signs into series (such as the 'oily sheen' or 'strange crystals') the event is made to emit additional sense. The subsequent question of the good or bad nature of that sense merely recapitulates the aspect of divergence. Instead of returning to the heart of the event, a slide is made across its width.

Rhineland

The effects of the Black Death had not yet subsided, and the graves of millions of its victims were scarcely closed, when a strange delusion arose in Germany, which took possession of the minds of men, and, in spite of the divinity of our nature, hurried away body and soul into the magic circle of hellish superstition. It was a convulsion which in the most extraordinary manner infuriated the human frame, and excited the astonishment of contemporaries for more than two centuries, since which time it has never reappeared. It was called the dance of St. John or of St. Vitus, on account of the Bacchantic leaps by which it was characterized, and which gave to those affected, whilst performing their wild dance, and screaming with fury, all the appearance of persons possessed. It did not remain confined to particular localities, but was propagated by the sight of the sufferers, like a demoniacal epidemic, over the whole of Germany and the neighbouring countries to the north-west. They formed circles hand in hand, and appearing to have lost all control over their senses, continued dancing, regardless of bystanders, for hours together in wild delirium. (Hecker, 1888 cited in Vermorel & Vermorel, 1989:120)

Whether it sprang from misery or homelessness caused by the heavy spring floods of the Rhine that year, or whether it was the spontaneous symptom of a disturbed time, history does not know, but the participants were in no doubt. They were convinced that they were possessed by demons. Forming circles in streets and churches, they danced for hours with leaps and screams, calling on demons by name to cease tormenting them or

crying that they saw visions of Christ or the Virgin or the
heavens opening. When exhausted they fell to the ground rolling
and groaning as if in the grip of agonies. As the mania spread to
Holland and Flanders, the dancers appeared with garlands in
their hair and moved from place to place like the flagellants.
They were chiefly poor—peasants, artisans, servants and beggars,
with a large proportion of women, especially the unmarried.
(Tuchman, 1978:259–60)

Dancing mania, or St. Vitus dance, disappeared as a mass activity
soon after it had arisen. There were a few outbreaks over the centuries, small contained pockets which flared briefly, before the phenomenon was consigned as an oddity to medical history. Given the
apparent epidemiology, and its emergence in the 'calamitous' 14th
century, the parallels between dancing mania and bubonic plague
are readily apparent. The shared model is of contagion. Infection
occurs through proximity—the 'sight of the sufferers'. The afflicted
are drawn into the dancing circles, where they remain until their
collapse. The dance itself spreads through transmission by human
hosts, in a route across Europe formed by a chain of available
bodies.[6]

The responses made to the dancing mania further resonate with
the experience of plague. Attempts would be made to exorcise spirits from the collapsed sufferers. Alternative festivities and ceremonies displaying public piety were held to ward off the spread of
the dance, in the same manner that they had been deployed against
the Black Death.[7] Dancing mania was oxbowed into a form whence
it could be safely isolated. The force of the dance became expended
as its material was increasingly divided. Plague and dancing mania
were thereby enacted as similar problematics and as equivocal solu-
tions. Or to put it another way, the same basic strategy was embodied with regard to the plague-event and the dancing mania-event.

'Strategy' here refers to a discontinuous process, distinct from
something like the pre-ordained implementation of 'policy'. This is
described by Foucault in the description of how 'contagion-discipline' as an essentially formless strategy moved across the 'penal
archipelago' from the military to the schoolroom and the prison via
the naval hospital (1977). No central programme directs the spread
of strategy, rather a fortuitous series of transmissions across practice is made, on the basis of temporarily shared models of formulat-
ing problems, and often on the basis of sheer chance (see Foucault,
1977; Rose, 1989). With regard to dancing mania, the staging of

processions can be located as a problem-solution formulation occurring in a conjunction of the discursive economies of religion and civic governance, pre-established by the plague.

Why then speak of strategy? Why not just describe religious belief of the time? By way of answer, another example from Foucault. In *The Archaeology of Knowledge*, repeated reference is made to typing the letters 'AZERT' on a piece of paper as an illustration of a statement—the basic unit of discursive formation—that simultaneously becomes such in its relation to 'something else'.[8] The typed letters correspond to the layout of keys on a standard French typewriter, but, for Foucault, it is not in their simple duplication that they become 'active' in a discursive sense. Nor is the relationship that of signification, where the typed characters correspond to material signifiers for the signified of the French typing series. It is instead in the way that the documentary fragment formed by the typed sheet of paper exists at an intersection of a secondary field of elements constituted by the typewriter keys, casing and fingers of the typist. The ordering of this non-discursive field supports and makes possible that of the discursive, which in its turn exerts a kind of holding power back on the initial elements.

The further example of the plot of a graph makes this apparent: the graph of, say, intelligence quotient (IQ), in itself refers to nothing. It rather marks the organization of a field of knowledge which quantifies any given population of individuals according to a set of principles. It also marks the intersection of a technology of psychological testing applied to a particular group of people in a specific place (school, workplace, interview procedure). In a later reworking of the illustration, Foucault goes on to show how the ordering of a filing cabinet with the preparation of files compiling information on individual cases comprises the non-discursive conditions by which the 'contagion-discipline' strategy is enacted, involved with a very specific kind of judicial knowledge of criminology and the delinquent (Foucault, 1977, 1978).

These examples suggest grounds for examining dancing mania not as a religious phenomenon, but in terms of the non-discursive elements of the dance itself, and the relation between the ordering of these elements and the countering organization of processions. The main component is the bodies of the dancers, arranged in circles, engaged in the flow of the dance. Following this are the various 'Bacchantic leaps', screams of possession, cries, convulsions and visions. These might be divided into two series, one of causes (bodies in relations) and another of effects (leaps, screams, visions).

Dancing mania would then appear to require, as its conditions, the simple form of a 'circling-grouping' strategy at the level of causes: bodies are drawn into a circle and participate in the dance.

From here the focus can be shifted to the relations between the dance and milieu through which it passes. This is akin to asking a wider question of proximate causal relations. Tuchman (1978) offers two related hypotheses: that dancing mania arises through the combination of poverty and homelessness amongst a downtrodden population, or that it represents a symbolic transformation of the disturbances of the time as played out by a particular European social group. Both formulations attend to the physical conditions of the dancers in their respective home environments. If the emphasis on strategy is retained, then the question becomes analogous to those asked by game theory: under what variables and conditions will the circling-grouping strategy be played out?

Smelser (1962) provides a catalogue of relevant conditions and variables, related to particular stresses and strains on the social fabric. These include models of events such as collective delusions and mass panics during cinema fires. Building on this work, Lazarus (1966) extends the scheme towards individual processes, by arguing that a model of strains and structural coping responses is a systemic feature of all kinds of organisms. Taking this approach, dancing mania might be distributed into a number of schemes, from the social effects of the plague and floods through to the personal appraisal of the dancing crowd as threat or challenge. Each could be modelled as a discrete game according to a small number of variables and rules of combination. 'Circling-grouping' could be seen to emerge and be maintained as a function of particular states of play of the games.

In spite of the attractions of such modelling, the problem it poses is that the dancing is not a uniform response made by the entirety of a relevant population, but something participated of by a heterogeneous range of persons, from a variety of differing environments. The dance occurs in a distributed, discontinuous form, beyond the limits of a particular game scenario. Given a slightly different inflection, the dance does not represent the result of the application of a rule to a limited series of variables. Rather, the rule is reinvented, or transformed as it is reapplied. Hence the composition of the dance changes, shown by changes at the level of effects—garlands appear in the dancers' hair, acts reminiscent of the flagellants become prevalent. It is merely at the strategic level of 'circling-gathering' that the dance appears to have some unity. Strategy is

72

the means by which the transformations in dancing mania can be analytically grasped as 'the qualitative forms of a single cast which is ontologically one' (Deleuze, 1990:59).

In understanding the dancing mania, one can posit that it represents an early example of mass hysteria, or to give it a more recent conceptual gloss, as an instance of 'shared stress'. This is to capture the event of dancing mania in a different discursive formation, to apply to it a bio-medical or psychological set of codings. What would it be, though, to grasp the event instead purely at the level of the non-discursive, with regard to its simple ordering of causes and effects? This would require a curious form of practical analysis that said nothing whatsoever directly of the event.

Another example may provide some direction. In late-nineteenth-century Paris, the North American dancer Loie Fuller ('The Lily Dancer') performed a number of technically stunning dances utilizing then novel materials such as electric lighting and huge panels of silk. Fuller's self-described technique was that of 'hypnosis', of becoming lost in the swirling of the material under the reflected light. The effect is the production of a movement seemingly without a subject:

> 'La Loie' moves through her images rather than playing them as roles, metaphorically. Constantly transforming themselves, these images succeed one another so rapidly that pieces named for their dominant imagery, such as the 'Lily dance', move beyond the representation of single images to represent, ultimately, movement itself. (McGarren, 1995:756–7)

A non-representational dance, then, that tends instead to capture a movement passing through various forms. What forms are these? What is the aboutness of this dance? Fuller works towards the staging of hysteria, a prevalent medical diagnosis of the time (Evans, 1991). This is achieved through a number of means. At the most mundane level, the staging of some of Fuller's poses bears clear resemblance to existing medical illustrations of the uterus (held to be the seat of hysteria), but at the level of elements brought into play, a more sophisticated diagramming appears. Fuller's dance depends upon her mastery of the new technology of electricity in lighting, just as the contemporary medical treatment of hysteria required mastery of electricity in therapeutic application. And in its execution, the dancing acts towards pure movement, dissolving structure, a kind of 'de-anatomization' of the dancing body (McGarren, 1995:771). This meshes with the shift from an explanation of hysteria in terms of uterine irritation to one of diffuse neurophysiological disorder favoured by Charcot, the leading French clinician of the time (Shorter, 1992).

If it is accepted that Fuller's dancing relates to hysteria, then it does so expressly by saying nothing about it. The dance grasps hysteria at the level of elements, the non-discursive ordering of electricity, neurophysiology and the uterus. Fuller diagrams causes and effects—pure movement—without adding to them an explicit discursive formulation. The question again: what would it be to diagram dancing mania?

Vienna

Hysteria is the archetypal model of functional (inorganic) conduct disorder. The term has a long history with a well known etymological connection to the uterus, hence women are represented as its principal subject.[9] This is articulated in two distinct ways. The first is with intense scrutiny and intervention upon the female anatomy, such as pressing upon or even removal of ovaries whose 'irritation' was thought to cause the onset of hysterical attack. This reaches its apotheosis in the 1870s with Charcot sketching and classifying various 'stigmata' (ie, localized loss of sensation, headaches, visual abnormalities) exhibited by hysterics under his care. A signifying regime was established that distributes 'four stages in every hysterical attack, three categories of hysterical stigmata, and twenty hysterogenic zones on the twenty-year-old female body' (Bernheimer, 1985:7).

The second articulation is essentially moral. Pinel had earlier dictated that hysteria arose because of a lack of proper restraint on the part of the sufferer, who allowed themselves an excess of sympathies. Rest or a return to the orderly procession of marriage and family life might calm flights of passion. The traditional reading of such advice is as a further exercise of already excessive social control. Both articulations combine in the spectacle of the 'demonstration', where the hysteric is called upon to produce *'la grande hystérie'* before an attentive audience. Charcot's *leçons du mardi* assume, in terms of contemporary iconography, a place somewhere between circus and court room, as judgements are pronounced upon the feats performed by pre-hypnotised patients. A chain of grimaces, poses and faintings proceeds in carefully sequenced manner.

Judgement is pronounced on the basis of the 'laws of hysteria'. As explicitly formulated by Charcot, these refer to the organic, hereditary basis of the phenomenon, buried within the central nervous system of the afflicted. But the focus on the female anatomical structure which he inherits suggests a second axiom, that of a semiotic process whose meaning is grounded in a sex-specific conception of life. The sympathies of the uterus and ovaries are linked, by this law, to gender relations within the social body (see Gatens, 1991). The ill of which the body speaks is simultaneously that of the female hysteric in the family or society at large, hence the treatment of one (gynaecological cauterization, ovariotomy, rest cures) affects that of the other as well.

Since Charcot, the laws pertinent to hysteria have been rewritten, or to be more accurate, hysteria has formed the substance for a constitutional struggle to write into law concerns of vastly differing natures. The interest here is in how one term ('hysteria') can enter into such struggles and so be endowed with a peculiar kind of history ordered by its participation with the search for transcendent law. In attending to this, it is inevitable that Freud is taken as the initial point of departure. With the *Fragment of analysis* relating to Dora, hysteria forms the basis for a series of manoeuvres wherein Freud plays out a number of authorial guises as detective, founder of psychoanalysis or moral authority (Marcus, 1985), but most importantly, produces groundwork for the tenets of psychoanalysis.[10]

The status of the document is unusual since it is a record of an incomplete analysis—a failure. Freud undertook analysis of the eighteen year old Dora (Ida Bauer) at the behest of her parents, following displays of depression, nervous coughs and other symptoms typically associated with *fin de siècle* hysteria. Her story rapidly unravels: Dora's father is attempting to offer her as exchange to the husband of his mistress (the K's) in order that their affair may continue. Freud does not dispute this account, but nevertheless feels a bisexual identification between Dora and Frau K is partly at issue. Dora rejects the conclusions and walks out on the analysis.

There are two major feminist readings of the case (see Moi, 1984). Either Dora is the victim of a patriarchal power game, dignified by the analysis, or she presents a spirited resistance to the events, culminating in the rejection of the males colluded against her. The legal force of the case, however, is in the translation of the events into the formulations of nascent psychoanalysis. In this respect the case is a 'disaster' (with Dora's exit) that is managed by

Freud as an instance of theory building, thus its actual success is irrelevant. Hence the original disaster—the hysterical events leading to Dora's presenting to Freud—and the original secret—what happened during a lakeside encounter between Dora and Herr K (the 'primal scene' of the case, Gearhart, 1985)—are displaced (see Table 1).

Table 1

Series	Disaster	Secret
Dora-Freud	Dora's hysterical symptoms	The lakeside scene with Herr K
Dora-Freud } Freud	The failure of the analysis	The laws of psychic identification
Dora-Freud } Freud } Lacan	The emphasis on transference	Language in the ortho-dramatization of patient's subjectivity
Dora-Freud } Freud } Lacan } Rose	The ambiguities in the theory of sexuality	The laws of desire

Two initial series can be noted. Dora-Freud is the original series, that of the analysis, whose expression would be that of the sense of the complex games surrounding Dora. The 'fragment' that actually exists, however, written some time after the analysis, constitutes a second series, Dora-Freud } Freud.[11] The first series comes to play the role of content to a very different kind of expression, that of revealing the hitherto secret laws of the psyche and the means of their decipherment. Hysteria is the term that links and moves the progression of knowledge, with the series being ordered such that events are recognized as a disaster in whose fragmentation a secret must be uncovered.

A third series is initiated by Lacan's *Intervention on transference*, which grasps Freud-Dora } Freud as content for a display of the 'dialectical reversals' that mark an analytic dialogue. At issue here is the manner in which Freud allows the elaboration of the notion of counter-transference between analyst and analysand to dominate his theoretical speculations on the Dora case. For Lacan, this acts to disattend to what is spoken, the words themselves being the proper reference point. If the focus on transference is the disaster, which is only a diversion from the proper 'orthodramatization of the subjectivity of the patient' (Lacan, 1985:103), then the secret is that of the twists as the 'word of the symptom' comes to enter analytic dialogue.

From here a further link may be formed by taking Freud-Dora }
Freud } Lacan as the content of an examination of desire.
According to Rose (1985), the hesitancies in Freud's theorizing of
female sexuality provided the grounds upon which the analysis
foundered. The combination with Lacanian discursive psychoanalysis effectively brings the question of hysteria into a further
expression. The form here being the objectifying and subjectifying
processes of desire and their respective difficulties for not only
Freud and the project of psychoanalysis, but also for Dora at the
scenes in which the diagnosis of her hysteria is enmeshed. A new set
of secrets are opened with the posing of 'the question of desire *as* a
question' (Rose, 1985:146).

The process of reworking the event of hysteria through the addition of series ensures a difference within continuity, whilst the perpetual reconstitution of a secret, through its very opacity, hints at
the development of a common thread (is it perhaps the same secret?
do all the secrets refer to some prior mystery?).[12] Although the original secret—what happened between Herr K and Dora at the lakeside—is ever displaced, it seems to inhere in the subsequent secrets
as a lesser case, an example drawn from an increasingly lower set.
Producing knowledge in this fashion seems to require not only that
the term that links series be suitably polyvalent, but also that it is
possible to interpret the previous series as involving a disaster of
sufficient magnitude—otherwise why bother instituting a new
expression?

Hysteria fulfils both requirements. As a phenomenon it becomes
enacted around the concealing of a secret within a private disaster.
Knowledge of hysteria then comes to take on this form of ordering,
a 'hystericization of psychoanalysis' (cf. Evans, 1991) occurs as the
production of knowledge becomes itself hysterical. As such it takes
on many of the tropes which are often assimilated with modernity
(hidden knowledge; depth; the discovery of law). It might then be
asked to what extent does this form of ordering knowledge correspond to the experience of contemporary sociality?

In a useful counter-example, dealing with the transformation of
economic discourse in late 1980s Australia, Morris notes the difficulty in observing 'the quality of antagonism between two opposing
figures who *sound* exactly the same . . . but who are now quite audi-
bly saying materially different things' (1991:81). The same economic terms are in the mouths of speakers in very different cultural

and political positions. Here there is no secret and no disaster that marks the alternative expressions, they are instead 'at once intelligible, seductive and a mark of profound dispossession' (Morris, 1991:78) for the observer.

The movement between expressions is, for Morris, 'ecstatic', in the sense of a transport across (social, discursive) space without the sense of having crossed any great distance. No longer the search for secrets but the illumination thrown by surface glare. Perhaps then, the constitution of the secret has some functional role internal to the ordering of knowledge, in that it provides a way of channelling attention towards some specific area of concern. The ecstatic ordering that Morris describes appears instead to entirely abolish vision as a critical trope (involved with bringing before 'the gaze'). All that remains is the hypnotic drone of different intonations of the same discourse. Hysteria and ecstasy are not then to be opposed, but are rather alternative mechanisms for producing knowledge by circumventing visibility.[13] The analytic task is then presumably that of elucidating the conditions wherein each emerge and come to function.

Kuwait

In 1991, the American Psychological Association (APA) organized a task force to contribute to the organizational task of managing the Persian Gulf War. They took their focus to be developing strategies for 'the return home, reunion, and reintegration of service personnel with their families and work' (Hobfoll *et al.*, 1991:848). Haunted by the Vietnam experience of traumatized veterans returning from a deeply unpoplar war, the APA decided to produce a series of guidelines to aid the identification of 'at risk' individuals. Attention was also allocated to children's 'special needs'. The rationale took the form of establishing how an effective network of support could be facilitated that would welcome military personnel back into a 'meaningful' position in the community: 'The burden of coping must not fall on the returning soldiers and their families alone. They fought for all of us. Psychologists need to carry this message as well' (Hobfoll *et al.*, 1991:853).

The task force adopted a model based around the stresses of traumatic events. Persons were to be considered at risk of later psychiatric disorder based on the number of threats or actual losses to which they were exposed and the number of resources (practical, emotional, psychological) that they had available to them with which to cope. This latter component is what makes the model more sophisticated than that of 'shell shock'. Initially, traumatized soldiers were thought to be suffering from organic traumas brought on by excessive noises and conditions (Shalev & Rogel-Fuchs, 1993). This came eventually to be superseded by an approach which emphasized a range of moderating factors, including behavioural genetics, conditioned responses, and 'maladaptive' patterns of conduct.

The recommendations split into identifying the warning signs (eg, 'shame over some failure', 'sleep problems', 'blunting of emotions') and providing guidelines for interventions. Much of this latter consists of exhortations to build a 'psychological sense of community' (Hobfoll *et al.*, 1991:851) through providing esteem-building emotional and material support. Much is made of the 'fit' of a person's style of coping to the environment. The kinds of styles prescribed depend very much on the kinds of individuals involved and their personal situations. But several coping styles are definitely proscribed—avoiding problems, blaming, excessive pessimism, isolation and drug and alcohol use are rarely successful in the long term.

With retrospect it is easy to mock these efforts. It may perhaps be testament to their effectiveness, but the problem of traumatized returnees has failed to materialize on a large scale. The issue is instead 'Gulf War Syndrome' or 'desert fever', a reported set of injuries to the nervous and immune systems widely supposed to be brought on either by a cocktail of chemical agents given to protect against nerve gases, contact with organophosphate pesticides or exposure to unconfirmed biological attacks. Complaints include memory loss, joint pain, constant headaches, fatigue, low-level flu-like symptoms and birth defects. Most of these are also plausible symptoms of extreme stress.

The problem is one of visibility. The APA drew up a system of effects based around stress. They hypothesized a particular problem contained within a stochastic set of possibilities and set up a network of probable observations and projected actions. In doing so they directed attention in a highly particular manner. The problem that emerged not only cut through the APA's expectations, but also had a dense character that was completely unsuited to the cognitive-behavioural framework in which they are embedded. The hierarchy of cognition>body>conduct that was carefully traced became destabilized by apparent organic damage relates to unsubstantiated practices (ie, actual exposure to chemical agents). It could only 'show up' as a distinct problem through an absence of effects in the network, as something that is 'non-obvious'.

It was not just the biological connection that proved elusive. The APA also failed to appreciate a changing political climate. It is in relation to time that the network proves especially ineffective. With a simple distribution of bodies in space, such as the task of fitting persons into trenches or aeroplanes (the original military task given to psychologists such as Terman), the success or failure of psychological technologies is not at issue, since the act is relatively immediate. Similarly, an IQ test *will* divide the 'correct' numbers of persons since it is constructed around a normal distribution and can therefore be applied to whatever grouping of bodies is of concern. Whether this is *just* is a different question. But as soon as there is any delay of reasonable length between the act of division and the possible actions and effects that may result, the problem of the 'non-obvious' emerges.

It may occur because the system of divisions cannot register that which operates below an established liminal threshold and so misses the 'more pedestrian traffic' (Lee & Brown, 1994) beneath its expectations. It may also happen because the divisions are themselves incapable of responding to an event that is ordered around an entirely different series (eg, biological rather than psychological; political rather than a matter of social support). In this case the construction of the network is inadequate for the task of prediction. Here it also proved unreliable in its orientation to both social history and collective memory. The APA depended upon an image of the USA as the nation that had sought to forget the Vietnam experience and abandoned its returnees. They sought to instil a sense of civil responsibility in a populace that would, it was reasoned, otherwise avoid such a calling. In doing so they proved inattentive to a decade of Vietnam revisions in cinema and popular culture. They misjudged the complex geopolitical series of CNN, daily surgical strikes and spoilings for new world order.

This mistake is not merely a miscalculation in psychological thought, but is directly involved with the APA's stance on posttraumatic stress disorder (PTSD) and the modes in which it produces such knowledge. In the USA, the Veterans' Administration medical system is a key means of researching PTSD. Young's (1995) ethnography of one institute in the system (specifically created to provide services to diagnosed PTSD sufferers) describes how such knowledge is shaped through a series of processes beginning with treatment and then continuing with the assimilation of results through a managerial hierarchy. Due to the psychoanalytic approach dominating the institute, particular attention is placed on both the adequate disclosure of traumatic memories, and on a successful 'working through' of previous experiences with therapists. The resultant knowledge is then subjected to a similar procedure when the therapist reports to the institute director. Successful ordering of memory (which is simultaneously its reconstruction) translates into adequate ordering of knowledge regarding PTSD.

Total management of the production process proves impossible. The voluntary clients of the institute—many of whom live in impoverished or precarious conditions—are expected to produce reasonable accounts. To remain within its relatively secure walls they must appear to be 'working through'. Young notes that this is the only perceivable change effected by the treatment programme, other than an expected change in conduct on entry to the institute (1993). In other words, the knowledge production is grounded entirely in the attempts of clients to construct what they perceive to be the 'correct' institutional rhetoric (ie, that of striving for truth). Producing the right kinds of memories, and more importantly positioning oneself in relation to truth and emotion, positions the client as content for further expression in the subsequent series of organizational discourse, leading, eventually, to the integration of knowledge by bodies such as the APA. By the point the Gulf-War report emerged, the original secrets held by traumatic memories were long deferred.

The reception of the non-obvious is therefore intimately bound to the functioning of a system of knowledge production that marks time and memory in a distinctive way. There is the assumption that, if sufficiently ordered, memory provides the keys to successful adaptation. One seeks a stable present by trawling through memories of disaster. The disaster is, in this sense, instructive. But this is to assume a neutrality, to give the disaster a being outside of its hailing *qua* disaster. Whatever the events are that come to be marked as traumatic, they only become a disaster with the intervention that recognizes them as such. The disaster is therefore certainly of the past, and indeed can really only be spoken of on the condition that it has already happened, but properly exists in its moment-by-moment constitution in the present.

So what did happen? What was the nature of the event that the APA reacted to? The question is badly put: it is the reaction as expressed by the stress-coping concept which made whatever happened an 'event'. The concept *is the event*, or rather it is the means by which a heterogeneous series of elements took on a particular kind of pattern which could gain standing as an event.

Of course, whatever happened was not no-thing. It could and will be effected as many different kinds of events, especially if the concept of Gulf War Syndrome gains legal recognition. What is at issue is not a word-thing problem, a difficulty with naming. It is instead a puzzle of articulation and visibility, a calligram in which concepts and the series of materials they hold together struggle against one another, where:

> visible form is excavated, furrowed by words that work from within, and which . . . spin forth the web of significations that christens it, determines it, fix it in a universe of discourse. A double trap, unavoidable snare. (Foucault, 1982:22)

Afterword

The problem I have attempted to articulate here is how it is that a concept takes place. This essentially non-representational problem needs to be differentiated from the many others that might be posed, such as around the 'correctness' of the concept, its veridicality or else the equity of settling upon this rather than that concept (say, stress rather than hysteria). These formulations all amount to a questioning of whether a given concept is *well placed* or not. They imply recourse to an ethics of problematisation that I am unwilling to explore here (but see Chomsky & Foucault, 1974; Munro, 1995; Brown *et al.*, forthcoming). To say, on the contrary, merely that an event *takes place* is to indicate that there is a certain work performed by a concept (a work, no doubt, of differentiation) and that this labour allows something to occur, such as the production of series, the dispersion of materials, the ordering of elements or the construction of a puzzle or calligram.

A concept is then inseparable from the event in which it takes place. The event of a medical emergency, the event of dancing mania, the event of *fin de siècle* hysteria, the event of the aftermath of the Gulf War. One might then be tempted to assign a precise time and date to the taking place of a concept (as in Deleuze & Guattari, 1987). Again, it is possible to approach concepts in many other ways, such as enquiring into the nature of the general conditions of their articulability. That is, what must be *in place* before the concept can *take place*. Yet this leads us further away from what is decisive regarding a concept: its machinery or the process of ordering which is proper to it. The method of recognizing secrets in the midst of disaster that is proper to hysteria, for example, or the transmission of a movement of circling-grasping that takes place with dancing mania. Conceptual machinery is always already engaged in a labouring for and of division: this is a secret and that is a symptom, here is evidence of poisoning and there is an incidence of stress, these people are coping badly and those have neurological damage. One might imagine a problem space criss-crossed by the trajectories of manifold concepts taking place (a hospital enquiry, a case of analysis, war returnees falling ill), creating spaces of dissensus and contestation. In short, the labours of dividing as conceptual machineries order, resonate or clash.

As such it would be unhelpful to envisage some form of democracy of concepts, over which the great, grand dualisms of social science would no doubt preside. We might do better to posit a convoluted web, network, typology, phylum or plane, over and through which concepts scurry as so many creatures in a burrow. Or else to think of a tangled mess of machinery, assembled from different periods and with very different uses, operating one upon the other. A confusion of difference machines, all labouring noisily. Indeed one might consider each of the machines assembled in this chapter as in the process of disassembling and dividing all the others (as stress reworks hysteria, but also as dancing mania disorganizes stress, or the interlocking of gulf war syndrome and hysteria, and so on). Or each of the pieces in a book 'about' the labour of division as resonating with and operating upon its neighbours.

It might then become somewhat less obfuscatory to say that the 'labour of division' can, as a concept, only have its being in *taking place*. Which implies the operation of a conceptual machinery, certainly, but also a space that is taken or occupied in the event of the concept. What is this place? Part of the difficulty in answering is that the taking place of the concept itself reworks the *concept of place*. In the tangling of conceptual machinery, archaic difference machines like the Cartesian cogito may enter into proximity with the most recent conceptual events of literary theory or medicine (hence the presence of something very old in the practices of the APA, or the persistence of hysteria in stress). Indeed here it probably makes little sense to speak of 'archaic' of 'recent'. What matters is that we are able to devise methods where this joint articulation of events becomes apparent, or at least is able to take place. Which is to say that the event of the 'labour of division' does not just happen, it must be made.

Notes

1 Rosch, 1995 describes this incident.
2 As Hay & Oken, 1977:120 put it 'stimuli are present to mobilize literally every conflictual area at every psychological developmental level' in such settings.
3 'Events have their place; they consist in relation to, coexistence with, dispersion of, the cross-checking accumulation and the selection of material elements; it occurs as an effect of, and in, material dispersion. Let us say that the philosophy of the event should advance in the direction . . . of an incorporeal materialism.' (Foucault, 1972b:231)\
4 One of the major claims by the deceased patient's relatives is for the right to conduct a proper funeral, which has been impeded by an isolation restriction placed upon the body, following the poisoning hypothesis.
5 Although the stress explanation was initially favoured by the medical authorities, their subsequent position shifted toward the revised poisoning hypothesis, which had the legal advantage of defending against claims of medical negligence.
6 The consensual view is that dancing mania (St. Vitus dance or chorea, Danse de St. Guy) was an outburst of mass hysteria, and hence not properly part of anatomical medicine. However, as Hayden, 1981 notes, the phenomenon remained an active part of folk-lore (celebrations in honour of St. John still occur) and the epistemic basis for the diagnosis of what is now known as Huntingon's chorea. Hayden suggests that the dance might have been based upon the jerking movements which characterize the disease. The medical use of the term 'chorea' (derived from 'chorus' or 'performance') is certainly derived from the medieval dance, which has to some extent hampered the re-presentation of such organic disorders as genetically determined.
7 'These processions took a form which continued to be used . . . for another couple of centuries. On matters of great importance to the city . . . the whole population became involved. Citizens, the Church hierarchy, and other religious orders, formed into groups to carry through the streets the holy relics located within the institutions of the city, and the banners of saints whose aid was being sought to intercede on behalf of the city and its citizens.' (Hatty, 1992: 161)
8 The following draws upon the discussion of the AZERT example in Deleuze 1988:11–12.
9 This in spite of Charcot's insistence that 'the word "hysteria" means nothing'. He pioneered the diagnosis of male hysteria, believing in a fundamental underlying hereditary nervous disorder, although this aspect of the phenomenon and, indeed, hysteria itself fell into disrepute after his death in 1893—see Shorter, 1992.
10 The text occurs mid-way between the writings on the unconscious ('The Interpretation of Dreams') and the initial theorizing of sexuality ('Three Essays on Sexuality')—see Moi, 1984.
11 Felix Deutsch saw Ida Bauer in his capacity as a psychiatrist in 1922, two decades after the termination of her analysis with Freud in 1900. The later series of sessions was revealed in an article—broadly sympathetic with Freud's original conclusions—in 1957 (reprinted as Deutsch, 1985). The importance of hysteria to psychoanalysis itself is noted by Freud in 1924: 'Obsessional neurosis and hysteria are the forms of neurotic illness upon the study of which psychoanalysis was first built, and in the treatment of which, too, our therapy celebrates its triumphs.' (Freud, 1974:297)

12 Simmel describes how secrets may act as modes of ordering; see Cooper, 1990.
13 For a provocative account of hysteria, signification and visibility, see Baudrillard, 1990.

References

Anderson, R.V. & Cotton, M.M., (1992) 'The Newcastle earthquake experience: The human context and its implications for disaster management in P. Hinton, *Disasters: Image and context*, Sydney: Sydney Studies.

Baudrillard, J.,(1990) *Seduction* (B Singer, trans.), London: Methuen.

Bernheimer, C., (1985) 'Introduction: Part one' in C. Bernheimer & C. Kahane (eds) *In Dora's case: Freud, Hysteria, feminism*, London: Virago.

Blanchot, M., (1986) *The writing of the disaster* (A Smock, trans), Lincoln: University of Nebraska Press.

Brown, S.D., Pujol, J. and Curt, B.C. (forthcoming) 'As one in a web: Discourse materiality and the place of ethics'. In I. Parker (ed) *Social constructionism, discourse and realism*. London: Sage.

Cooper, R., (1990) 'Organization/disorganization' in J.S. Hassard & D. Pym (eds) *The theory and philosophy of organizations*, London: Routledge.

Deleuze, G., (1988) *Foucault* (S. Hand, trans.), Minneapolis: University of Minnesota Press.

Deleuze, G., (1990) *The logic of sense* (M. Lester, trans), New York: Columbia University Press.

Deleuze, G. & Guattari, F., (1987) *A thousand plateaus: Capitalism and schizophrenia* (B. Massumi, trans.), London: The Athlone Press.

Deleuze, G. & Guattari, F., (1994) *What is philosophy?* (G. Burchell & H. Tomlinson, trans.), London: Verso.

Derrida, J. (1978), *Writing and difference* (A. Bass, trans.), London: Routledge.

Derrida, J. (1982) *Margins of philosophy* (A. Bass, trans.), Hemel Hempstead: Harvester Wheatsheaf.

Deutsch, F., (1985) 'A footnote to Freud's "Fragment of an analysis of a case of hysteria"' in C. Bernheimer & C. Kahane (eds) *In Dora's case: Freud, hysteria, feminism*, London: Virago.

Evans, M.E., (1991) *Fits and starts: A genealogy of hysteria in modern France*, Ithaca: Cornell University Press.

Foucault, M., (1972a) *The archaeology of knowledge* (A. Sheridan, trans.), New York: Pantheon.

Foucault, M., (1972b) 'The discourse on language' (R. Sawyer, trans.) in M. Foucault, *The archaeology of knowledge*, New York: Pantheon.

Foucault, M., (1977) *Discipline and punish: The birth of the prison* (A. Sheridan, trans.), Harmondsworth: Penguin.

Foucault, M., (1978) 'About the concept of the "dangerous individual" in 19th-Century legal psychiatry' (A. Baudot & J. Couchman, trans.), *Internal Journal of Law and Psychiatry*, 1, 1–18.

Foucault, M., (1982) *This is not a pipe* (J. Harkness, trans.), Berkeley: University of California Press.

Freud, S., (1974) *Introductory lectures on psychoanalysis* (J. Strachey, trans), Harmondsworth: Penguin.

Funkenstein, D.H., King, S.H. & Drolette, M.E., (1957) *Mastery of stress*, Cambridge: Harvard University Press.

Gearhart, S., (1985) 'The scene of psychoanalysis: The unanswered questions of Dora' in C. Bernheimer & C. Kahane (eds) *In Dora's case: Freud, hysteria, feminism*, London: Virago.

Haas, J.E. & Drabek, T.E., (1970) 'Community disaster and system stress: A sociological perspective' in J.E. McGrath (ed.) *Social and psychological factors in stress*, New York: Holt, Rinehart & Winston.

Hatty, J. ,(1992) 'Coping with disaster: Florence after the Black Death' in P. Hinton (ed.) *Disasters: Image and context*, Sydney: Sydney Studies.

Hay, D. & Oken, D., (1977) 'The psychological stresses of Intensive Care Unit nursing' in A. Monat & R.S. Lazarus (eds) *Stress and coping: An anthology*, New York: Columbia University Press.

Hayden, M.R., (1981) *Huntington's Chorea*, Berlin: Springer-Verlag.

Hobfoll, S.E., Spielberger, C.D., Breznitz, S., Figley, C., Folkman, S., Lepper-Green, B., Meichenbaum, D., Milgram, N.A., Sandler, I., Sarason, I. & van der Kolk, B., (1991) 'War-related stress: Addressing the stress of war and other traumatic events', *American Psychologist*, 46(8), 848–55.

Lacan, J., (1985) 'Intervention on transference' (J. Rose, trans) in C. Bernheimer & C. Kahane (eds) *In Dora's case: Freud, hysteria, feminism*, London: Virago.

Lazarus, R.S., (1966) *Psychological stress and the coping process*, New York: McGraw Hill.

Lee, N. & Brown, S., (1994) 'Otherness and the actor network: The undiscovered continent', *American Behavioral Scientist*, 37(6), 772–90.

Marcus, S., (1985) 'Freud and Dora: Story, history, case history' in C. Bernheimer & C. Kahane (eds) *In Dora's case: Freud, hysteria, feminism*, London: Virago.

McGarren, F., (1995) 'The "symptomatic act" circa 1900: Hysteria, hypnosis, electricity, dance', *Critical Inquiry*, 21(4), 748–74.

Moi, T., (1984) 'Psychoanalysis and desire: The case of Dora', *Desire: ICA Documents*, 1, 3.

Morris, M., (1992) *Ecstasy and economics: American essays for John Forbes*, Sydney: Empress.

Munro, R. (1995) 'The strings of belonging: textual labour and the individual "in" division'. Papers distributed for the first *CSTT Workshop on The Labour of Division*, Keele University.

Pronko, N.H. & Leith, W.R., (1956) 'Behavior under stress: A study of its disintegration', *Psychological Reports*, 2, Monograph Supplement (5), 205–22.

Rosch, P., (1995) ' Is hysteria catching? Don't blame it all on "stress" ', *Stress Medicine*, 11(2), 71–4.

Rose, J., (1985) 'Dora: Fragment of an analysis' in C. Bernheimer & C. Kahane (eds) *In Dora's case: Freud, hysteria, feminism*, London: Virago.

Rose, N., (1989) *Governing the soul: The shaping of the private self*, London: Routledge.

Shalev, A.Y. & Rogel-Fuchs, Y., (1993) 'Psychophysiology of Posttraumatic Stress Disorder: From Sulfur fumes to behavioral genetics', *Psychosomatic Medicine*, 55, 413–23.

Shorter, E., (1992) *From paralysis to fatigue: A history of psychosomatic illness in the modern era*, New York: The Free Press.

Smelser, N.H., (1962) *Theory of collective action*, London: Routledge and Kegan Paul.

Taylor, A.J.W. & Frazer, A.G., (1982) 'The stress of post-disaster body handling and victim identification work', *Journal of Human Stress*, 8(4), 4–12.

Tuchman, B.W., (1978) *A distant mirror: The calamitous fourteenth century*, London: Macmillan.

Vermorel, J. & Vermorel, F., (1989) *Fandemonium!*, London: Omnibus Press.

Young, A., (1993) 'A description of how ideology shapes knowledge of a mental disorder (Posttraumatic Stress Disorder)' in S. Lindenbaum & M. Lock (eds) *Knowledge, power and practice: The anthropology of everyday life*, Berkeley: University of California Press.

Young, A., (1995) *The harmony of illusions: Inventing Post-Traumatic Stress Disorder*, Princeton: Princeton University Press.

Section II
Organizing division

Introduction

Equating the labours of division with the 'anatomizing urge', Karen Dale contrasts the work of the scalpel and the mirror as the two instruments that create identity in a 'culture of dissection'. In following this idea, her chapter has two movements. First, the 'cutting' of the scalpel divides the world into ever smaller parts. Following Descartes, the scalpel is made essential to penetrating beneath the surface and 'rendering visible' that which is usually hidden. The predominance of the visual replaces the earlier dominance of the text, creating a transparent relationship between what we 'see' and the underlying 'reality' of the world. Dale then develops her theme to suggest how death is sequestered as 'deviance'. Paradoxically, for Baudrillard, this brings about a culture of death: 'by abolishing that which cannot be abolished death makes its symbolic mark everywhere'. Baudrillard's point here recalls Foucault's placing of a 'shadow' on the analytic of the identical.

The second movement of the paper follows the mirror, which plays a key role—in contemporary surgery literally a keyhole role—in facilitating self-reflection and the development of a new sense of identity, heightening the possibilities for self-control. So much has been argued variously in the work of Elias, Mead and Foucault, but Dale goes on to develop how 'identity' becomes increasingly aligned with the 'identical'.

In this respect, her analysis on the 'anatomization' of women further helps bring out the links between Foucault's focus on normalization and a more general movement towards 'mechanical reproduction':

> . . . penetration and incision can never give access to knowledge of the Other, to subordinated, subjective, lived, embodied knowledges, it can only reflect back the dominant, normalized, disciplined knowledge. In this way the mirror becomes a tool for

the normalizing principle. It reflects back, not unique images of the individual, but replicated copies of the norm.

Dale's argument is that a culture of dissection is marked by a conflation of (human) reproduction with (mechanical) replication. Thus, although her analysis perhaps has more in common with Cooper than Strathern, it could be emphasized that this is just the sort of conflation that an 'adding culture' would make when its analytic of identity eschews complementarity in favour of augmentation.

For Parker, the labour of division as a cut is also seen at work within the organisation or firm. Drawing on the idea of process rather than structure, verbs rather than nouns, Parker wants to see organization as a mobile process that operates through a labour of division. Division within an organization not only orders, it also does disordering work, unsettling the categories of identity in which workers and managers seek to come to rest. Organizational division is itself divided along a number of lines. Parker discusses three of these, spatial/functional, generational and occupational/professional. It is around the dividing of division, its labour, that identity work takes place within the organization.

That this labour of division is a contested process is clear from Parker's account. Where one settles (within an organization) is really about how mobile one can be in negotiating one's place (often by contrasting it with the place of others) within the desiccated spaces made by the labour of division. While none within an organization are immune from such a process, able to stand outside, those who can occupy the 'space' closest to where the division comes down as a cut, are best able to avoid being cut off, rather they might be said to be at the cutting edge within the organization. It is they who are most easy to move with the disorganization that division does rather than have it move against them.

Tony Watson's chapter is also concerned with division within organization and the issues that they raise for managers' identities. The identity of the manager is an ambivalent one, one that is internally cut by different positions that have to be assumed in relation to different parts of their work. This identity work is work that goes into dividing and undividing self. According to Watson, this identity work can be seen in interaction and self-enquiry, such as in answering questions like, 'am I a good manager?' Questions like this reveal that in such 'middle-of-the-night' thoughts, identity is always in the middle, in the space of labouring. Boundaries and margins are not always found at the edge, cut off from the rest, they are spaces of traffic through which we labour with categories of identity through which we try to perform some sense of a coherent self.

The discursive resources that managers draw upon in this labouring work of self, relates to the labour of division within an organization and the organizational culture that it generates. By contrasting cultures such as i) *empowerment, skill and growth* with ii) *control, jobs and costs* Watson argues that the manager has to perform self differently. Managers confront what Watson describes as 'the double control problem' trying to use themselves as a vehicle for exerting their employer's control over others, while at the same time having to negotiate its control over their own lives. How well this is done will indicate whether a member of an organization is a good or bad citizen. To be a manager is to be a division-labourer as is revealed through the self-reflections and theorizations that managers adopt when answering the questions of the ethnographer. It is through reflection on the work of division that a sense of unity comes to be constructed.

Identity in a culture of dissection: body, self and knowledge

Karen Dale

Introduction

This chapter explores the idea that the effects of one particular 'labour of division'—the development of a distinct discipline of human biology based on dissection—have been central to the development of the dominant 'western' tradition of knowledge.[1] In this context, I apply the phrase 'labour of division' to refer to the work of the early anatomists, who did indeed have to labour to transform their knowledge base from one which relied on the authority of handed-down texts to one which drew on the slicing up of human cadavers. Although this 'anatomic disarticulation' (Foucault, 1970:269) is now a commonly accepted facet of science, it originally involved a confrontation with deeply held religious and societal traditions and taboos about the sanctity of the human body, and the meaning of life and death.

I argue that this 'labour of division' cut deep into the heart of what is understood by the scientific method and philosophical rationality, the two arteries of our dominant intellectual tradition. Not only did the anatomists establish a discrete disciplinary area around their work, they also provided a pattern for the search for knowledge that I characterize as the 'anatomizing urge' (following Sawday 1995). Jonathan Sawday has described the Renaissance 'culture of enquiry' as a 'culture of dissection', involving an 'incisive recomposition of the human body, which entailed an equivalent refashioning of the means by which people made sense of the world around them' (1995:xi). The tools of the 'culture of dissection' are the two items held in the hands of *Anatomia*, the personification of the body and our knowledge of it. These are the scalpel and the mirror (Sawday 1995:183).

From the time of the scientific revolution, the scalpel has come into its own, creating the human body as a place for invasive investigation, fragmentation and re-organization. As Sawday comments regarding medicine: 'anatomization takes place so that, in lieu of a formerly complete "body", a new "body" of knowledge and understanding can be created. As the physical body is fragmented, so the body of understanding is held to be shaped and formed' (1995:2). This urge comes to invade almost all areas of knowledge, not only bio-medicine, by its power as a metaphor and as a form of representation. In this respect, the 'slash' or oblique (/) marks out the dualisms upon which 'western' thought is founded (Foucault, 1970:268; Plumwood, 1993).

In the mirror's reflection we see our own selves. Through invasive investigation, the scalpel cuts to the bone, whilst the mirror allows the reflection back of the 'inner self' which has been thus dissected. In other words, the 'anatomizing urge' as the dominant form of knowledge not only affects our thinking, it also shapes 'western' ideas of human identity. The chapter argues that the Enlightenment heritage has given us a world of identity where we have come to make an assumption of a wholeness and oneness to the self. But the mirror can also be taken as a form of replication, the production of identical mirror images. In this schema—from which developed a world of mass production and simulacra—those which do not resemble the original and possess its qualities are cast aside as deviant. Although on the one hand we have the Enlightenment individual endowed with Reason and Rights, the opposing tendency of 'normalization' (Foucault, 1977) is also to be found. Here those who are different are stripped of individual identity and rights, and their ability to reason is questioned. In this spirit, a divided, gendered world of knowledge is created.

Thus it is not simply that there are divisions and differences. What is important is where the cuts and incisions are made and how the resulting parts are re-organized and re-ordered. Power, discipline and hierarchy play a major role in the 'culture of dissection'. Whose labour is valorized? Whose identities predominate over others? These are significant questions we need to ask. We need to consider why there have been cuts between certain relations, categories, concepts and what power relations have been invested in them. In relation to this, re-connecting cut threads can be subversive of the dominant tradition. We also need to consider what differences have been emphasized, whilst others have been occluded. Who or what have been forced into sameness or marginalized as

Other? Reflecting back the dominant onto itself, recursion, repetition and mimicry can then be subversive tools.

In this chapter I do not seek to further incise the field, but to reconnect some of these threads cut apart by the 'culture of dissection'. It is ironic, for example, that although the 'anatomizing urge' developed through the study of the human body, it fostered the division of the body as material object from mind as cognitive subject. As will be discussed, the body has also become associated with the female gender and with nature—both subordinated concepts in 'western' thought—and the mind with the male gender and culture, especially science (Easlea, 1983; Jordanova, 1989). These categories have also been cut off from each other and placed in hierarchized relations. Here I would like to try to re-cover some of these severed connections between body, self and knowledge. However, as Mallarme commented 'we are condemned to meaning' (quoted in Hoskin, 1995:142), and in constructing our meanings we also incise and organize the world. This indicates the difficulty of writing in a 'culture of dissection'.[2] To inscribe a page with text is to participate in this culture. For what we do in writing as academics is to foreground and umbrate, underscore and ignore, select out and put in, embolden and fade out, excise and incise on each and every page. It is not only as readers that we 'gut' a piece of text by lovingly looking at its entrails. To write anything is to fillet. We need to recognize this difficulty. Any attempt to play with concepts, exploring a web of meanings and identity (Griffiths, 1995) and being diffuse or recursive in expression, is disciplined by the conventions of the academic text, the need to communicate and the constraints of deadlines and word limits. I will return again to this matter in the conclusion.

The scalpel

I begin the discussion of the anatomizing urge with Descartes who, it has long been argued, is of paramount importance to understanding the development of 'western' science. Along with his formation of a coherent Method of Scientific Inquiry based on the fundamental principle of human Reason, his thought has also significantly shaped the re-organization of the modern conception of the human body.

In the *Discourse on Method* Descartes reveals his interest in how we can develop a method of reasoning about the world. The key to understanding was the recognition that mathematics gave us the secret of the universe. Building upon this insight he goes on to develop his four rules of logic which are thus:

> The first was never to accept anything as true if I had not evident knowledge of its being so; that is, carefully to avoid precipitancy and prejudice, and to embrace in my judgment only what presented itself to my mind so clearly and distinctly that I had no occasion to doubt it.
>
> The second, to divide each problem I examined into as many parts as was feasible, and was requisite for its better solution.
>
> The third, to direct my thoughts in an orderly way; beginning with the simplest objects, those most apt to be known, and ascending little by little, in steps as it were, to the knowledge of the most complex; and establishing an order in thought even when the objects had no natural priority one to another. And the last, to make throughout such complete enumerations and such general surveys that I might be sure of leaving nothing out. (Descartes, 1637 [1954]:20–1)

Simple components are seen as providing the basis upon which knowledge develops in what is a variant of foundationalism. Yet this is a complex epistemological system. Certainly Cartesianism (along with Bacon's experimentalism in *Novum Organum* of 1620) has been important in the forming of the 'culture of dissection'. But what we witness here is metaphysical realism, in the sense that reality has an objective structure unaffected by human understandings. It is also a form of objectivism, when taken with the belief that this reality is accessible to human knowledge. It further assumes epistemological individualism, for humans gain knowledge of the world as individuals not as socially constituted groups. There is also a clear rationalist bias, for knowledge is gained through reason and when this reasoning is based upon the senses (especially that of sight) this leads to empiricism. Finally, there is a universalistic assumption here too, for reason is available to all human beings (though decidedly not to animals) should they wish to conquer the impediments of value bias.

From the point of view of the present argument, the key things to note are that the Cartesian Method relies upon division of the world into small, understandable components. For Descartes, reason proceeds by splitting the whole into the parts. Thus he splits the mind from the body, because the use of rationality by the mind internally allows the mind to look outside the body at external matter. Self-consciousness is the property of mind and not the body. It is superior to that thought of which animals are capable, for they have no soul nor any capacity for reason. Animals are machines not blessed with a soul and therefore are automata. It is the possession of mind rather than a body which Descartes sees as crucial to his Method. In order to develop the powers of pure Reason, one must escape the visceral and the irrational and seek Reason.

Descartes was not solely interested in the rational for its own sake, but in how it is applied to understanding the workings of the material world. He himself was interested in anatomy and attended the public anatomy 'theatres' where he searched for the source of the soul, looked at animal hearts and studied the development of the human foetus. Description and measurement are key in this world-view, and the further development of knowledge was particularly founded on making more of the world visible to the human eye and thus to the mind. In anatomy we see the movement to practical dissection replacing the authority of the text: in this the scalpel is essential to penetrating beneath the surface and rendering visible that which is usually hidden. A variety of technologies have been developed in order to aid this process of visualization, from Kepler's compound microscope in 1611 to present day electronic and laser imaging techniques (Stafford, 1991:24). It is therefore interesting to note that Descartes published on optics in his philosophical essay of 1637.[3] The predominance of the visual assumes a directly transparent relationship between what we see and the 'reality' of the world.

In *The Order of Things*, Foucault connects the development of anatomy with a new way of relating to and categorizing Life. Instead of the Classical taxonomy where there is a great natural order based on the external description of things from the simplest and most inert to the most complex and living: '[t]his space has now been dissociated and as it were opened up in depth. Instead of a unitary field of visibility and order, whose elements have a distinctive value in relation to each other, we have a series of oppositions, of which the two terms are never on the same level . . . ' (1970:268). As Plumwood (1993) argues, the resultant dualisms such as the Cartesian mind/body split are not only significant in 'western' knowledge because they lead to a conceptual divide between concepts and structures which are related in much more complex ways, but because they impose a hierarchical relationship between the two entities which are set in opposition against each other. Through this means we have the active privileging of the mind over the body, of culture over nature, of male over female, and so on. This encourages the exclusion and silencing of the subordinated category. The use of the incisive 'slash' or oblique cannot, as some authors perhaps intend, return the terms to harmony or symmetry, but rather acknowledges the formation of a certain form of knowledge which is dominant, valued, whilst other forms are subjugated. It is this metaphor of the scalpel and its incision which clearly marks off the sciences (and the social sciences, which set out to emulate the success of the natural sciences) for it highlights the importance of penetration and revelation which science still sees as key virtues.

In popular depictions of *Anatomia*, she is shown as armed with scalpel and mirror. This representation indicates the connections which there are between these forms of knowledge and the development of the understanding of the individual and hence of identity which we now have in the west. As we have seen, the scalpel indicates the pervasiveness of the desire to cut beneath the surface, to make visible that which is hidden, to be incisive. On the other hand, the mirror indicates our desire to know ourselves, to be self-reflexive, to have a coherent idea of our own identity. Yet to see ourselves from the inside is a profoundly disturbing activity for to observe our insides—intestines, viscera and organs—is to face the personal in ways which presage death and disorder (Sawday, 1995). Before discussing further the mirror and its relations to identity, I want to consider deviance in the context of the relations between dissection and death.

Dissection, death and deviance

Thinking and writing about death in the late 20th century has become profoundly discomforting. Average life expectancy in the west has gone up and '(f)or the majority of people, death approaches slowly over years of gradual decline and its final advent is supervised by qualified personnel in systematically organized settings where technical facilities for prolonging life are to hand. Similarly, disposal of the dead, like the process of dying, has been rationally organized' (Mulkay, 1993:31). Thus the experience of death has been largely privatized (Mellor, 1993) and set apart, institutionally and emotionally, from the rest of 'life'. Yet the anatomizing urge and its organizing processes are intimately bound up with death. It is the legacy of this key labour of division which itself makes looking at death so uncomfortable to us, for death is both separated off from and yet a defined presence in modern life: truly a/part. Baudrillard argues that death has become a state of abnormality: 'Death has become incurable deviance' (Gane, 1991:113)—it has been ghettoized. But, paradoxically, this has brought about 'a culture of death: by abolishing that which cannot be abolished death makes its symbolic mark everywhere' (*ibid.*).

The historical and cultural construction of death, as of the living body, is fluid. Each form of social organization produces images of the dead human body which come to play a role in the management of the human body whilst it is alive. And here the medieval anatomist plays a central re-organizing, indeed almost revolutionary role. Anatomy meant confronting the oldest taboo—that around death—by counterposing the abstract idea of knowledge to the material physicality of the corpse. There is a close relationship between the scalpel and that other instrument of Reason, Ockham's razor, 'which castrates and traces the taut thread of abstraction and reason' (Baudrillard, 1993:124). Death became subordinated to the noble pursuit of science, although we still acknowledge the taboo, as for example in the 1994 scandal around Copenhagen University's forensic laboratories charging members of the public to look at corpses.

The development of anatomy cannot be seen simply as the progress of an objective scientific discipline accumulating greater knowledge of the human body; rather it was part of a complex web of changing social, spiritual and cultural meanings (Turner, 1990:11; Sawday, 1995). Dissection was not generally accepted as a legitimate scientific technique until the 19th century (Lupton, 1994:45), for it not only disrupted the physical body but also disarticulated beliefs around life and death, the nature of the soul, and the fear of the bodily interior (Lupton, 1994:45; Sawday, 1995). To start with, anatomy was closely bound up with criminal investigation, execution and public dissection. The infamous 'murder act' of 1752 in England could be seen as part of this process of cultural location, instituting 'penal dissection' where, as an alternative to the body being gibbeted, the body would be taken to the surgeons and anatomized. It was intended to evoke horror in the viewing public at the violation of the body and the denial of burial. There had been public dismemberments before, but Foucault argues that the point of departure was that it was now linked to the idea of a greater public good in keeping with the rational philosophy of punishment (1777:48). The other side of the fear and horror invoked by dissection is the fascination with it as demonstrated in the popularity of the anatomical 'theatres' which gained fashionable success throughout 17th-century Europe. These public demonstrations were 'ritualistic expressions of often contradictory layers of meaning' (Sawday, 1995:63) involving the confrontation between the living and the dead, the symbolic power of scientific knowledge over the individual, the representation of society's progress where the criminal is subordinated to the good of the community and the structural coherence of the universe (see Sawday's analysis of Vesalius' *De Humani Corporis Fabrica*). It was only after the move away from public executions in the 18th century that anatomical investigations could begin to be seen as 'disinterested' rational science.

Dirty work is often associated with those who have dealings with the dead, and those who murder and cause death are often vilified (cf. Ackroyd and Crowdy, 1990 on workers in abattoirs). Anatomists had to obtain corpses on which to work, and as the discipline grew so did the requirement for fresh dead bodies. The general public became deeply suspicious of grave robbers and the representatives of the anatomists who frequented the gallows on behalf of a select slice of society. If the hanging proved inefficient and a body began to revive, anatomists would often murder it themselves because of the body's value to science. Thus the early anatomists anonymised themselves in their diagrams for fear of a public outcry against their transgressive invasion. Valverde's picture of 1556 on the self-flayed body (figure 1) is of relevance here, for it shows the need to hide the identity of the anatomist from the public who saw anatomization as an anathema. In this picture the dissected corpse participates in its own dismemberment, eagerly holding up its own skin to display the secrets beneath. But this also indicates to us the simultaneous fascination and repulsion of dissection—the desire to know what lies under the skin, but the fear of it being one's *own* skin.

Thus the scalpel and its close association with death has its own consequences for how we understand our own identities in this world. Mellor argues that in high modernity people are 'ultimately having to take individual responsibility for the construction of meaning as well as the construction of identity. In this context, death is particularly disturbing because it signals a threatened "irreality" of the self-projects which modernity encourages individuals to embark upon, an ultimate *absence* of meaning, the *presence* of death bringing home to them the existential isolation of the individual in high

TAB. PRIMERA DEL LI b. SEGVNDO

Valverde flayed figure from *Historia de la composicion del cuerpo humano* (1556). Reproduced by kind permission of Wellcome Institute Library, London.

modernity' (1993:19–20). It is this anxiety over the unpredictability, irrationality and potential meaninglessness of death that fosters the organization of death and its separation from public life (*ibid.*: 20–1). In the following section I consider this construction of identity, for although the scalpel as agent of death seems to overwhelm the mirror in which we see reflected our own identity, the two tools of the 'anatomizing urge' remain hand in hand.

The mirror

As Norbert Elias (1978) has shown in *The Civilising Process*, the development of the mirror in medieval Europe occurs in parallel with the growth in the concept of the individual. Thus the German word 'ich' only appears on the stage when, around 1500, members of the aristocracy became conscious of themselves as individuals separate from the community. And in this separation, the mirror plays a key role in allowing self-reflection and the development of a new sense of identity. By allowing the individual body to be seen by its Self, the development of self-consciousness arises. This is crucial in the process of individuation where human beings come to have a sense of their separation, physically and psychologically, from the Other. G.H. Mead (1934) was to talk of the distinction between the 'I' and the 'Me' in terms of this separation, for once there is self-consciousness, there is the necessary distinction between the inside and the outside, the depths and the surface. Here is where the sense of self as both subject and object comes from. Here is where the objectification of self, as separable from the community in which it is to be found, originates. If we play around with the concept of 'identity' and dissect it to produce 'id'/'entity', we can focus on the sense of self as individual and 'id'iosyncratic, and also as a whole and complete 'entity'. Thus the notion of identity seems to emphasize the completeness of the self, yet total separation from the Other. Thus the scalpel and the mirror have been used to divide between self and Other. With 'identity' this sense of self *reflection*, of being able to see oneself as others do and of looking at the self from 'outside' owes much to the metaphor of the mirror. Once the self is aware of its own existence, control of self becomes possible. Thus for Elias, self control, and for Foucault, self discipline, become possibilities when the mirror allows us a glimpse of a self-possessed 'individual'.

In this way, the 'culture of dissection' produces a form of identity which is under powerful pressure towards conformity, both through the self-disciplining of the individual and through the disciplining and marginalization of the Other. In other words, 'identity' seems to become closely allied to 'identical'. Although the Enlightenment emphasis on the individual with rights marks in some ways an individualistic turn of thought regarding the self, other developments have served to emphasize that the individual with rights is actually standardized, mass produced from an identical mould—and consequently those who do not fit the mould are not accorded these rights or perceived as self-determining, they are not permitted to have self-identity. It is argued that this rests on the process of 'normalization' which Foucault (1977) proposes is key in 'western' society. Normalization is the process by which the eccentricities of human beings in their behaviour, their appearance and their beliefs become subject to measurement and, if necessary, corrective straightening. Just as a sense of self as separate and different begins to threaten to blossom, then the rise of disciplinary technologies nips it in the bud. The encouragement is to become self-correcting.

Normalization is both a form of identity construction and a form of knowledge construction, as Foucault makes clear. The body of the individual and the body of society are divided and differentiated only so that they can be standardized and disciplined into conformity: 'The perpetual penality that traverses all points and supervises every instant in the disciplinary institutions compares, differentiates, hierarchizes, homogenizes, excludes. In short, it *normalizes*' (Foucault, 1977: 183).

In Bauman's study of the Holocaust we see the brutal society-wide organization of the anatomizing urge. The mass production of the identical is matched by the mass destruction of the Other. In Bauman's analysis we can also see the close association between the 'culture of dissection' in the creation of a new, uniform 'Aryan' identity and processes of rationalization and 'scientific' knowledge. First there is the clear social and physical separation of those considered deviant (Jews, gypsies, disabled people and homosexuals). These are separated according to a view of a norm which is suitable for the creation of a particular image of society. Then there are the efficient processes of differentiation and destruction which involve the separation of roles and tasks, ends and means, between people, between layers of hierarchy, between the private person and the public Nazi. As Bauman argues: 'Definition sets the victimized group apart (all definitions mean splitting the totality into two parts—the marked and the unmarked), as a *different* category, so that whatever applies to it does *not* apply to all the rest' (1989:191).

The incision between male and female is also typical of the culture of dissection, for it supposedly rests on incontrovertible and essential bodily differences. The speculum, a mirror specifically designed for penetration, is used predominantly by men to reflect upon, and penetrate within, women.[4] For the speculum, says Irigaray, 'is not necessarily a mirror. It may, quite simply, be an instrument to *dilate* the lips, the orifices, the walls, so that the eye can penetrate the *interior*' (1985:144). Thus the speculum is the mirror located on a penetrative arm—it combines the qualities of mirror and scalpel. As will now be discussed, the gender dimensions of the mirror and the scalpel are in need of articulation.

Reflection, gender and replication

The female category is cut out in the culture of dissection as a container of all that is Other to scientific and philosophical rationality: it is associated with the body, nature, emotion as opposed and divided from reason, science, culture and the mind. Thus women and the feminine had to be marginalized, controlled and excised by the penetrating advances of masculine science (Easlea, 1983; Jordanova, 1989; Lloyd, 1984). However, within this anatomization of the female, the opening up of the woman give to man forms of control and knowledge over the source of his own and her sense of identity—as supplement to him—and also of the great mystery of life. It encourages much greater understanding and control of the reproductive potential and problems associated with women's bodies so that the protection of *his* offspring (given the property rights culturally associated with fatherhood) is better ensured. The speculum allows close observation of reproductive issues by penetrating almost to the seat of the reproductive act—the womb. Laid bare and specularized, the female patient loses all subjectivity and becomes a passive recipient of, even client for, penetration. The completeness of self, the id's entity, becomes lost in the hands of the surgeon wielding speculum and scalpel.

The identification of woman's physiology also allows man to seek out, record and come to manipulate women's pleasure for his own ends, often it has to be said to allow even further penetration of the female body. It is but a short step from the scientific investigation of the female interior to the commercial pornographic exploitation of this hidden 'knowledge'—and in the 'harder' versions the violent disarticulation of 'soft' (female) flesh becomes explicit, in the worship of parts which is integral to the anatomizing urge. Williams (1990) points out that in pornography the image maker seeks to portray the female orgasm and render it visible to a male audience. This is often accomplished by holding up a mirror and displacing the female orgasm into the male ejaculation—the so called 'cum shot'. However, 'this new visibility extends only to the knowledge of the hydraulics of male ejaculation. . . . The gynaecological sense of the speculum that penetrates the female interior here really does give way to that of a *self reflecting mirror* . . . ' (quoted in Grosz, 1994:199, emphasis added).

Thus penetration and incision can never give access to knowledge of the Other, to subordinated, subjective, lived, embodied knowledges, it can only reflect back the dominant, normalized, disciplined knowledge. In this way the mirror becomes a tool of the normalizing principle. It reflects back, not unique images of the individual, but replicated copies of the norm.

In 'western' society and knowledge, I would argue, replication, in the sense of simple cloning, repetition, copying, has become a central concept. This is related to the modernist focus on the machine as a way of understanding the world. Thus we return to normalization, the idea of *mechanical reproduction* where again we have the mass production of the identical mirror image. The power of the ideas of replication and mechanical reproduction are bound up with the dominant conceptualization of the human body which emerged from the discipline of anatomy. During the Enlightenment, the body was reconstituted as a machine; a reinvention of a body which fitted with the world-view that developed from the Copernican revolution. In the same way that the movement of the planets becomes understood as a mechanistic process, so too do the elements of the human body: in 1628 William Harvey announces that the blood is circulated around the body through the pumping motion of the heart. Thereafter the major conceptualization of the organ is that the heart *is* a pump. And, indeed, recently surgeons have developed the ability to entirely replace the heart with an electrical pump (*Sunday Times*, 29 October 1995). The body is seen as a mechanism endowed with functions which provide its *raison d'être*. The machine-body was dynamic, the parts interconnected—but they operated according to the laws of mechanics not needing an intellect of its own. Thus the body became objectified, a focus of intense curiosity, but entirely divorced from the world of the speaking and thinking subject. 'The development of the machine image dramatically transformed the attitude of investigators towards the body's interior, and towards their own tasks of investigation. They no longer stood before the body as though it was a mysterious continent. It had become, instead, a system, a design, a mechanically organized structure, whose rules of operation, though still complex, could, with the aid of reason, be comprehended in the most minute detail' (Sawday, 1995: 31). In this way, fear of the body and particularly its dysfunctions could be partly offset against the belief that it worked to a rational set of laws. Anatomy also provided the representation of the body-machine as a system of interchangeable, standardized parts. From here it is but a small step to see the main mechanism of the body to be that of an accurate copying of these parts. For example, in many accounts of genetics inherited disease and disability are seen as the breakdown of this replication process. In this way the scientific narrative can be neatly divided from social and subjective aspects of reproduction. Thus on the one hand the effects of poverty or pollution on reproduction, for instance, do not warrant consideration; on the other, the lived, embodied experience of the parents, especially the mother, of abortion, pregnancy and birth, become irrelevant.

I would argue, therefore, that the culture of dissection is marked by a conflation of (human) reproduction to (mechanical) replication. Here a number of incisions around body, gender, self and knowledge coalesce. In the latter half of this century reorganization of human reproduction has turned the process of 'labour' into a factory.[5] The unique individual experience of giving birth is disciplined and organized into the form of the assembly line. The cutting out of the Other in the Holocaust involved the mass destruction of the Other; in reproduction the denigration of the Other (mOther?) is achieved through mass (re)production. The emphasis has come to lie with the *product*—the humanistically laudable outcome of a healthy mother and child (with as many 'defective' products as possible having been cut out of the system earlier, aided by modern techniques to see beneath the surface of the skin). But the *process* itself is de-humanized. Emily Martin (1987) has shown that modern maternity is organized around the dominant ideas of industrial society—standardization, hierarchy, 'active management' of resources and time. In looking at the labour of division which surrounds the organization of reproduction, we see again the play of the scalpel and the mirror. The scalpel cuts between the mother and the foetus, between the woman's experience and the cultural construction of Motherhood. Both technology and medical expertise expropriate the child, allowing it to be individuated and alienated from its symbiotic relationship with its mother. The mother is almost removed from reproduction by a labour of division in which the child is foregrounded. It now stands out from its mother as an Enlightenment individual with rights and an identity. But this identity has developed at the cost of de-identifying mother with child (Taylor 1993) and is an identity based on the mass production of exact copies. The mother herself is also to be replicated as a mirror image of the highly ideological cultural category of 'Mother'. The cultural constitution of 'Mother' in 'western' societies, with its connotations of nurturing, selfless 'sole caretaker', isolated and insulated in the home, is key to the maintenance of patriarchy: 'the relationship between mothering and patriarchy can only be understood if we look not only at how women reproduce Mothering, but at how Mothering reproduces Woman' (Rossiter, 1988:15). This is predicated on the mother-child relationship, and the control of the woman's body.

Ultrasound pictures of the foetus are used to engage this cultural construction of Mother from the moment of conception rather than from birth and also to construct the foetus as a separate individual from the mother. For ultrasound, although it involves no physical cut, is the modern mirror image of the scalpel. 'Fetal imagery epitomizes the distortion inherent in all photographic images: their tendency to slice up reality into tiny bits wrenched out of real space and time' (Petchesky, 1993:610). Modern technologies *claim* to render visible that which is en-wombed; but, the image of the foetus requires an interpretative framework which makes sense of the fuzzy image, this interpretation being itself the vehicle for the highly politicized discourse surrounding reproductive rights (Taylor, 1993:601). Along with other reproductive technologies, it becomes part of the control of the female body.

Both mother and Other are also increasingly written out as normalization takes place around an exclusively male norm. Brian Easlea (1983) argues that men attempt to appropriate the creativity of reproduction. From Aristotle's view of women as mere ovens in which the creative, heroic sperm is placed (Grosz, 1994) to the contemporary comic *VIZ* wherein the parthenogenic myth is advanced so that women are seen as disposable because men come to reproduce each other (Hearn, 1994), the(m)Other is silenced and rendered invisible. Irigaray argues that woman has only two roles in relation to the male norm—as 'reproductive material' and as 'duplicating mirror' (in Burke, 1989:228), and these are seen as simultaneously coming into play in the modern organization of reproduction. Again we see the pervasiveness of the culture of dissection, as the scalpel excises that which does not accurately reflect the mirror of normalization.

Conclusions

In this chapter I have argued that dominant conceptions of body, self and knowledge have been shaped by a 'culture of discretion' which is characterized by both incision and replication.

To conclude, I would like to explore tentatively the potential subversion of the identical from within, by looking briefly at some of the work of Baudrillard, Irigaray and Butler. I suggest that their perspectives might collectively form the basis of a way of writing within a 'culture of dissection' which will not create a new series of incisions, but play with new connections, recursion and mimicry.

Baudrillard argues that the stage of reproduction—of the production line—is subsumed by one of simulacra, since there is no longer an original: 'all forms change from the moment that they are no longer mechanically reproduced, but *conceived according to their very reproducibility*' (1993:56). Thus reproduction is turned back on itself. 'At the end of this process of reproducibility, the real is not only that which can be reproduced, but that which is always already reproduced: the hyperreal' (1993:73).

In the context of the theme of replication in this chapter, Baudrillard's suggestion is fruitful. In the place of the identical as output, as in mechanical reproduction, processes of simulation *begin* with an idea of the identical. If the orders of simulation play on this—so that difference is no longer eliminated—difference is added in order to provide identity. Thus:

> The entire analysis of production will be swept aside if we stop regarding it as an original process, as *the* process at the origin of all the others, but conversely as *a* process which reabsorbs every original being and introduces a series of identical beings. Up to this point, we have considered production and labour as potential, as force and historical process, as a generic activity: an energetic-economic myth proper to modernity. We must ask ourselves whether production is not rather an intervention, a *particular* phase, *in the order of signs*—whether it is basically only one

episode in the line of simulacra, that episode of producing an infinite series of potentially identical beings (object-signs) by means of technics. (1993:55)

The idea that we are able to liberate ourselves from a restrictive analysis of political economy perhaps overstates the matter, but we seem no longer determined by it.

Irigaray argues that there is only one sex—the masculine—and one discourse—the philosophical logos. The domination of these come from their power '*to reduce all others to the economy of the Same*' (1985b:74). Thus women are 'this sex which is not one', for 'women can never be understood on the model of a "subject" within the conventional representational systems of Western culture precisely because they constitute the fetish of representation and, hence, the unrepresentable as such. Women can never "be", according to this ontology of substances, precisely because they are the relation of difference, the excluded, by which that domain marks itself off. Women are also a "difference" that cannot be understood as the simple negation or "Other" of the always-already-masculine subject . . . they are neither the subject nor its Other, but a difference from the economy of binary opposition, itself a ruse for a monologic elaboration of the masculine' (Butler, 1990:18). But within this system women are the 'duplicating mirror' for the masculine, which allows the logos, the subject to reproduce itself (Irigaray, 1985b:75).

Within this phallogocentric order, Irigaray argues, it is not sufficient that women demand a redistribution of power, since this leaves in place the power structure itself. Instead, she suggests that 'mimicry' might be more subversive, by 'convert[ing] a form of subordination into an affirmation', 'to make "visible", by an effect of playful repetition, what was supposed to remain invisible: the cover-up of a possible operation of the feminine in language' (1985b:76). Thus replication may be turned back on itself in order to show the mechanisms which produce the assembly line of identical images. Similarly, Butler argues that: 'Gender should not be construed as a stable identity or locus of agency from which various acts follow; rather, gender is an identity tenuously constituted in time, instituted in an exterior space through a *stylized repetition of acts*', thus it is 'a construction that regularly conceals its genesis' (1990:140). But, as with Irigaray's mimicry, by a 'parodic repetition' (*ibid.*: 141) of the performativity which is gender, it is revealed as a 'regulatory fiction' (*ibid.*). Butler suggests that this false relationship between simulacrum and 'original' can be expressed through such gender transgressions as butch/femme and transvestite performances.

These are two very different perspectives, but they indicate the possibility of subverting the power of normalization and its creation of identical mirror images through reflecting these processes back on themselves, thus de-naturalizing them. A subversive reversal of the conflation between replication and reproduction can be illustrated through Angela Carter's *The Passion of the New Eve*. Here the male subject, Evelyn, is surgically reconstructed as a woman and becomes pregnant, thus retelling the story of Eve, but simultaneously parodying the incisions between male and female, disrupting the assumptions of the body derived from the anatomizing urge. Sewn together, Baudrillard's simulation and Irigaray's mimicry might also show the beginnings of a way to write in a 'culture of dissection' which does not further incise and penetrate, but rather is playful and suggestive.

Notes

1 While keenly aware that 'western', used as a shorthand, is a relativist concept which has developed through colonialist and ethnocentric assumptions, I mark it out to indicate a reflexivity over the active *construction* of this 'western' history which is seen as representing a unique rationality, the progress of Reason, whilst simultaneously obscuring its inclusions and exclusions (see for example, Morley and Robins, 1995).

2 I am grateful to Rolland Munro who pointed out the difficulty of 'writing in a "culture of dissection"'. It is indeed difficult, since I do not wish to suggest a superior reading which itself incises the Other and is set up as the most penetrating insight into the problem. Gibson Burrell (1997) has reflected on the subversive possibilities of silence, though as academics this is a problematic stance to maintain!

3 Much more detailed and subtle analysis of optocentrism is to be found in Martin Jay's (1993) *Downcast Eyes* and a collection edited by David Michael Levin (1993), *Modernity and the Hegemony of Vision*. This was also a time when politically that which was hidden, seen to be secret and mysterious was being cut out of society. Descartes himself was in 1623 widely thought likely to be a member of the 'invisible college' and his name associated with witchcraft scares. His interest in solitude (and hence, it was thought, secrecy) was a decided disadvantage in this climate. To overcome this problem, Descartes showed himself often in Paris to demonstrate to all who were interested that he was a visible and a known person.

4 Despite the subversion of its use by feminist women reclaiming knowledge of their bodies during the Women's Liberation Movement.

5 Replication smacks not only of the factory and mass production, but of the laboratory. There is not space in this chapter to discuss this fully, but there are certainly links between the early 'anatomy theatres' and the laboratory. This is an

interesting aspect of the development of social organization which has not yet been explored. It is relevant to note here that in discussions of the new reproductive technologies, women's bodies have been characterized as 'living laboratories' (Rowland, 1992). The laboratory also emphasizes replication of experiments to gain a degree of certainty over a chaotic world. But here, too, order gives way to disorder, homogeneity to heterogeneity, conformity to creativity. In studies of science laboratories there is an acknowledgement, even by the scientists, of the individual 'craft' skills of science compared to mechanized reproduction, the different conditions under which experiments are undertaken, the 'finger factors' which mean that replication is not so straightforward (see, for example, Gilbert and Mulkay, 1984). Thus the control which is implied in the creation of the identical is not so easily achieved. Nor is it so easy to control the identical once it has been created. However, as Latour and Woolgar (1979) illustrate, these aspects are written out of the 'inscription devices' which constitute the product of the laboratory.

I would like to thank Gibson Burrell for pointing me towards Sawday's *The Body Emblazoned* as an inspiration in the first place and for his invaluable comments on various versions of the chapter. I would also like to thank Michelle Minto at the Wellcome Institute Library for her help in the reproduction of the Valverde print.

Bibliography

Baudrillard, J., (1994) *Symbolic Exchange and Death*, London: Sage.

Bauman, Z., (1989) *Modernity and the Holocaust*, Cambridge: Polity.

Burke, C., (1989) 'Romancing the Philosophers: Luce Irigaray' in Hunter Dianne (ed) *Seduction and Theory*, Urbana and Chicago: University of Illinois Press.

Burrell, G., (1997) 'Linearity, Text and Death' paper presented at the EIASM Conference, Leuven, 4–6 June.

Butler, J., (1990) *Gender Trouble*, New York: Routledge.

Carter, A., (1982) *The Passion of the New Eve*, London: Virago.

Clark, D., (ed.) (1993) *The Sociology of Death*, Oxford: Blackwell.

Descartes, R., (1637) [1954 transl. and edited Elizabeth Anscombe and Peter Thomas Geach] *Philosophical Writings*, London: Nelson's University Press/Open University Press.

Easlea, B., (1983) *Fathering The Unthinkable*, London: Pluto.

Elias, N., (1978) *The Civilizing Process: the history of manners*, Oxford: Blackwell.

Foucault, M., (1970) *The Order of Things*, London: Routledge.

Foucault, M., (1977) *Discipline and Punish*, London: Allen Lane.

Gane, M., (1991) *Baudrillard's Bestiary: Baudrillard and Culture*, London: Routledge.

Gilbert, N. and Mulkay, M., (1984) *Opening Pandora's Box*, Cambridge: Cambridge University Press.

Grosz, E., (1994) *Volatile Bodies*, Bloomington: Indiana University Press.

Hearn, J., (1994) 'The Name of the Pose', *Journal of Gender Studies*, 3, 1, Mar., 69–75.

Hoskin, K., (1995) 'The viewing self and the world we view: beyond the perspectival illusion', *Organization*, 2/1:141–62.

Irigaray, L., (1985) *Speculum of the other woman*, Ithaca, NY: Cornell University Press.

Irigaray, L., (1985b) *This Sex Which Is Not One*, Ithaca, NY: Cornell University Press.

Jay, M., (1993) *Downcast Eyes*, Berkeley: University of California Press.

Jordanova, L., (1989) *Sexual Visions: Images of gender in science and medicine between the eighteenth and twentieth centuries*, London: Harvester Wheatsheaf.

Latour, B. and Woolgar, S., (1979) *Laboratory Life*, Princeton: Princeton University Press.

Levin, D.M., (ed.) (1993) *Modernity and the hegemony of Vision*, Berkeley: University of California Press.

Lupton, D., (1994) *Medicine as Culture*, London: Sage.

Martin, E., (1987) *The woman in the body*, Milton Keynes: Open University.

Mellor, P., (1993) 'Death in high modernity: the contemporary presence and absence of death' in Clark (ed.).

Morley, D. and Robins, K., (1995) *Spaces of Identity*, London: Routledge.

Mulkay, M., (1993) 'Social death in Britain' in Clark (ed.) *The Sociology of Death*, Oxford: Blackwell.

Petchesky, R.P., (1987) 'Fetal Images: the Power of Visual Culture in the Politics of Reproduction', *Feminist Studies*, 12, 2.

Plumwood, V., (1993) *Feminism and the Mastery of Nature*, London: Routledge.

Romanyshyn, R., (1989) *Technology as Symptom and Dream*, London: Routledge.

Rossiter, A., (1988) *From Private to Public: A Feminist Exploration of Early Mothering*, Toronto: The Women's Press.

Rowland, R., (1992) *Living Laboratories*, London: Cedar.

Sawday, J., (1995) *The Body Emblazoned*, London: Routledge.

Stafford, B., (1991) *Body criticism*, Cambridge, Mass.: MIT.

Taylor, J.S., (1993) 'The Public Foetus and the Family Car: From Abortion Politics to a Volvo Advertisement', *Science as Culture*, 3, 4, 601–19.

Turner, B., (1990) 'The Anatomy Lesson: A Note On The Merton Thesis', *Sociological Review*, 38, 1–18.

Williams, L., (1990) *Hard Core*, London: Pandora Press.

Dividing organizations and multiplying identities

Martin Parker

> It is no linguistic accident that 'building', 'construction', 'work' designate both a process and its finished product. Without the meaning of the verb that of the noun remains blank. (John Dewey cited in Strauss and Corbin 1990: 259)

I take it that 'organization' could also be added to this list. As others have noted, the word obviously has two different referents—one a noun, the other a verb (see for example Law, 1994; Cooper and Law, 1995). In the most general terms, structural theory concentrates on the noun, seen as the more or less stable 'outcome', or 'precondition' of human actions. The nouns are those structures 'inside' or 'outside' our heads that constrain (or—depending on the 'purity' of the structuralism—even obliterate) human agency. Capitalism, patriarchy, bureaucracy, the state, imperialism, discourse, ideology, *'langue'* and so on can, according to this way of thinking, be conceptualized as 'iron cages' with a certain kind of facticity to them. Not material things certainly, but things with effects that are analogous to material constraint or grammatical rules. Agency theory, on the other hand, tends to concentrate on the verb—processes of organizing. Organizing here refers to making more or less stable patterns—the use and continual revision of recipes, interpretive frameworks, accounts and so on that allow human beings to act as if the 'buzzing, blooming confusion' is ordered. In the most general sense, but again depending on the 'purity' of the theory of agency concerned, 'outcomes' are dissolved into a flow of interpretive practices. There is nothing stable here, simply a stream of revisable methods for sense making, for doing *'parole'*, for organizing.

This diagnosis of the two poles of social theory is probably overdrawn but certainly widely accepted (see Dawe, 1970 for a classic article on the problem). It has also, of course, led to many attempts to repair or dissolve the supposed breach—within sociological theory the work of Elias, Bourdieu, Giddens and, more lately, Archer and Mouzelis. What is common to the work of these authors, and others, is an attempt to develop a theory of nouns as verbs and verbs as nouns, of 'being' and 'becoming' depending on each other in some way (Cooper and Law, 1995). Whilst I certainly don't intend to try anything as ambitious as a general post-dualist theory in this chapter, I do want to illustrate some practical ways in which ordering can be seen as a performance and not an end. In this sense, actors' (and researchers') conceptions of what an 'organization' is could be seen as moments within endless organizing processes.

This chapter argues that the division of labour, which is a pre-condition of social ordering, results in a labour of division which continually dis-orders. More specifically, I argue that the specialization of function which is found in all organizations produces multiple and contested identities for organizational members. The chapter is based on a research project in which I wanted to put forward a non-functionalist and non-managerialist way of thinking about 'organizational culture' (Parker, 1995a). Using case study material from a health district, a factory and a building society I suggested that culture in organizations should not be seen as (only) a sharing of meanings—a dominant formulation in management writing on the topic—but also as a pattern of differences related to divisions within the organization. In other words, I wanted to suggest that a theory of organizational culture must also recognize 'the culture of department X', 'engineering culture', 'the culture of the older managers' and so on as fragments that are themselves consti-tutive of 'the culture of the organization'. For the purposes of this chapter however, I want to take two terms—identity and division—and use them to develop this argument with a particular focus on identification and dividing—the labour of making and re-making self and other.

Division and identity

In a very obvious sense, formal organizations are sites of division. As Adam Smith's classic example of pin-making illustrated, special-ization of task is the central principle of modern capitalism. Durkheim's embedding of this concept in a teleological framework further suggested that specialization, the differentiation of persons, was the central principle (and problem) of modernity itself. It is only through task specialization that complex social structures can exist at all, yet the fragmentation of affiliations that results threatens to dissolve the normative glue that supposedly holds the social contract together. In the contemporary organizational context, the development of division has extended tasks to include a wide variety of activities arranged laterally and hierarchically. The extension of 'required' functions—marketing, production, design, purchasing, stock control, accountancy, personnel—and the further sub-division of those functions—advertising, public relations, customer care—together with the vertical extension of status and reward differentials now provides an elastic web in which organization persons can be suspended. These divisions of labour (combined with certain material technologies) allow organizations to be globally co-ordinated, exercising remote control effects over time and space that would otherwise not be possible. However the extension itself presents problems of surveillance for the manager. Putting it simply, the more complex the organization, the easier it is for individuals to engage in practices that are subversive, costly or peripheral to the interests of those who are supposed to be 'in control'.

So, for the manager who wishes to avoid an organizational version of *anomie* we have seen repeated attempts to argue for the importance of (re)strengthening normative coercions. A common theme in the contemporary literatures on culture, motivation, leadership, selection, quality and so on (as well as the earlier works of Taylor, Mayo, McGregor *et al.*) has been the attempt to sponsor a version of organizational *Gemeinschaft*. Direct control is costly and the world is increasingly complex. Thus, so the story goes, in order to be successful managers must ensure that their employees believe in the shared mission of the organization. After all, as many social theorists now suggest, self-surveillance is the most effective control technology. For the purposes of this chapter I wish to suggest that the key assumption behind these varied literatures and practices seems to be that division is the problem and that new articulations of identity are the answer. Division, according to this reading, equals 'segmentalism'—beliefs and consequent behaviours that are oriented to one part of the organization rather than to the whole (see Watson, 1994 for a useful discussion). The problem here can be illustrated as that of the organizational member who fights for their territory, department, occupation or whatever without regard for 'the bigger picture'. The organization then ceases to become a body of people oriented towards a common goal and becomes a battleground for sectional interests. Many strategies that attempt to transcend the battleground fail because they are interpreted in diverse ways that result in collective frustration and failure. The suggested treatment for this diagnosis is the construction of a form of identity that would transcend segmentalist interests—an organizational identity, common culture, sense of community, morale, mission statement and so on. Organizational division is defined as pathological and the actor is made whole through unity with others.

If we leave the 'treatment' aside for a moment, I suggest that what we have here is a very suggestive theory of the divisions of identification that result from organization. Organizing does division-ing in order to produce organizations. Hence, organizing produces identities—sites that enable particular classifications of similarity and difference. Identification in this sense is something like 'perspective'—a particular site from which certain things are ident-ified as this and not that. However, the differences between these identities then disrupts the stability of organizing itself. To put it another way, the unintended consequence of organizing is the continual undermining of the very organizations it seeks to produce—the verb continually disrupts the stability of the noun. Now in general terms this is certainly a fairly poststructuralist claim. Notions of the signified, of fixed meanings, are continually dissolved by the unceasing and unstoppable spillage of signifiers. Organization and disorganization depend on each other, which probably means in practice that attempts to prevent 'segmentalism', in order to organize more 'efficiently', continually undo themselves.

So, organization entails an unending process of contested classifications. Deciding what counts as similarity and what counts as difference is the key to drawing boundaries that bring into being organizations. This must involve division—a claim of separation—as well as identification—a claim of similarity. It is worth noting here that social psychologists have written about the varied ways in which people classify others. For example, Tajfel (1978) suggests that the recognition of, and preference for, 'similar' persons helps to affirm a social identification but hence results in the formation of subgroups. More generally, positive and negative social categorization is argued by Tajfel to be an inevitable feature of human groups since it is an element in the construction of personal identity. Setting the implicit functionalism of this approach aside, what I take from this is that there are a huge number of materials that might be used to decide what difference makes a difference—gender, skin colour, dialect, sexuality, clothing, age, yellow armbands and so on. In Levi-Straussian terms, what is 'good to think with' is a locally contingent issue. Further, the symbolics of these differences will be context dependent because sameness and otherness will be deployed in different ways in different contexts. In other words, a person does not only have one identity but engages in a continual process of identification, or as Munro puts it, a 'consumption' of meanings and materials (1996).

Another, older, language seems to provide similar insights, though it sets them within a more noun-like theory. As Gouldner (1957) and Becker and Geer (1960) argued, individuals have a variety of *role* commitments, some of which will be manifest and others latent at different times. These notions of role conflict or strain are translated into the organizational culture in the 1980s by the few authors who have attempted to theorize culture as difference. The piece I have found most suggestive here is Van Maanan and Barley (1985) who use a Venn diagram representation to illustrate how different senses of culture—management, worker, professional, departmental and so on—might cross-cut each other within one organization. More recently, Anthony Cohen has written about this as a matter of identity, rather than role or culture. For him, 'segmentalism', multiple identification, is a fact of organizational and social life—'a person identifies with different entities, and with different levels of society for different purposes.' (1994: 93)

This line of argument suggests that any (noun) formulation of a person's understanding of an organization—their role, culture, identity or whatever—also needs to theorize it as a (verb) process of making claims about membership categories. The categories will be instantiated as suggested unities and differences between others inside and outside the boundaries of the formal organization. In addition, these claims are multiple—one person does not have one identity and one identity is unlikely to be located in only one person. Following Van Maanan and Barley, I attempt to illustrate this crudely in Figures 1 and 2—though remember that the material constraints of ink, paper and two dimensions tend to make these pictures much more 'solid' than I would like them to be

Figure 1 is a 'snapshot' of one organization divided and unified by three hypothetical identification categories derived from 'outside' its formal boundaries. Firstly, certain members of the organization share beliefs and values with members of the same profession or occupation working in other organizations which distinguishes them from other professions and occupations within the

118   © The Editorial Board of The Sociological Review 1997

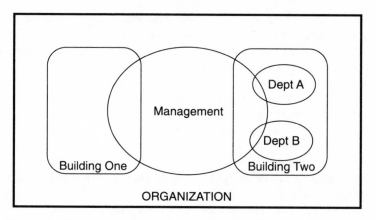

Figure 1 *An organization with some 'externally' derived divisions*

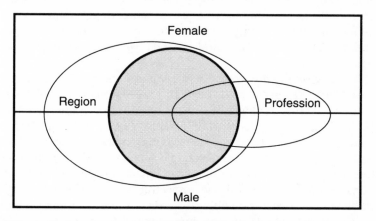

Figure 2 *An organization with some 'internally' derived identity divisions*

organization. Secondly, the organization is located in a particular geographic region which distinguishes it from organizations operating in other regions. Finally the organization, region and profession are cross-cut by assumptions about gender that pervade the wider society.

Figure 2 is a 'snapshot' of the same organization divided and unified 'internally' by three more hypothetical identification categories. Firstly, it operates from two buildings, which divides members into two potential spatially derived categories. Secondly, one of the buildings contains two departments which again can function as markers of difference. Finally, the managers in both buildings and departments are unified by a common hierarchical position and hence distinguishable from other members.

Putting both diagrams together it is possible to imagine a female professional manager working in department A of Building Two for this organization based in a particular region. Any of these division-ings, and lots of others too, may be relevant to her at particular times because they all potentially suggest identities based on some kind of sharing—and hence some kind of difference. The common beliefs, values or languages of the organization 'as a whole' may be the relevant ones sometimes, but are unlikely to be all the time. That being said, it seems that certain commonalities also seem to be more enduring than others—femaleness is likely to be a more durable classification than membership of department A, for example. A central feature of this proposal that I will explore empirically is that many of these affiliations may be contradictory in their allegiances and imperatives—whether to act a a manager or an inhabitant of building two may provoke a real dilemma. In general terms though, this is a model of what *can* be used, not what will be used.

Insisting on the processual dimension also means that these categories are only given form through their continuous deployment and that what is used will be historically variable in interpretation. If the Chief Executive or staff canteen moved from building to another, then it is likely that the meanings attached to that building would also change (see for example Young, 1989). In summary then, this formulation of identification and dividing in organizations is processual, plural and respectful of contradiction (despite the image of structural solidarity given by the diagrams). In the next section I will try to show how some of these concepts helped me think about the three organizations I researched.

Some divisions of division

The line of argument followed above suggests that any model of organizational identity needs to recognise multiple potential lines of dividing within a unity which in itself is a division and so on. However, it is vital to note that the pattern of fractures recognized or reproduced by one member will be different from that of another member—there is unlikely to be total or durable agreement on the grounds of 'us' and 'them'. This is not to say, however, that accounts of organizational division are unpatterned. In my research it seemed to me that there were broadly three types of claim that were commonly made—spatial/functional, generational and occupational/professional (for more detail on two of the organizations see Parker, 1995; Parker and Dent, 1996).

Before exploring these a little, it might be helpful to point out that all of my three organizations shared other commonalities too. They existed within a state and society which can be described as capitalist and patriarchal, and in which there are prevalent ordering assumptions about the meaning of age, professionalism, management, technology and so on. Whatever the ontological status of these assumptions, the talk and action documented in my case studies clearly showed that actors behaved as if they had ordering potential. At the same time, it is clear from my cases that members in each of the three organizations responded to these generalized pressures in different ways. Each organization ordered unique symbols, concerns and practices that made particular sense locally. Transposing talk and action from one organization to another would result in confusion precisely because of the importance of this particularity. Understanding the identification and dividing of one organization hence involves both detailing both specificity and generality—appreciating what made the organization both different and the same. In this regard, it seemed helpful for me to suggest three methods by which members appeared to translate the general into the specific (see Figure 3).

Spatial/Functional	Geographic and/or departmental dividing—'them over here, us over here'.
Generational	Age and/or historical dividing—'them from that time, us from this time'.
Occupational/Professional	Vocational and/or professional dividing—'them who do that, us who do this'

Figure 3 *Three Divisions of Dividing*

It seemed that the classifications of time, space and person shown in Figure 3 were common ways to classify the identity of self and other and hence materialize a particular assertion about the distinctiveness of a particular individual or group. It is important to note that the three forms are not distinct, more than one may be used simultaneously and occasionally the use of one is dependent on assumptions about another. The contexts in which they are deployed depend upon local histories and understandings but their use seemed generalizable to all three organizations. I will now explore them in a little more detail, using examples from my three organizations.

Spatial and functional divides

In all three organizations—a health service district, a factory and a building society—there were assertions of divisions based on space. In the health service district it was suggested that those working at the Regional level were different to people in the district. Within the district it was suggested that the hospital centre had concerns that were not the same as those working in the smaller hospitals or units—elderly, mental health, community and so on. Within the hospital centre members proposed that the Royal Hospital's culture was subtly different to the City Hospital's culture. In the factory a major divide was also expressed in spatial terms—the top site and the bottom site—and in the building society similar assertions of difference were made about head office and branches. Yet these spatial differences were not usually of importance in themselves but were deployed as evidence of other organizationally relevant divisions. Of course, in many organizations, spatial divisions are also functional divisions and the use of spatial binaries usually involves assertions about the different character of different functions. Hence within the district, region was regarded as managerialist, centralized, absorbing too much of the available resource and marginalizing the problems of the periphery. Within the non-acute units of the district, the hospital centre was seen to have the same failings as region. Within the hospital centre, Royal respondents saw the City as having a lower medical status and a more managerialist orientation whilst the City respondents saw the Royal as having poorer accommodation and less efficient management. Within the factory the bottom site managers saw the top site as too accountancy- and design-focused, the reverse was that the bottom site was regarded as too insular and production-focused. Similarly, in the building society, the head office regarded the branches as needing more control, whilst the branch managers saw the head office as imposing too much control and not understanding the problems of the real world.

Not all of these divides had immediate implications. The distinction between the City and the Royal, for example, was rarely mentioned by doctors and seemed to be more a matter of vague historical allegiance. Other spatial/functional divides appeared as far more pressing. In the building society, for example, it would have been almost impossible to conduct an interview with a branch manager without them criticising the staff in head office because it was a matter of continual concern to them. What this seems to indicate is the importance of some kind of us-and-them polarity with space being used as a shorthand for other issues—'them over there are like that, we over here are like this'. As well as this being a device that could be used on a wide level to encompass large divisions within the organization it could also be used to indicate a more localized sense of difference. Consider this story from a bottom site manager at the factory.

> The number of times they come down here with such stupid,
> pathetic ideas, they don't come any more. (. . .) I'll give you an
> example. [*Someone*] bought a panel down here and there was no
> holes in it. Now that may not be significant to you but to me as
> an enameller the point is if there's no holes I've got nowhere to
> hang it. Which means that the man who bought it down has got
> to run through the furnace with it in his hands. And he insisted
> that there could be no holes in this panel. So I give him a mouth-
> ful and basically told him to go away and come to his senses.

The quote tells us that the speaker based 'here' has an expertise that 'they' (who are not often here) do not have. This leads them to do and say things that are 'stupid'. If they really understood the problems of 'here' they would not do and say these things. What is important is that the 'here' can be both used and understood on different levels. The assertion can be classified as one of the general difficulties of communication between top and bottom sites but it is also referring specifically to the enamel shop itself. The enamel shop manager constructed an 'us-and-them' as 'the enamel shop' against 'everyone else'. His department had particular problems and skills that no-one else understood or appreciated. In a similar way the marketing manager in the factory asserted a difference between his department, which understood the vagaries of a competitive market, and everyone else, who looked inwards and thought products sold themselves. Whether used as large or small scale assertions about 'here' the spatial referents are used to indicate something about the relative understandings of the two groups, to assert that rationality can be found here and irrationally there. I will now explore another dimension along which divides were expressed within the case studies—that of age.

Generational divides

> Old age and treachery will overcome youth and skill. (Poster in senior district manager's office)

Another divide common to all three organizations was the use of generational identities—new managers and old administrators in the district; new engineers and old engineers in the factory; new managers and old managers in the building society. I will begin by looking at how an older generational identity can be used as a way of criticising 'now' and then move to look at how a new generational identity can be used to sponsor change.

The dominant theme within an older generational identity was the idea that the organization was currently in danger of throwing away its past—its real mission or heritage. New style management, technology, professional practice or whatever were inadequate because they did not recognize what customers really wanted, what the organization should be doing or what had worked well in the past. The older group had often been with the organization for some time and were less likely to have formal qualifications. In two cases, the factory and the building society, they also related their particular skills to the idea that the people of the local areas, Tidsbury and Moortown, had given the organizations a particularly valuable heritage. They also often held positions of power, were more conscious of the organization's history and were keen to stress that their years of experience were an asset that could not be gained through college or shorter tenure within the organization.

> The one thing you've got with a graduate—you know he's intelligent. But if you accept that he's more than that I think this is where mistakes are very often made. They think somebody that's just graduated from a university, you bring him out there and stick him into something and he's going to be a whizz kid and that's just not on. (. . .) If you take it that he's going to come in and he's going to change 163 years of experience—he's not going to do that. (Factory manager)

Implicit in such a view was that these new people were in danger of sweeping tried and tested values and practices away and this may not be a good thing.

> We've gone away from the old bureaucratic organization's rule
> of precedent. Now in some ways that was an unnecessary
> constraint but in other instances the precedent was used because
> it was sensible. It indicated what had worked in the past and, by
> that definition, what might not work. We just have to be careful
> that we don't go too far out on a limb with some of what we're
> about and chop the limb off while we're on it. (District manager)

This distrust of change was often indicated by this kind of mea-
sured criticism, or sometimes very faint praise (in the building society) or occasionally in open hostility to the change agents who were
attempting to introduce these ideas (in the factory quote above).

An essential component of this generational divide was a nostalgia for a time when things were more certain, when the organization produced quality products or services for grateful customers
and really cared about quality. This was exemplified by the district
manager who asserted that 'this isn't the service I came into', or the
factory manager who compared their old products to the new ones.

> We've got an old cooker in our little museum somewhere up the
> top. It's a cast iron Hercules and it cost about three pounds in
> 1899 or something like that. Now if I got that Hercules down
> here and our latest [*product*] with all the technology we've put in
> it and you give me a leg of pork (. . .) I could do that ham on the
> Hercules, it might take a little bit longer. (. . .) I could make you
> a cup of tea and make a piece of toast on that hotplate and the
> grill just as good as the [*new product*].

In the building society there was a similar nostalgia amongst older
managers for the time when:

> Things were very straightforward, repetitive, you learnt
> something and you were confident that it was hardly likely to
> change much at all. Whereas now things are very different.

As I suggested above, in two of the cases this nostalgia was also
connected with ideas about the particularity of the organization's
geographical location. For the factory it was the close knit community of Tidsbury—'It used to be a little foundry in a little
village'—or the traditional values of the building society were supposed to be based on 'the traditional thinking of a thrifty country-
folk of the day'. In both cases it was as if social change was
affecting these 'communities' for the worse and if the organization
forgot its roots in the imagined community it would be losing a central part of its reason for existing.

The importance of nostalgia has occasionally been mentioned by others writing on organizations. Gouldner briefly referred to what he called the 'Rebecca Myth', the idealization of past events or leaders (1952:346). More recently Gabriel has written about the importance of 'organizational nostalgia' (1993)—a longing for home, for past events, certainties and triumphs. Anthony (1994) and Lilley (1995) have noted that organizational change inevitably involves the re-writing of history—the changing of assumptions about the appropriateness of what was done in the past. Understandings of history seem to be powerful resources within organizations which can serve as a countervailing pressure to change. In all three of my organizations it was as if the older members felt that they were happier in the old days—things may have been hard but there was pride in a job well done and a sense of community.

> There's not many left now, but there was forty people done fifty years service and their families and their grans and their dads had worked here. They were vulcanized. Vulcan industries had been good for Tidsbury. (Factory manager)

Seemingly opposed to this nostalgia was a younger or new generational identity that was positively oriented to change. This group were likely to have been with the organization for a shorter period of time and have formal qualifications for their sector, profession or occupation. They did not usually hold senior management positions and were less concerned with the organization's history or uniqueness.

> To me the health service is a business, it's just in a business of people's care rather than the business of manufacturing nuts or bricks or bolts or whatever. (District administrator)

In addition, in two of the cases (the factory and the building society), these were people who were not natives of the area. In the factory, a group of graduate project engineers fitted this characterization fairly closely. They regarded the older engineers as conservative, under-qualified and currently doing a bad job of running the factory.

> At the moment no-one knows what's going on. Tickets all over the place. [*Products*] falling off the end of the line because there is no-one there to take them. (. . .) You've only got to sit in the office to see what problems they've got. People are running around all over the place.

The younger engineers saw the organization differently because they believed that they were not burdened with assumptions about how things should be.

> Since I don't have much industrial experience, or I haven't been in industry, I don't have a narrow mind (. . .) That's the only advantage I have over the people with twenty to thirty years experience.

By implication, the older generation were narrow minded and change meant persuading them that the new ways were appropriate, teaching them that things could not carry on as they had in the past.

> The older engineers are realizing that they have to change. I think there was a short of resistance initially but now they are realizing that they have to change.

Similar assertions can be found in the building society. In this case the younger generation meant anybody who was appointed since the last general manager retired. Those who were appointed by him were again conservative—'dinosaurs' as one manager put it—and doing a bad job of running the organization.

> There are a number of areas in head office where people have become so cloistered and institutionalized in their own departments that they haven't got an awful lot of common sense, and I say that with some feeling.

The younger head office managers and the branch managers felt that they better understood the problems of the organization and the strategies that were needed to make it prosper.

> We've got to move with the times because the whole financial world has been shaken up over the last few years out of all recognition. And if you don't gear up to change you're going to get left behind really.

Hence in both the factory and the building society a generational identification was also being deployed to sponsor change, to suggest that things needed changing and that the younger generation held the key. This could be characterized as a faith in the future rather than a faith in the past, the articulation of an assumption that what had worked in the past would not work anymore.

So, I suggest that a generational identity, like a spatial/functional one, is a resource that organizational members can deploy to orient themselves for or against a particular issue. Bate characterizes the two sides neatly—

> . . . the elders, those who claim tireless validity for their way of life and struggle to maintain this by pursuing defensive, stability oriented strategies. (. . .) the champions of change, the young turks, disrespectful of authority and indifferent about history, hell-bent on the pursuit of offensive strategies that will bring down the old regime . . . (1994:149)

Like the spatial/functional identity, it involves an identification and dividing of 'them and us'. They don't understand because they are the wrong age, because they don't share our special understanding of what will work for this organization. They are conservative but we are radical, or, they are naive but we are experienced. I should stress that I am not trying to ironize either of these claims. Whether the past was 'really' better or worse than the present is not a matter that can be adjudicated upon. It is enough to note that an understanding of organization must recognize that members' understandings of the divisions of their organization's history are vital in shaping their understandings of the present. As with the spatial/functional divides, the generational divides seem to signify something else. They summarize the difference between whose who understand and those who do not, between those who know what the organization should be doing and those who do not.

Occupational/professional divides

In addition to spatial and generational dividing there seemed to be another way in which difference could be articulated, that of an occupational or professional identity. I am treating the two terms as essentially similar here, though I would argue that the former is the inclusive term with the latter being a particularly intense and powerful form of job related identity (Bloor and Dawson, 1994). Unsurprisingly perhaps, this was clearest in the health district with the clinicians using their professional identity to resist the incursions of managers.

> Now if [*a manager*] comes to me and says 'your hernia waiting list has gone shooting up, and that's bad', my first reaction is to hit him on the nose and say 'well what the hell do you know about it? Do you know how many colo-rectal carcinomas we've had? Do you know how long they stay in a bed? Do you know

how long it takes to operate on them? Do you know the average age of them and the medical problems associated with those patients? They are absorbing all my energies and time. Of course I've got a bloody great hernia waiting list. Have you looked at the number of surgeons we have here? What have you done about trying to increase the number of surgeons?'

There seem to be two elements in this quote. One is a claim that the professional has an expertise that their managers do not. This expertise is based on a training and experience that can not be replaced or controlled by management, technology, new ideas and so on. The second element is a claim that only the professional really understands the central purpose of the organization—making patients better, producing large numbers of products or whatever. Even in the building society, the organization with least obvious 'professionalisation', the three trained accountants—one of whom was the general manager—used the notion of an 'audit environment' both to resist change and point to the suggested central task of the organization. As the internal auditor said:

People here have criticised us for being too conservative, for not getting on to new ideas, but I think there's a lot to be said for being careful. Profitability is important but you've also got to bear in mind the risks.

A professional identity, with its imagined identification outside the organization—doctor, engineer, accountant—could hence be used as a resource to resist change, as well as a claim to special understanding of what the organization should do.

Of course generational and occupational identities could be related—the older factory engineers were both experts because they knew about production but also because they had 'shop floor education' and 'engineering genes if you come from Tidsbury'. This is hardly surprising because implicit in defensive occupational claims is the assumption that they were listened to in the past but that the new order marginalizes them and elevates the knowledges of others. The history of different professions is clearly also relevant here as an indicator of their legitimated power. As is well established, doctors have a long history of professionalization whilst engineers and accountants have begun to make such claims more recently (Armstrong, 1987, 1987; Dent, 1993). The extent to which a particular group in an organization can call upon a professional identification is hence related to wider assumptions about the credibility of such a claim. On the other hand, the extent to which spatial/functional or generational identifications can be called upon is not as contingent on such external validation, being instead a more localized claim that would not necessarily have legitimacy outside the organization.

The examples given so far suggest that an occupational identification is a unified one that can be used to resist or sponsor change; but there were also examples in which a divide was being talked about within an occupation, between emergent professional engineers and craft-oriented engineering managers. In the factory, all the bottom site managers were often opposed to the accountants and designers on the top site but they were also clearly divided into the older 'shop floor education' engineers and the younger academic engineers. The key to this set of positions was certainly still related to claims about professional expertise but in this case they were claims that had not been heeded in the past because of what was effectively defined as an insufficiently professional approach by the older engineers, hence their connection to a generational identification. Reformulating the organization along the lines suggested by new systems engineering suggested that both the older engineers—who 'think if you've not in work with jigs and fixtures and machine tools you're not really an engineer as such'—and the top site accountants—who wanted 'to identify every screw, nut, washer'—had incorrect assumptions about how the organization should work. For the younger engineers the organization could best be understood as a series of abstract systems in which information, people and things moved around. Such a system could be efficient or inefficient and such a judgement could only be made rationally if the procedures of systems engineering were followed. Identifying oneself as a 'professional production engineer' meant promoting, not resisting, change and convincing others that this is a valid strategy.

A similar but more generalizable example of claims to be constructing a professional identification can be seen in the case of management. The professionalisation of management is a process that has gained considerable momentum over the last twenty years and again involves claiming access to a unique body of knowledge. In the health district, and to a lesser extent in the building society, there was mention of the move from 'administrator' to 'manager'. This particular linguistic and conceptual shift is not limited to these cases, it has been noted by other commentators on management (Johnson, 1983; Cox, 1991; Clarke and Newman, 1993; du Gay,

1994). If administrators were conservative bureaucrats who followed established rules and procedures then managers are dynamic leaders who remade the organization.

> They're going to react much more quickly to the demands of people than they would be if it was bureaucratic. (District manager)

The development of management as a professional identification hence again involves asserting claims to centrality, to a particular expertise that other groups do not have. In the district this meant asserting that doctors may be good at clinical things but they should not have formal management power. Similarly with IT professionals, it is a manager's job:

> (. . .) to identify the problems and ask the people with the expertise to tell me whether the systems can actually answer those problems. (District manager)

Hence neither doctors nor IT professionals could 'manage' because they did not have the skills or experience.

Strong echoes of this development of a distinctive management identification can be found in the general manager of the building society attempting to reduce the power of his board because he did not want to be a 'paper fetcher and carrier', whilst his younger head office managers were sponsoring 'management development' and his branch managers criticising the rule-bound 'administrators' at head office. In all three cases new style managers were being articulated as those who caused change to happen. As noted above, to adopt a management identification means being for 'excellence', 'quality', and 'dynamism'—being able to use contemporary management thought in a 'proactive' way to develop a common culture. It meant being against conservatism and insularity, against the established assumptions of groups who felt change could not or should not, happen.

> It was a company that was all these little islands and people did their own thing and the director was king and even another director almost wouldn't want to go into another director's bit of the empire. And that's been swept away. So [*the factory*] now is a team of people with a common goal.

Most importantly perhaps, it meant being able to understand the 'real' needs and environment of the organization. As noted above, being a manager meant understanding the turbulence of the organization's market, being able to look outwards and into the future and see things that those who only looked inwards could not see.

As might expected, the assertion of a distinctive management identification did not go unchallenged—though the challenges themselves sometimes, ironically, worked to talk into existence professional management, even if it was not manifested in the respondent's organization in particular. In all three case studies there were examples of employees denying that a particular occupational group were really 'managers' at all. This was clearest in the health district, with doctors asserting that those who called themselves managers were really administrators because they worked within a bureaucratic and welfarist structure and could never make profits to reinvest. Similarly in the factory, the new engineers asserted:

> They use the term manager to mean foreman. (. . .) 90 per cent of the managers here would be termed supervisors elsewhere.

The implication was that these 'managers' were not performing management tasks and hence did not deserve the title. Finally, in the building society, branch managers criticised the 'glorified typists' who 'shouldn't be in charge' and again used the term 'administrator' with derogatory connotations. In each of the cases, the claim to a professional management identification was being denied and instead it was being suggested that these people were 'time-servers', 'bureaucrats' or 'rule followers'. As I suggested, implicit in such claims is the recognition of precisely the management identification that was being claimed. It was not being denied that there could be dynamic entrepreneurial leaders, simply that these examples did not fit the bill and should therefore not be granted that status. Hence denying a professional identification to a particular group did not mean denying the existence of that profession as a whole and neither did it necessarily imply a particular orientation to change. After all though the doctors wished to deny managers' claims in order to resist their incursions, the new engineers and branch managers were doing the same thing to explain why their changes were not being adopted more rapidly.

My final example, which illustrates that a professional identification can be used to sponsor change, is the case of the information technology professionals in the health district. In this case the emergent professional identification had almost no relation to an older one—such as 'administrator' in the building society—but was instead being developed from first principles. It relied on assumptions about the importance of a particular kind of material technology—computers and associated objects—and the importance of expert guidance on their use. As with the managers, the IT professionals had to distinguish their expertise from that of managers and doctors, to demonstrate that they could do things that neither of the other groups were capable of doing. Like the new engineers in the factory, they used a specific body of concepts and language to model information flows around the organization. The argument was made that this was a politically neutral service, they were not acting for clinicians or management but for the wider benefit of the organization and its clients. As the head of health information said:

> I am a box and string maker. We make empty boxes with strings and they put what they want in the box and pull the strings the way they want to pull them.

In other words, no-one else can make the boxes and strings but after we've made them what 'they' do with them is their business. As was often stated, both managers and doctors were often afraid of computers and hence did not realize just how useful they could be. In a way that was similar to the new engineers; justifying a claim to be an IT professional meant persuading others that they needed information, that the organization is best seen from an information systems point of view. 'We' have the expertise and 'they' need convincing both that we have it and that they need it.

To conclude this section, I suggest again that professional identifications are resources that can be deployed around particular organizational issues. Like spatial/functional or generational claims they provide a shorthand for saying 'we understand and they do not'. Again, as with the other identifications, they can be used both to sponsor 'change' (new engineers, managers, IT specialists) or to hinder it (doctors). This fits well with the idea that professionalism is a collective strategy for social mobility by establishing a monopoly over a particular service (Johnson, 1972; Parry and Parry, 1976). Using a professional identification meant protecting or sponsoring the centrality of a particular group to the organization. Hence it also meant asserting that one particular group best understood the real needs of the organization in a particular area (medicine, computing, production engineering or management) and that other groups (managers, old engineers, accountants, doctors and so on) did not. In other words, to use a professional identification is to comment on the inability of others just as it elevates the expertise of self.

Discussion

In this chapter I have argued that dividing is central to the identification that members deploy in doing organization. In other words, modern organizations are always sites of labouring over divisions. Various resources can be called on to articulate these senses of dividing and I have suggested that they can be broadly classified as spatial/functional, generational and professional. In each of these cases a marker of difference is used to articulate a distinct view of what the organization should be doing and suggest that the other group does not understand the 'truth' about the institution. In addition to this I have suggested that the three kinds of claim can be deployed in a combination of ways, using a spatial claim does not preclude the use of a professional claim simultaneously or on another occasion. Hence the older factory managers could classify themselves spatially as 'bottom site managers' but also as generationally different to the younger engineers in being 'older engineers'. The younger engineers could make the same spatial/functional claim for a production focus but also differentiate themselves professionally as 'new engineers'. It is essential to note that the deployment of claims to difference is a matter of context. An organization member was able to use a combination of these division-ings in different ways to articulate senses of who they were and who others were. Orientations to change, to the past, to the 'mission' of the organization could all be expressed with different combinations of claims. Yet who was 'us' and who was 'them' for a single member could differ according to the context in which they were talking—who they were talking to, what was being discussed, what had happened that morning and so on. This certainly results in a complex picture of the organizing of identification but I would suggest that this is preferable to more simplistic claims about group A and group B. After all, it is surely naive to suggest that some people or groups within an organization are for change and others are not, or that this department thought X and that department thought Y. Organization is a contested process, a continually shifting set of claims and counter claims and there is surely no place or time from which it can be finally captured and presented as fact.

Of course, if we accept a broadly post-structuralist view of language then any claims to explanation are partial. However, to add to this it should also be noted that some claims do seem to have more persuasive power than others, especially when they are put forward by high-status or well-resources members or groups within the organization and/or because they echo claims being made by high-status or well-resourced individuals or groups 'outside' the organization. After all, politicians, state functionaries and management gurus are in the business of making 'us' and 'them' claims too. Organizations are populated and influenced by actors who occupy different power positions depending on their access to wider sets of rules that effectively legitimate certain actions and beliefs but not others (Whittington, 1994). Organizational identifications are hence not a democratic, stable outcome of multiple claims, but a continuing process of articulating contested versions of what the organization should be doing, who it should be responsible to and who does what work for what reward. The sense members make of their organization (and that I make of it) is therefore bounded by the context of these more pervasive, yet still contingent, divisions— between men and women, the old and the young, managers and workers, professionals and administrators and so on.

A development of this claim would be that any organization's pattern of identifications and divisions is unique, yet all these patterns are likely to be constructed through similar dividing strategies. Using a linguistic metaphor foregrounds precisely this kind of assertion. Grammar is a set of rules which allow linguistic practice to take place, we all agree on these rules, without them there could be no shared language. Yet, the use of these rules does not commit us to agreement on the definition of particular terms or the substance of any given linguistic interaction. Analogously, organization (the process of organizing) is a set of rules that allows organizations (more or less stable institutions) to be produced. This does not mean, however, that there is stable and enduring agreement on the meaning of particular material and social elements (technologies, administrative structures, products) or on what the organization has, is or should be doing. As I suggested at the start, in theoretical terms this metaphor suggests that the structuralist question 'how is social order possible?' should be asked at the same time as the agency question 'what are the rules of disorder?' How is an organization recognized by its members and sociologists as a (more or less) agreed-upon entity, but yet also a 'plurality of heterogeneous mentalities' (Bate, 1994:136) or 'temporary and fraught coalition of coalitions' (Watson, 1994:111)? To put it another way, within an organization there must be areas of consensus to enable the complex co-ordination of people, buildings, paper, machines and so on that allow organization to take place. However, as is demonstrated by any reflection or research on organizational practice, there will also be considerable dissensus because these complex processes themselves produce very divergent opinions on the costs and benefits that accrue to different actors within and without the organization as it is formally understood. Organization is an endless process of identifications and divisions—not *either* one *or* the other.

Further, these identifications and divisions, like languages themselves, spill across state and geographic boundaries, while they are cut through with regional dialects as well as vocabularies of occupation, tender, class, ethnicity, age and so on. Defining 'a language' is hence not a simple matter of suggesting a physical boundary. Similarly with identification. After all, as Robin Cohen has argued, 'British identity' is not confined to the boundaries of the British state and is internally divided along a multiplicity of lines (1994). The same argument might be made for any other formulation of identification as something contained within a space, category of people, period in history and so on. Identity is hence a term which must necessarily always be located as the 'identification of X' where X is deemed by an individual or group to be a classification that has descriptive or explanatory force for them at that time. But identifications are also divisions—a cut that divides 'us' from 'them'. Beyond certain requirements of durability and distinctiveness, a huge variety of identification claims are therefore supportable and specifying exactly what the 'bottom limits' of such claims might be is very difficult. Minimally, it must involve more than one person and provide some evidence of a durable and agreed sense of collectiveness. Beyond this the plausibility of such claims depends entirely on whether they are deemed credible, given durability, by the definer, the defined and the audience. As Anthony Cohen suggests (1994:93), just as segmentary lineage structures are resources for deciding who is 'us' and 'them' in matters of 'grazing herds, feuding, contracting marriages, making war, and so on', so is organizational segmentation used for different identification work at different times. In modern organizations, 'identity' is a form of self and other re-cognition that continually divides and disrupts the stability of its noun form through the multiple ident-ifications that follow from the division of labour.

To conclude, what I have attempted to do in this chapter is to attend to three local organizations of identities in order to provide descriptions of organizing processes that reflect the practices and classification systems of actors. This involves understanding the huge variety, and contested nature of, 'us' and 'them' claims that are the necessary and continual outcome of organizing processes. In some cases the organization will be 'us', but in many others ideas about similarity and difference will call upon dividings or identifications from other sources. I would reiterate that there is no neat managerial answer to this disorganization of organization. Identification is the product of division and division the product of identification. For organizations, like any human organizing process, there is no vision without division.

Acknowledgements

Thanks to the editors for their very helpful suggestions on the revising of this chapter.

References

Anthony, P., (1994) *Managing Culture*, Buckingham: Open University Press

Armstrong, P., (1986) 'Management Control Strategies and Inter-Professional Competition' in D. Knights and H. Willmott (eds) *Managing the Labour Process*, Aldershot: Gower.

Armstrong, P., (1987) 'Engineers, Managers and Trust', *Work, Employment and Society*, 1/421–40.

Bate, P., (1994) *Strategies for Cultural Change*, Oxford: Butterworth-Heinemann.

Becker, H. and Geer, B., (1960) 'Latent Culture', *Administrative Science Quarterly*, 5:304–13.

Bloor, G. and Dawson, P., (1994) 'Understanding Professional Culture in Organisational Context', *Organisation Studies*, 15/2:275–95.

Clarke, J. and Newman, J., (1993) 'The Right to Manage: A Second Managerial Revolution', *Cultural Studies*, 7/3: 427–41.

Cohen, A., (1994) *Self Consciousness*, London: Routledge.

Cohen, R., (1994), *Frontiers of Identity*, Harlow: Longman.

Cooper, R. and Law, J., (1995) 'Organisation: Distal and Proximal Views' in *Research in the Sociology of Organisations*, 13:237–74.

Cox, D., (1991) 'Health Service Management: A Sociological View' in J. Gabe, M. Calnan & M. Bury (eds) *The Sociology of the Health Service*, London: Routledge, 89–114.

Dawe, A., (1970) 'The Two Sociologies', *British Journal of Sociology*, 21:207–18.

Dent, M., (1993) 'Professionalism, Educated Labour and the State: Hospital Medicine and the New Managerialism', *Sociological Review*, 41/244–73.

du Gay, P., (1994) 'Colossal Immodesties and Hopeful Monsters', *Organisation*, 1/1:125–48.

Gabriel, Y., (1993) 'Organisational Nostalgia' in S. Fineman (ed.) *Emotion in Organisations*, London: Sage.

Gouldner, A., (1952) 'The Problem of Succession in Bureaucracy' in R. Merton *et al.* (eds) *Reader in Bureaucracy*, New York: Free Press.

Gouldner, A., (1957) 'Cosmopolitans and Locals', *Administrative Science Quarterly*, 2:281–306.

Johnson, N., (1983) 'Management in Government', in M. Earl (ed.) *Perspectives on Management*, 170–96, Oxford: Pergamon Press.

Johnson, T., (1972) *Professions and Power*, London: Macmillan.

Law, J., (1994) *Organizing Modernity*, Oxford: Blackwell.

Lilley, S., (1995) 'Disintegrating Chronology', *Studies in Cultures, Organisations and Societies*, 2:1–33.

Munro, R., (1996) 'A Consumption View of Self: Extension, Exchange and Identity' in S. Edgell, K. Hetherington and A. Warde (eds) *Consumption Matters*, Oxford: Blackwell.

Parker, M., (1995a) *Organisational Culture in Context*. Unpublished PhD, Stoke-on-Trent: Staffordshire University.

Parker, M., (1995) 'Working Together, Working Apart: Management Culture in a Manufacturing Firm', *Sociological Review*, 43/4:518–47.

Parker, M. and Dent, M., (1996) 'Managers, Doctors and Culture: Changing an English Health District', *Administration and Society*, 28/3:335–61.

Parry, N., and Parry, J., (1976) *The Rise of the Medical Profession*, London: Croom Helm.

Strauss, A. and Corbin, J., (1990) *Basics of Qualitative Research*, London: Sage.

Tajfel, H., (1978) (ed) *Differentiation Between Social Groups*, London: Academic Press.

Van Maanan, J. and Barley, S., (1985) 'Cultural Organisation', in P. Frost, L. Moore, M. Louis, C. Lundberg and J. Martin (eds) *Organisational Culture*, Beverly Hills: Sage, 31–53.

Watson, T., (1994) *In Search of Management*, London: Routledge.

Whittington, R., (1994) 'Sociological Pluralism, Institutions and Managerial Agency' in J. Hassard and M. Parker (eds) *Towards a New Theory of Organisations*, London: Routledge, 53–74.

Young, E., (1989) 'On the Naming of the Rose', *Organisation Studies*, 10/2: 187–206.

The labour of division: the manager as 'self' and 'other'

Tony J. Watson

Introduction

Do join me in the space which our editors have allocated to me in their editorial labour of division and engage with this story I have to tell. But in accepting, for a moment, your identity as reader and mine as writer, note that I said 'engage with' this story. This means moving beyond these identities so that we not only subvert the division of reader and writer but transcend it in order to *work together* on a story about managers. We will necessarily work separately too, however. Whether reading or writing, each of us brings to a story our own experiences of life and self in organizational settings and what we know of managers. And we will also bring forward what we might have read in other divisions of this book or from chapters in other books. Allowing categorical divisions to appear and fade in this way is not just part of my introductory recognition of the divisions with which we are both working. It is, first, to apply to ourselves the sort of deconstructive work that we are about to do to others. We can call it *work*, yet it is work which, true to its own spirit, recognizes its *playing* with categories. And this is what the manager does too—or so my story will have it. Will yours? Let's see.

Why is the manager an important figure for study? One answer to this lies in the very ambiguous situation of this organizational employee who is treated to the identity of 'manager' by virtue of the fact that he or she can be distinguished from 'the managed', and yet who is in many ways more 'managed' than those whom they allegedly manage. Being a manager at the same time as not being a manager, we might add, is similar to that other ambiguity where the managers find themselves playing the part of a hard-headed officer of the corporation at the same time as acting out the part of a warm-hearted organizational colleague. Sustaining both 'parts' involves a lot of category work, a lot of identity play. If we are interested in looking at how identities are shaped and maintained in contexts where divisions of labour are also being shaped and sustained, there is no better category of the 'modern' person to look at than that of the manager employed in a contemporary work organization. Work organizations are settings in which attempts are made to shape activities and, increasingly, this involves attempts to shape the subjectivities of those who are employed. If organizations are task-based institutions, they nevertheless require a degree of human commitment and identification with the institution and this commonly requires those directing organizations to seek the investment of something of their very selves by the employees of the enterprise.

The people charged with bringing about this commitment and identification with the institution are those employed as managers. But note the words just used: 'those *employed* as managers'. As we have already recognized, managers are employees themselves. In addition to managing 'others', managers are managed. And, to cope with this (and everything else in their lives), they have a third task: that of managing themselves . . . managing their *selves* . . . shaping and reshaping their self-identities. Like everybody else they have to work and play at 'who they are', at 'putting themselves up as persons'. This involves a simultaneous process of labouring to *make* and to *unmake* division as they order and re-order their worlds.

Identity work and the emergent self—Margaret's musings

My story is about some of the identity work which people employed as managers engage in. I want to make visible the ways in which some of the managers with whom I have worked labour both to divide and undivide and do this within an ever-emergent sense of self. But how is this possible?

As a researcher I observe people doing managerial work. And I can draw limited inferences from this. But these are likely to be very limited. All that I can really do—like any other social investigator—is to listen to what my 'subjects' have to say and attempt to make a 'reading' of their words in the light of my own theoretical predispositions and concerns (Geertz, 1973; Watson, 1995b). I do not do this in the representationalist tradition of social analysis

(Rorty, 1980; Chia, 1996), claiming that I am eliciting straightforward 'reports' of individuals' states of mind, personalities and shifting identities. Instead, I engage in conversations with individuals involved in managerial work with the intention that my questions, comments and challenges offered to the individual in the course of that conversation will prompt them to engage in 'identity-work' as they 'present' themselves to me—and indeed to themselves. There is clearly a particular view of the person here which derives from the long tradition of symbolic interactionism, linguistic philosophy, social constructionism (ivism) and the emerging strand of discursive social psychology (Gergen, 1992; Shotter, 1993; Harré & Gillet, 1994). The effect of all of this is, as Potter and Wetherell put it, to 'displace attention from the self-as-entity and focus it on the methods of constructing the self'. This means that 'the question becomes not what is the true nature of the self, but how is the self talked about, how is it theorized in discourse' (1987:102). The concern is with 'how a subject may be *constituted* on any occasion in talk or writing' (Edwards and Potter, 1992:128).

The focus of this activity must be set in its broader sociological and historical context. And this can be done through recognizing that the simultaneous process of a person *talking* and *becoming* is part of a dialogue which each person continually has with the culture, or cultures, within which they live. We do not work out who or what we are on our own. Our sense of self, our notion of who and what we are, is, in effect, an ongoing achievement of conversations which go on 'in our minds'. There is no 'core' self on which we build as we move through life—at least no core which is more than a recurrent theme in a story which we have built over time in the light of the material, biological and other circumstances through which we have lived. As Bruner puts it, when somebody tells us about their life, 'it is always a cognitive achievement rather than a through-the-clear-crystal of something univocally given' (1987:13).

The conversations in our minds typically involve the putting of one story about ourselves, or the world, up against another. More generally these conversations involve putting up one *argument* against another and then a further argument against that one, and so on. Thinking about our self, putting ourselves up as a person, is a rhetorical process of arguing or debating about ourselves (Billig, 1995). But these 'arguments', propositions, stories, do not just invent themselves in our minds. They are drawn into our self-creating process from our social and cultural context. They may be taken immediately into our thinking process from the words of another person with whom we are in dialogue at that moment but, equally (and often at the same time), they will be taken from our *cultural knowing*—from what we have seen, heard and read over our remembered life. Thus Margaret attempts to construct for herself a self-notion of a 'good manager':

> Am I a good manager? Yes, I think I am. This is what my boss is saying by giving me a big PRP (performance related pay) bonus. But my staff see me as a creep. So perhaps I am not a good manager. Can I be a good manager if my people think of me like that? Possibly. How? Well, as long as I get them to turn out the goods—and that's what a good manager does—it doesn't matter (and, anyway, I only have my secretary's word that the department call me a creep). Hang on, though, I've just been on a course which identifies the good manager as someone who achieves continuous improvement. Have I done that? Oh dear, I fear not. So perhaps I am not so good. But then again, I have been invited to the MD's strategy forum. He only invites to that the people he thinks are really good. If he thinks I am good— that will do for me. I am a good manager. But, what if . . .

I have in part invented this illustration of a private thinking process; but my fiction is based on a conversation in which Margaret was telling me about what she referred to as her 'middle-of-the-night thoughts and reflections'. These reflections are just one tiny aspect of her continuous self-making labours, one relating both to a preferred external identity as a 'good manager' as well as a preferred private self-evaluation as such. This person is *making-up self* but is making it up in dialogue with 'others'. These 'others' are past, present, future, imagined, actual, and potential human contacts. But our culture does not just provide us with imagined or remembered 'others' to help us construct our worlds and our selves. Cultures 'operate' discursively (Foucault, 1980); they both 'offer to' people and 'impose on' them sets of concepts, expressions, terms and statements which frame 'realities'. And within these discourses are specific notions which can be drawn upon when a specific argument is shaped. In the above illustration, two clear examples of these *discursive resources* are the notion of 'the creep' and the notion of 'continuous improvement'. The individual is drawing from the various cultural and discursive contexts in which they live to help them in the reality-constructing labours.

An implicit division utilized by Margaret in her internal conversation is that between a 'good manager' and a 'bad manager'. In effect her own 'self' is divided when, against the notion of her being a good manager as defined by the PRP bonus system, she sets a notion of her as a bad manager in so far as the staff are labelling her a 'creep'. This divided self is repaired by turning to a third concept of a 'good' manager, one in which the good manager is one who 'gets the goods out'. But no sooner is the wound healed than a further one is opened. The voice of a training-course presenter is remembered arguing for a concept of the 'good manager' as one who achieves 'continuous improvement'. Margaret feels that she is on the wrong side of the division implied here; she is a 'non-continuous-improver'. But this division is then dealt with, or avoided, by turning to an alternative one—one where she can feel herself to be on the better side. This is the division between those who are invited to the managing director's strategy forum and those who are not. Margaret labours hard at the labour of division, continuously dividing and combining categories as her *emergent self* is worked upon.

At the end of the day: the life and death of Arthur

The notion of persons drawing on *discursive resources* from the various cultural contexts in which they have been involved to do identity-work is especially well illustrated in a brief statement made by Arthur:

> At the end of the day I live or die by what I do for the
> competitive advantage of the business.

The first phrase, 'at the end of the day', is drawn from a general colloquial tradition in the UK to imply that one is speaking about the basic principles underlying the area of activity being discussed and, at the same time, implying 'quite the opposite: a gritty realism and a recognition of the stark short-term realities of "getting the goods out of the door" or "the meal on the table"' (Watson, D.H., 1988:175). The phrase holds within itself a division—that between the principled and the pragmatic—which it also repairs. The expression is being drawn from an ancient cultural tradition as a discursive resource which helps Arthur say, 'Look at me, I know what things are really about; nobody fools me and I don't fool myself; I know the rules of the game. I know what life is about and all its harsh realities'. Arthur is asserting himself as an 'individual': when the reckoning comes, it is *he* who stands alone and will count the gains and the losses.

The end-of-the-day trope is built upon with the second one about living or dying—with all its echoes of military glory, bravery and religiosity. There is then a switch to a much newer discursive tradition, that of contemporary business-school-speak. This helps present Arthur as someone who is up-to-date with business knowledge. But, with all its implications of competition, winning and losing it links into the two older tropes to suggest an individual who is both a down-to-earth realist and a noble fighter in the battles of the business world. Every element of this tiny piece of skilled everyday rhetorical self-construction (Nash, 1989; Watson, 1995a) can be scrutinized and 'read' to tell a story about how Arthur draws from his culture, social experience and educational history to do identity work at a particular time, in a particular place, in conversation with a particular person (someone he knew to work in a business school, for example, but someone who, at this stage of acquaintance, had not yet revealed his personal distaste for the language of 'competitive advantage'). Even the expression 'the business' has considerable import.

Why did Arthur use the term 'the business' instead of 'the company' or 'the firm' or 'ZTC plc'? My close involvement in this organization (as an ethnographic researcher and participant observer) enables me to make a particular reading of these words which relates to the issue of how identity work can be related to issues in the labour of division. The company had seen a whole series of 'cultural change' initiatives over the two or three years prior to the occasion on which this individual was speaking to me. Central to this had been a series of initiatives known as BIP—the Business Improvement Plan. And the key notion which this attempted to spread among the employees was that each person, at every level in the hierarchy, was an important 'contributor to the business' who was continually developing their skills so that each—as an individual—could, at the same time, improve themselves (through 'personal development' and through enhanced rewards based on skills acquired) and improve the performance of 'the business'. There was a whole panoply of terms associated with this initiative which existed with other initiatives like DOC (Developing Organizational Capability) and the PDP (Personal Development Programme). I came to conceptualize all this as an *empowerment, skills and growth discourse* (this uneasily existing alongside a *control, jobs and costs discourse* (Watson, 1994:114–18). The person whose words we are analysing was one who, as he put it (drawing on yet another discursive resource from the 'empowerment, skills and growth' discourse), had 'fully bought in to DOC, BIP and all that'. Part of his having 'bought in' was his subscribing to the language of 'the business'. He had incorporated into his self-identity, we might say, the notion of his being a 'contributor to the business'. In the statement of self we are examining he is expressing himself as a 'warrior for the cause'. He is presenting himself as a simple soldier who will live or die as his army goes over the top in the battle for business supremacy. But things are not as simple as this, of course. There are particular tensions associated with the occupation of 'manager' which have to be handled by persons as individuals.

Handling the double control problem—the life and identity of Brian

Every manager has to handle what I have called a *double control problem*—a concept that occurred to me when looking at the equivocal stance adopted by many managers with regard to managerial 'fads, fashions, buzzwords and flavours of the month' (Watson, 1994b). I suggested that the awkward tendency of managers to shift between a fondness for and a rejection of managerial fads has to be understood in the light of the *double control* aspect of managers' lives. This is 'because managers who embrace these notions (whether they be rhetorical devices to persuade people to act in certain ways or are actual practices and techniques) are simultaneously trying to exert control on behalf of the employing organization and exert control over their own life by using these ideas and actions *to make sense of their own lives and their place in the scheme of things*. The managers we are looking at here should not just be seen as handling the issue of controlling their own private concept of 'who and what they are'—the element of manager talk that we have concentrated on so far. The people we are looking at are employed as managers and are therefore required also to 'control' the activities of *others*.

Indeed a key part of the whole cultural change exercise undertaken by the company was one which identified managers as 'change champions'. And this, in effect, meant working to change not just the activities of other employees but the whole way they thought about their employment. Arthur, in speaking so as to express his personal work identity as a 'contributor to the business', is associating himself with a discourse which encourages non-managers likewise to shift their subjectivities in a direction which makes them similarly 'members of the business' rather than merely employees of the firm. This manager is using discourse ideologically, then, in attempting to create meanings for others as well as for himself—meanings in which power tends to be obscured and in which the division of labour is made much more ambiguous. It is made more ambiguous with reference to the *vertical* division of labour than it was when only managers focused on supposedly coordinating 'the firm' and left the workers to carry out the tasks which managers devised. And the *horizontal* division of labour is obscured or made more ambiguous than it was when each employee, managerial or otherwise, had a job and a 'function' as opposed to being required to develop and deploy skills in the light of what everyone could recognize as the 'needs of the business'.

All of this means that there is a major challenge to the manager's concept both of what their job is and of who they are as a person. Having 'collected' large numbers of accounts from managers about their work and what we might call their 'self understandings' both in the ethnographic setting of my study of ZTC and in less closely contextualized conversations and interviews carried out in subsequent and ongoing research, I see a pattern where persons strive simultaneously to *identify and deny* a division between themselves as managers and others as non-managers. We can see an example of this in the following piece of dialogue between a manager and myself. This conversation occurred during a tape-recorded interview with Brian, a man whom I had come to know reasonably well from working alongside him in ZTC on one or two projects. I asked him a broad question about what it meant to him to be a manager;

> I don't give a lot of thought, most of the time, to the role of being a manager here. Sometimes I think that the only real significance of being at a managerial level is the car that I drive. That is important—don't let anybody kid you that it is not. But you find yourself, now and again, asking what is different about you that puts you in the car-driver category. I mean, this is something I found myself thinking about the other day. A lot of the time I try to act with my people as if we are just colleagues working together—the only difference being that I carry out certain co-ordinating tasks. You know, I go 'Come on chaps we need to get these figures sorted for the meeting tonight; we'll all be in the shit if we don't have it cracked'. Do you get me?

Yes, but 'being a car driver'?—go on.

Yes, where was I? Oh yes. Well if all I am doing is just another job in the department—a co-ordinating and geeing-up job—then the question arises as to why I get into a company car at the end of the day and the others don't.

Brian can be heard here (or 'read' if you prefer) questioning the idea of difference. As a division-labourer he is working on his *legitimacy* as a division-labourer, both in the eyes of themselves and others. The interviewer is the particular 'other' here, of course, but in part the interviewer stands for a more generalized other and plays a 'looking glass' role in Brian's self-management. Brian can be seen as joining the researcher in puzzling about the nature of his role in the organization. He is debating with me about his role, yes, but he is also arguing with himself. Like Arthur, Brian uses the expression 'at the end of the day' and, at one level, this is used in a direct and literal sense to refer to the time of leaving the factory each evening. However, at the connotive level, there is an implication that the 'question' which arises about why he drives a company car when others do not is a rather fundamental one. We will see in a moment how the conversation developed. But let us, first, look at his words in more detail. It might be helpful to note that the term 'car driver' was sometimes used in the plant to mean somebody at a sufficient level in the hierarchy to have a company car as part of their 'reward package'. And the size and type of car was an important indicator of one's status within the managerial hierarchy itself.

Brian presents himself as someone who is thinking about his role in the division of labour prior to this conversation: he was thinking about these matters 'the other day'. His understanding is framed in terms of the horizontal division of labour, rather than that of a vertical hierarchy; he is a 'colleague' with *his people*. The very use of the term 'my people', of course is letting the claim to colleagueship slip away somewhat. He is aware that he is not really just a colleague doing what he calls 'certain co-ordinating tasks'—at least this is suggested by his statement that he tries 'to act' as if this is the case. He tells us the sort of things he says to his staff, 'come on chaps', and he implies that 'we are all in this together' with the use twice of the plural pronoun 'we'. Manager and managed are all in the same boat, all on the same side—if the problem is not 'cracked' then 'we'll all be in the shit'. Brian is handling a *division*—the division between manager and managed—by stressing the opposite of division: *unity*. In doing this he is adopting an utterly standard ploy used by every manager and political leader down the ages: one in which the leader implies to the led that they are all part of an organic unity, all part of a team, all members of a family. This type of metaphor for the organization (or polity, or army, or church) is one which often tries to convert a potential to dominate into a facilitating authority by making the 'vertical' division between the 'managers' and the 'managed' appear more like a type of 'horizontal division'. Thus the manager/leader figures herself or himself as the mother or father of the 'family' or as the captain of the 'team'.

In acting towards staff as someone who simply does 'a coordinating and geeing-up job', Brian is adopting an utterly standard managerial tactic. But there is more to this than initially meets the eye. Further labour of dividing and undividing is required to 'integrate' this activity into Brian's notion of self. It is clear from what he goes on to say ('the question arises as to why I get into a company car . . . and the others don't') that if the claim to colleagueship is a form of ideology-speak or propaganda then he is not one who easily 'believes his own propaganda'. But is his utilizing of a 'we are all really the same, chaps' discourse simply a matter of cold calculation and nothing to do with his preferred longer-term self-image? There is no reason in principle why this should not be the case, but my research suggests that managers are not easy with such a notion of themselves. They are conscious of an ever-present, if implicit, division between an insincere person and a sincere one, between a hypocrite and an honest person, between a manipulator and an honourable individual. Brian for example responds to my invitation to answer his own question with a further attempt to evade the issue of his part in a hierarchical division of labour.

> You could regard the car, along with the higher salary that I get, as a reward for my having a higher level of skills than the others—I am more experienced and have proved myself as capable of getting the others organized, keeping things moving, er . . . But . . .

> But?

> No, it isn't just that. It's responsibility. Responsibility is the key. When it comes down to it, I am responsible for what goes off in the department. I am answerable. It is me who's in charge of things and it's me who'll get hauled over the . . . er . . . it's me who gets the bollocking if we don't hit the targets.

You are in charge?

Of course I am. Yes, I suppose so.

You sound uneasy about it.

No I'm not. Yes, perhaps I am. I was.

Go on.

I am not the type who wants to be above other people, if you know what I'm saying. Yet I know at school I always wanted to be a prefect. I'm a bit complicated really. We are all different, aren't we? It is just how I am.

Could you explain that to me a little more?

I am not sure if I can explain it to myself. But I have pondered on it. I sometimes get quite bothered: I want to be liked and respected by the lads (and the lass, er, lady—my secretary) as, you know, like them. But I have something in me that, at the same time, makes me want to be—not above—but the one who is different—could I say as the one who wants to make a difference ... to things, I mean?

I'm not sure I am following you.

OK, the way I am is that I don't seek glory or anything like that but if there have got to be people who are bosses and people who are bossed, then I am not going to be one of the bossed. OK?

I think I follow that.

Hang on. No, rub that out. Stop the tape recorder. No, that's not me. 'Bosses' and that—that's not me, that's not the way I like to think.

Brian seems to be working hard here at the verbal labour of division and at identity-making. He seems to have a notion of himself as someone who is 'not above others' but who, in effect, is unhappy unless he is in some way different from or 'in charge' of others. At first he stressed 'responsibility' rather than accepting that he is 'in charge'. And immediately he had used these words he seemed on the point of withdrawing them. When, a little later, he found himself speaking of being a 'boss', he indeed attempted to retract his words. He wanted them 'rubbed out'. And he is as near to explicit as we might ever get in such a conversation about this relating to his self-identity. While not using this form of words, he draws on three 'lay' or 'everyday' discursive resources which function equivalently to the social scientist's concept of self-identity. The first of these is the notion of 'types': 'I am not the type who wants to be above other people'; the second is his expression 'the way I am' ('is that I don't seek glory') and the third emerges in his exclamation 'No, that's not me' ('that's not the way I like to think').

Conclusion

In this small insight into the life of Brian we see him engaging in a process of theorizing about himself. It is almost as if he is setting up and testing hypotheses about himself as he engages in what amounts to a debate with his interrogator as well as a debate with himself. Talking, thinking and being all come together in the process of self-examination, self-expression and self-creation. These words are Brian's unique account of his particular *ever-emergent* self. Yet, in my research, I found a pattern in many of the accounts which other managers gave which resemble this in an important respect.

Managers frequently used expressions such as 'the sort of person I am' and such self-concepts can be seen as pulling together the pragmatic aspects of the way they go about their work (especially those aspects involving relating to others) and the personal morality which, to various degrees, they feel they can bring to bear on their work (see also Watson, 1996). They would generally, I think, concur with the statement made by another manager who said,

> To be the sort who is a bastard at work—only caring about hitting the month end target regardless of the people they manage—and a good sort at home, is completely unacceptable as I see it. You'd be a Jekyll and Hyde. I mean, it's not human, is it?

To be divided in this way would be to involve losing all integrity, all wholeness, all humanity. Identity-work is needed to make clear to the world that there is no division between the manager as a human being and the manager as a functionary. The labour of division is as much about denying division or overcoming it as it is about making it. Nothing can be achieved without categories, but categories can be dangerous. This applies both to categories within self-making processes as well as to social categories which the manager has to handle in their occupational efforts.

The individual manager engaged in the labour of division, combined as it is in their occupational role with a labour of creating enough unity to bring about productive co-operation, frequently emerges in my research as a person striving to find pattern, consistency, integrity in what they do and what they are. The managerial labour of division, then, is also a labour of unity. It is a labour of constant self-creation and self re-creation. It is a labour of managing one's self as well as a labour of managing others. The talk we have examined in this chapter has enabled us, in part, to engage in an 'analysis of the linguistic micro-practices which define and shape . . . modernist discourse' (Chia, 1996:191). But it has also enabled us to engage with aspects of the private selves of particular human beings who are continually *making* and being *made by* that discourse. Managers endlessly strive to cope with the challenges of simultaneously managing *self* and managing *the other* as they engage with the never-ending tasks of casting and recasting divisions within that most modernist of institutions, the bureaucratic work organization.

References

Billig, M., (1995) *Arguing and Thinking: a rhetorical approach to social psychology*, Cambridge: Cambridge University Press.

Bruner, J., (1987) 'Life as Narrative', *Social Research*, 54:11–43.

Chia, R., (1996) *Organisational Analysis as Deconstructive Practice*, Berlin: de Gruyter.

Edwards, D. & Potter, J., (1992) *Discursive Psychology*, London: Sage.

Foucault, M., (1980) *Power/Knowledge*, Brighton: Harvester.

Geertz, C., (1973) *The Interpretation of Cultures*, London: Fontana Press.

Gergen, K., (1992) 'Organisation theory in the post-modern era' in M. Reed and M. Hughes (eds) *Rethinking Organisation*, London: Sage.

Harré, R. & Gillet, G., (1994) *The Discursive Mind*, London: Sage.

Nash, W., (1989) *Rhetoric: the Wit of Persuasion*, Oxford: Blackwell.

Potter, J. & Wetherell, M., (1987) *Discourse and Social Psychology: beyond attitudes and behaviour*, London: Sage.

Rorty, R., (1980) *Philosophy and the Mirror of Nature*, Oxford: Blackwell.

Shotter, J., (1993) *Cultural Politics of Everyday Life: social construction, rhetoric and knowing of the third kind*, Milton Keynes: Open University Press.

Watson, D.H., (1988) *Managers of Discontent: trade union officers and industrial relations managers*, London: Routledge.

Watson, T.J., (1994a) *In Search of Management: culture, chaos and control in managerial work*, London: Routledge.

Watson, T.J., (1994b) 'Management "flavours of the month": their role in managers' lives', *International Journal of Human Resource Management*, 5:889–905.

Watson, T.J., (1995a) 'Rhetoric, discourse and argument in organisational sense-making: a reflexive tale', *Organisation Studies*, 16:805–21.

Watson, T.J., (1995b) 'Shaping the story: rhetoric, persuasion and creative writing in organisational ethnography', *Studies in Cultures, Organisations and Societies*, 2:1–11.

Watson, T.J., (1996) 'How do managers think?—morality and pragmatism in theory and practice', *Management Learning*, 27:323–41.

Introduction

To think of division in spatial terms is usually to think of the Euclidean space of geometric shapes with clearly defined regions, territories and boundaries. It is to think of centres and margins, an issue that has come to dominate much spatial theory over the past decade. In this section all three chapters offer an alternative to Euclidean ways of thinking about space and its clear lines of sight. All chapters address the issue of complex topologies and the uncertainties of folding space, or what Marcus Doel has described as 'scrumpled geographies'. To see space as complex topology rather than a clearly defined set of regions challenges the way that space is represented.

In the chapter by John Law and Ruth Benschop, this issue is analysed through a series of visual representations of space in painting and the ontological politics that underlies these ways of representing. Starting with Uccello's *The Battle of San Romano*, they argue that the Renaissance tradition of linear perspective operates through the conventions of narrative Euclideanism. The painting illustrates a narrative and that narrative is held in place by the geometry of the perspective of the picture and the way of seeing that it performs. Narrative Euclideanism operates through a labour of division between subjects and objects. Perspective interpellates the viewer as subject who confronts the external world of objects represented in the picture through narrative form.

It was not until the 17th century, the period that Foucault has called the classical age, that art begins to challenge this narrative Euclideanism. Through the example of Vermeer's painting *View of Delft*, Law and Benschop argue that a more topologically complex relation between depicted objects and viewing subjects is created here. The absence of a single viewing point constitutes the viewing subject as an 'unmarked subject', a God eye that can see all from many different positions. The eye travels in a topologically complex space, it reveals that the subject and the object are more complex in their constitution than is represented in the narrative Euclideanism of the Renaissance.

While these differences can be discerned between Uccello and Vermeer, Law and Benschop argue that they still share a way of representing that performs a labour of division between subjects and objects. In more contemporary painting, this division is less clear. Looking at Rémy Blanchard's *Le chat dort, les souris dansent* they argue that in such contemporary painting we can see a deconstruction of this separation between subjects and objects and an attempt to represent heterogeneity and ambiguity instead. The narratives told by the picture are not static or singular, they are ambiguous and unimaginable. In this painting representation is about impossibility and discontinuity.

Finally in Tim Leurah Tjapaltjarri and Clifford Possum Tjapaltjarri's *Napperby Death Spirit Dreaming*, Law and Benschop see in this example of Australian Aboriginal art a complete break with the western traditions of representation in art. In particular, there is no separation of subject and object in this painting: they remain folded together, the picture becomes a depiction of the agency of objects that are synonymous with subjects. They argue that looking at how representation works reveals its ontological presumptions and that this revealing of the ontology of representation opens up a space for ontological politics.

While Law and Benschop consider the complex topology between subjects and objects, Kevin Hetherington addresses the topological relationship between spaces and places in his chapter. He argues that we should see places, not as the representations of sites by subjects and the expression of their subjectivity, but as material assemblages in which the heterogeneity of things comes to be ordered and named. Places, Hetherington argues through the metaphor of the ship, are heterogeneous placings of things that come by virtue of mobile arrangements, to be ordered into a system of difference and for those differences then to be named.

Places are made up of the material effects associated with placing, arranging and naming. Hetherington goes on to explore this argument by looking at that seemingly most subjective of places 'home'. He does this by reading Bachelard on the poetics of space, against the grain of Bachelard's humanism (1969), to reveal how much the felicitous and intersubjective poetic image through which we come to know places, is dependent on the agency of a material-

Section III
Spacing division

ity such as that found in the artefacts that make up a home or photographic snapshots. Place, in effect, becomes for Hetherington both material and semiotic. He shares with Law and Benschop the argument that subjects and objects are folded into one another and that agency is an effect of both rather than the exclusive privilege of the subject.

In Steve Hinchliffe's paper this idea of folding is also taken up, through the metaphors of disturbance and fluidity. Hinchliffe begins by looking at how nature gets folded into the home, in particular, by looking at the division between inside and outside and the traffic between such spaces. Boundaries are not fixed, they move in time and space and are called up through materials. Hinchliffe's intention is to disturb—to disturb the foundationalism and binarisms that underlies our representation of space. Home working is ambiguous in its boundary work; keeping out nature in the form of germs through the design of objects into the introduction of fresh smells to purify the home by bringing nature in. The main part of the chapter explores these complex topologies through a study of a housing estate in Hvalsø, Denmark, and the introduction of energy-saving devices into the home. Hinchliffe shows how we can think about home through the topology of the network and the way that this comes to contradict that of the region. He shows that to think of space as regions alone is to miss the conditions of possibility afforded by the network that makes the space. This was what environmental activists achieved, in trying to make home-owners see that their homes were not bounded regions cut off from the outside but inter-connected with other spaces. The making visible of the relational spaces of networks that are lost to regional space is also a way of making visible power effects.

Hinchliffe goes on, however, to show that the network metaphor has its own limitations, not least that it tends to treat the heterogeneous materials that make it up as somewhat static, structured and formalistic. He argues for a more fluid understanding of the relations that make a space and the possibilities for variation and uncertainty that this allows. Fluids, however, are not free flowing and without friction, they have a viscosity that allows things to stick, albeit temporarily. Fluidity and the folds we can see in a viscous liquid, albeit not through the conventions of a western 'linear perspective', are a way of seeing how space is constituted and divisions made, a theme further developed in section four.

Resisting pictures: representation, distribution and ontological politics

John Law and Ruth Benschop[1]

addressing a picture with a general rule feels rather like addressing a peach with a billiard cue (Baxandall, *Patterns of Intention*, 1985, p. 12)

To represent is to perform division. To represent is to generate distributions. Distributions between painter and observer, between a depicting surface and object depicted, between places located on a surface, between that which is depicted and that which is not. To represent is to narrate, or to refuse to narrate. It is to perform, or to refuse to perform, a world of spatial assumptions populated by subjects and objects. To represent thus renders other possibilities impossible, unimaginable. It is, in other words, to perform a politics. A politics of ontology.

This chapter explores four visual depictions and the different ways in which these make subject/object distinctions, narratives and spatialities. Our object is to lever these different modes of performance apart to create an area of play in which we may learn something of the politics of subject/object division, of narrative, of spatiality. Along the way we may learn about a politics which tries not to legislate about such divisions but, rather, explores the labour of division. Two of the visual depictions are taken from the great *corpus* of Western 'high art': paintings by Paolo Uccello and Jan Vermeer. The other two are contemporary. One is a painting by Rémy Blanchard, from France. The second, by Tim Leurah Tjapaltjarri, takes us to a recent tradition of Australian Aboriginal art. These four paintings do not simply differ from one another in their generation of distributions but also come from different times and places, differ in the status attached to them, and where we have to go in order to see them. We will not focus extensively on these other differences—but they make the approach towards each painting a little different, and mean (or so we hope) that we avoid falling into the trap described by Bryson above.

Our method is straightforward. We use each successive depiction as a yardstick to magnify differences between it and the subsequent painting. In this way we pay a necessary tribute to the ways our representations of these four depictions are constituted by technologies of representation. Thus the moves we make from picture to picture are neither innocent, nor fully dictated by their inherent structure. Instead they are part of a political exploration of representation, which is also a progressive trail: in time, from then (the fifteenth century) to now; in space, from here (the Western world) to there (Australia); from incompleteness to wholeness; and from the concealment of ontological work to its exposure.

Narrative Euclideanism: the rationalisation of sight

The first visual depiction is the painting (Plate 1) by Uccello of *The Battle of San Romano* (c.1435 to c.1455; National Gallery, London).[2] An art-historical account of this kind of painting tells that it *illustrates a narrative*,[3]—in this instance a battle in which the Florentines beat their opponents.[4] This painting shows an event that has occurred in the real world. Painter, viewer and object have been organized around and through this painting in the manner of the new perspectivalism of the Italian Renaissance.

The story told by art historians (including contemporary Italians themselves, and most notably Alberti), runs approximately so.[5] On the one hand there is a world, on the other, an observer. A faithful representation of the world understands the point of view of the observer as an eye that looks through an imagined windowpane onto the world. The canvas becomes the imagined windowpane. The world that is transformed to fit onto the canvas/windowpane is a Euclidean volume. The objects making up the world may be viewed through that window in accordance with a set of geometrical rules. Representation is a matter of projection from the observer's eye of the geometrically determined three dimensions of the world onto the two-dimensional surface of the windowpane. This means, *inter alia*, the construction on that surface of a vanishing point. Together with that construction, a series of transformations is made of the three-dimensional which allow a geometrically appropriate conversion of a perspective on a volume into a surface. Such is the theory: an application of humanist reason to the problem of representation.[6]

Paolo Uccello's *The Battle of San Romano* may be taken as an early application of the visual reasoning of linear perspective to depiction. According to Gombrich, Uccello seems to be playing with the forms and colours that make the surface of his painting. The 'blocky' horses make, as it were, statements about the projected volumes that they occupy in the world behind the representational windowpane. We also see Uccello experimenting with foreshortening, for instance, with the vanquished soldiers lying on the ground, their feet towards the observer. In addition, the fact that the painting as a whole is constructed with a vanishing point that assumes distance in the world is witnessed by the fall of the lances, pointing, as they do, to the perspectival vanishing point.[7] So what we see of those volumes varies in size as a function of perspectival projection and the imagined distance from the observer. Conversion is possible from the two dimensions of the painting to the three dimensions of the world according to the logic of Narrative Euclideanism. The two-dimensional resources that Uccello offers us make it possible, at least in principle, to reconstitute the volumes from which they were derived.

The observer, the world and its representation

We can tell stories about the art-historians' way of looking at Uccello's painting, stories of Italian Renaissance perspectivalism. Although the versions vary, for our purposes they can be aligned reasonably well. To summarise, it may be said of the *observer* that she:

is a *point*, constituted by the rules of perspective.

is a point at which matters are *drawn together*. A series of transformation rules render matters coherent at that point.[8]

is a point that is *not included in* the world that it observes. Subject and object are separate.

has only a single *perspective* on the world. She does not see everything at once, although inexhaustible other partial perspectives are possible.

is to some extent in a *relationship of control* with the world. Within the logic of Narrative Euclideanism the flat surface of the canvas is converted into a potential experimental site. Depictions could be re-arranged to re-present other thereby generated volumetric worlds.[9]

It may, in turn, be said of the *world* that it:

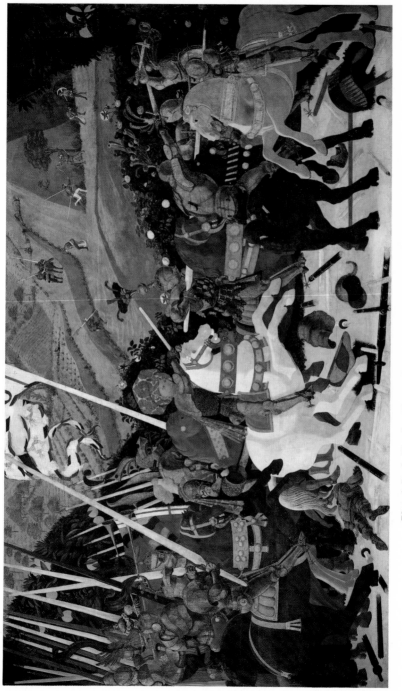

Plate 1 Paolo Uccello: *The Battle of San Romano.* Probably about 1450–1460. Reproduced by courtesy of the Trustees, The National Gallery, London.

Plate 2 Jan Vermeer: *View of Delft*. Amsterdam: Mauritshuis, The Hague.

Plate 3 Remy Blanchard: *Le chat dort, les souris dansent.* (When the cat is away the mice do play). Gronigen: Groniger Museum, The Netherlands. Photograph by John Stoel.

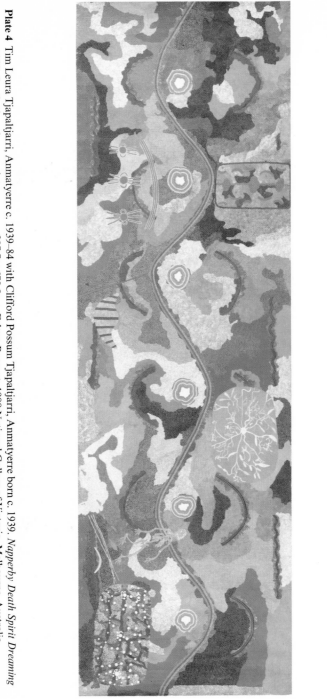

Plate 4 Tim Leura Tjapaltjarri, Anmatyerre c. 1939–84 with Clifford Possum Tjapaltjarri, Anmatyerre born c. 1939. *Napperby Death Spirit Dreaming* 1980. Synthetic polymer paint on canvas 207.7 × 670.8cm. Felton Bequest, 1988 National Gallery of Victoria, Melbourne, Australia.

is *separate* from the observer.

is a *volume* containing objects, which is three-dimensional and *Euclidean* in character.

exists *prior* to its depiction, awaiting discovery.

contains objects which have *continuities*. They pass through time revealing substantial geometrical stability—or differences—explicable in terms of object-interactions, collisions, etc.

has a need for *narrative*, for stories that illuminate the character and displacement of objects in the world.

Finally, it may be said of the *representation* that it is:

illustrative because the world and its narratives are separate from the depiction. They pre-exist their depiction. The stories are as it were out there, in reality. Depictions illustrate that world—a world apart.

limited, finite. It is a revealed perspective on the world. As we've already noted, other perspectives are possible. This means that the world is *inexhaustible* with respect to representation. Other constructions are always possible.[10]

Resisting narrative Euclideanism

It is often suggested that the geometrical art of narrating the Euclidean world of the Italian Renaissance became, in one guise or another, the hegemonic set of framing assumptions for much depiction in the West through to the nineteenth century.[11]

This claim may be nuanced in several ways, for instance, by including the cartographic geometries that generate views from nowhere.[12] But such nuances do not disqualify the claim completely. Thus though it is possible to find exceptions—and we will explore some of these below—geometrical ontologies have been naturalized in many contexts to the point where the (narrative) ways in which they constitute subject, object and spatiality are difficult to resist. For certain purposes they have performed themselves through, and into, us. Contemporary Westerners have, to a large extent, been constituted as Euclidean subjects at least when they think about representation.[13] Indeed, the naturalization has proceeded to the point where the conventions of perspective are often treated as a part of the order of things. A single mode has worked itself into places which might be—or even are—made in other ways.

An immediate consequence of this is that it is difficult to avoid treating the Italian discovery of linear perspective as the proper way of relating to representation—indeed as a discovery of the nature of reality rather than as an invention.[14] But it is possible to resist this, and a number of recent art historians and many artists do just that.[15] Our interest in joining that resistance is quite specific. We wish to resist the *ontological naturalization* implied if we allow that linear perspective is part of the order of things. We want to remind ourselves that Narrative Euclideanism may be imagined as invention rather than discovery (Edgerton, 1976:6).[16] If linear perspective is a way of *constituting* subjects and objects, rather than revealing relations that are given in the order of things, it follows that subjects, objects and spatialities do not have to relate in that particular way. Studying other depictions will help to discover other possible forms of the labour of division between subject and object, other ontological possibilities. It will help to rediscover, in short, that representation is not only about epistemology but also about ontology. Such rediscovery or resistance is thus a *technical* matter, a matter of colliding representational details.

Descriptive assemblage: planes and grains

The attempt to make space by imagining alternatives to Narrative Euclideanism takes us first to the work of Svetlana Alpers. In *The Art of Describing* (1989), she argues that much classic Dutch art constructs itself, its objects, and its subjects, differently from Italian Renaissance perspectivalism. So let's move to the 17th century Netherlands. Look at this painting (Plate 2) by Jan Vermeer, his *View of Delft* (c.1660; Mauritshuis, Den Haag). We are looking across the river to a townscape, the roofs of Delft. Alpers, talking also of other Dutch art, makes an argument in four parts.

Such paintings she says, *describe*, a depiction which is not, however, to be understood as the illustration of a narrative.[17] In Uccello's *The Battle of San Romano* a story is being told about the glories of a battle and, by implication, of the part the Medicis play in that battle. The Vermeer is different. There are people, but action there is not. The painting does not depend on, or appear to demand, a story. One might add that the picture is less obviously humanist than its Italian counterpart. 'Man' is not the measure of things. Which is not to say that Vermeer doesn't have room for the human, or to suggest that his art fails to constitute subjectivity and objectivity.[18] Rather, he is going about the matter in a different way.

Alpers' second point is that in this kind of painting no particular point of view is adopted. The *View of Delft* is not obviously geometrically perspectival. There *is* no viewpoint. It may best be understood as a view from nowhere. Nowhere in particular. To explain this, Alpers suggests that Dutch painting derives in part from the conventions of cartography: the various Western cartographic projections derive, most often, from a view from nowhere. For cartographic conventions may not be *perspectival*, but they are projections none the less. Global volumes are projected onto the flat surfaces that we call maps. These maps conserve certain relations, for instance those of area, distance, altitude or orientation (though all cannot be conserved simultaneously, choices must be made). The distinction between observer and representation is geometrical here again, but the rules are different.[19] Maps create a form of subjectivity distinct from Narrative Euclideanism. These particular cartographic constructions resonate with what Donna Haraway in another context has called 'the God trick' or the 'unmarked category'.[20] The unmarked category refers to a centred subject without a location. This centred subject sees (the important aspects of) everything, but is itself nowhere (to be seen). The question is whether this is what the Vermeer painting is up to. Is it creating a distinction between subjectivity and objectivity that generates an overview of the world from nowhere? Is it playing a trick that resembles Narrative Euclideanism in its distribution of object and subject? A distribution which assumes that there are object-volumes which can be caught in a system of geometrical transformations and can then be projected onto a surface? A trick that differs from Narrative Euclideanism in its dependence on a form of all-knowing subjectivity from nowhere?

Alpers argues against this interpretation. She shows how the *View of Delft* resembles the depictions of cities commonly found on the margins of the 17th-century maps familiar to Vermeer.[21] These representations of cities *are* views from nowhere. But *'nowhere'* is not an unmarked location constructed by the application of geometrical means. Something is going on which has more to do with the desire for travel. The wish to *move*, and to find out what may be seen in the course of that movement. The wish to learn about places with the help of engravings, and without the need to leave home (Alpers, 1989:152). Alpers' argument is that Vermeer is transforming this tradition of virtual travel. As an instance of transformation, in the painting of Delft he drops the roofscape from its conventional point high up in city depictions—with the effect of creating an overwhelming sky.

Third, Alpers' distinguishes Dutch painting from Narrative Euclideanism by claiming that in the latter '[t]he world stain[s] the surface with color and light, impressing itself upon it; the viewer neither located nor characterized' (Alpers, 1989:27). In the unlocated and uncharacterized viewer we recognize Haraway's God-trick. But perhaps not quite. The painting becomes '[a] surface on which is laid out an assemblage of the world' (Alpers, 1989:122). Note that term: the painting is an *assemblage*, she argues, of textures and surfaces, which have material, or visual/material attributes. These attributes may be detected by a moving eye, that changes its regard. An eye that sees as it travels. An eye that sees in a manner that is continuous with its subject matter.

Alpers' fourth and final point is to note that the *View of Delft*, like many Dutch paintings, isn't framed. It stops at the edges of the canvas. The edges seem to be placed arbitrarily, they could easily have been somewhere else. The picture is neither a window on the world not a story illustrating a separate reality. It is 'an unbounded fragment of a world that continues beyond the canvas' (Alpers, 1989: 27). In her terms, it is 'optical' in character rather than 'geometrical', because the eye moves around, discovers textures and surfaces, and translates them onto the canvas.

The observer, the world and its representation

What do Alpers' stories about Vermeer tell about the way subject and object are distributed? What is the character of representation, of the spatiality that is being arranged? And where, if anywhere, is there narrative?

Both the Uccello and the Vermeer *distinguish* between subject and object. A distinction is being made between what can be seen (and its depiction) on the one hand, and that which sees on the other. In addition, there is a suggestion of continuity in the external world. The world is always already out there, quietly waiting to be discovered by an inquisitive eye. Objects in the world have some kind of duration. But at this point the similarities start to give way to differences.

The Vermeer suggests that *space is topologically complex*. The travelling eye sees, but it does not reduce itself to a unified practice of perspectival transformation, with its singular assumptions about volumes and projections. The Vermeer does not generate a coherent cartographic view from nowhere. Vermeer's complex topological space is closely related to the way subject and objects are distributed. Subject and object are much more interconnected than in Narrative Euclideanism. Compare, for instance, the paintings and drawings of Pieter Saenredam which often create an alternative to the Italian system of perspective—the so-called 'distance point' approach which was formalised by Viator in 1505 (Alpers, 1989: 53 ff). In this approach, vision and the eye are the point of departure, but they are not constituted as a geometrical vantage point outside the painting/windowpane. The eye is located on the surface of the canvas, *not outside*. Then two 'distance points' are created on either side of the eye/surface. 'It is solely' writes Alpers, 'to people and objects in the work, not to the external viewer, that these three points refer' (Alpers, 1989: 53). The subject is located in the same plane as its objects. The subject is *among* the objects, in the world. Or, the subject is also an object.[22]

Objects are not limited and definable volumes located in a world itself constructed as an inclusive boundary-free Euclidean volume. Instead, the world *and* its objects are constructed as a set of intersecting surfaces, planes and lines of sight. All these construct many possible points of view. As noted above, a topologically complex space is created in which the eye moves. This moving eye discovers, from one point of view to another, the surfaces that impress themselves upon it, the surfaces and the relations between them as they overlap or butt up against one another.[23] Many commentators on Dutch art have commented on the obsessive, almost tactile concern with textures, fabrics, clothes, weaves, the materiality of surfaces.[24] This is what happens when the eye roves through the world. Surfaces impress themselves upon it, not only in their spatial attributes but also in their feel—which is transmuted to vision. The vision of the texture of a rich fur, or a sheet of paper.[25] Objects are made as sets of surfaces with discoverable relations between them. These surfaces have orientations, but they also have material attributes like the grain of a piece of wood, or the reflected gloss of a brooch.

But the subject is complex as well as the object. The subject in Vermeer's painting is not a straightforward God-trick, but is rather a set of movements of the eye. The eye of the observer, we have already noted, lies alongside objects. It takes the impression of the surfaces over which it travels. And thus, 'it' is not single. There are many points of view, many spatial and textural impressions. Alpers writes: 'The many eyes and many things viewed that make up . . . surfaces produce a syncopated effect. There is no way that we can stand back and take in a homogeneous space' (Alpers, 1989:58). The painted subjects are at once the viewing subjects: both are effects that move across the surfaces of a representation like Vermeer's *View of Delft*. These painted/viewing subject make a series of different connections between objects. Like the objects, subjects might here best be understood as assemblages.[26]

Deconstructive excess: uncomfortable ambiguity

Paolo Uccello's *The Battle of San Romano* displayed the making of subjects, objects, and the spatial organization of the world by geometrical means. These subjects and objects stand in narrative relation to one another, the eye of the observer outside the depicted world. In Vermeer's *View of Delft* the depiction of space is linked to virtual travel. The space is organized by the movement of the subject-eye as it passes through the world. This movement through space makes subjects and objects by means of juxtapositions and impressions. Uccello and Vermeer differ, but both approach a world that is larger than the eye can behold, larger than the painting can represent. Again, they not only share some representational traits, but are also both well-known and highly regarded. On the walls of the Groninger Museum in the Netherlands hangs a painting by Rémy Blanchard (Plate 3) which does not have a prominent place in the annals of art-history: *Le chat dort, les souris dansent* (When the cat's away, the mice do play) (1982). In the middle of the painting we see a white, sleeping cat. Around the frame of the picture—in a sense making the frame—is a series of mice. They have grey fur, made it seems from the material used for cheap children's puppets. Their eyes, red and orange, are made from slices of French bread.

As a representation this painting doesn't seem very *literal*. In fact, it is more or less *impossible*. The figures are not depicted perspectivally as volumes in a Euclidean space. Neither are we in a world of assemblage, although perhaps this is a little less remote for here too the textures—the fur of the mice, the contentment of a sleeping cat—indeed impress themselves upon us. But is that all we can say about the painting?[28] Rather than reading art history, in this case we sat in front of the picture in the Groninger Museum and looked at it, waiting and watching. Most immediately, the painting is about a white cat, and about the lurid circling mice. A kind of ghost figure in pale violet and blue rises from the sleeping cat. It is a sad, ghostlike figure, but also with a hint of the demonic. But we are unsure *what* it is—this is the first ambiguity.[29] Perhaps it is the cat's dreaming self. But if the figure is a dream, then what does it 're-present'? Unlike the cat, the 'dream' has his eyes wide open. Is this figure staring at the mice? Staring in reprimand, admonishing them for playing 'when the cat's away'. Does it seek, but fail, to still them because the cat is asleep, away? Rather than its dreaming self, the figure may be the cat's other side. Against the white goodness of the sleeping cat, its undomesticated aspect. The demon within. What exactly is the link between the good cat, the dreaming demonic figure, and the eerie grey mice?

These tentative explorations of what this painting represents, do not fit into the schemes we have thus far explored. Indeed, they suggest that this painting makes another kind of representational possibility, that of ambivalence or impossibility. Take, for example the connection between the cat and the mice. The cat cancels the mice. They can only exist—play—because the cat is away, asleep. But the cat is not away, it is right there. There is another ambivalence. The centre, the cat—away, asleep—creates its frame, the mice who can therefore play. The cat, however, also seeks to deny its frame, those mocking mice, running round and round. The mice present the borders of the cat's possibilities, they are—literally—its limits. But at the same time the cat is sleeping right through it all, and thus denies those limits.

Each of these ambivalences suggests a specific narrative. A Freudian account might settle the connection between cat and mouse in terms of superego and id. The cat represents a moral conscience, which is momentarily absent in sleep. The mice then are the id, having wicked fun in the cat's dreams. Anton Ehrenzweig might give an art-theoretical version of the Freudian account, discussing a tension between conscious thought (currently asleep) and the creative child's attention with its 'low level' scanning (represented by the mice).[30] A Durkheimian version might note that 'mouse-crime' is necessary in order to define the limits of 'cat-law'. These narratives, although providing ways of understanding the painting, are arbitrary as to where they begin. It doesn't seem to make a lot of difference whether they start from the cat or from the mice, from centre or periphery. They also seem to end arbitrarily. How many times do we need to shift from cat to mice in order to provide an adequate account of the painting?

This arbitrariness suggests that another kind of story might be appropriate. Lyotard's version of post-structuralism *starts* with undecidability, rather than concluding with it.[31] The undecidability implied in a Lyotardian story cannot be assimilated. In such a story order makes disorder, but disorder also makes order. The two *necessarily* go together, but they do so impossibly. They could never know one another fully, or at the same time.[32] They could never be represented together, because each is unimaginable, excluded by the other. Applying this post-structuralist narrative to Blanchard's painting expresses the impossible relations between the cat and the mice, the picture and its frame, and the shifts between them. It displays a form of representation that insists on the continuity of relations in order to make impossible discontinuities.[33]

The observer, the world and its representation

How does this post-structuralist account translate into the way the observer is constructed by this painting? What kind of world are we encountering, and in what way is this world shown to the viewer? What does an ontology of unassimilable ambiguity, of unavoidable excess, look like? Blanchard's painting makes sense and then it does not. The continual shifts make it an uncomfortable painting, so maybe the right way of exploring it is to do so uncomfortably.[34]

The painting lays bare its own workings. Instead of solving the problem of how to differentiate between different objects and between subjects and objects, it makes it manifest.[35] By displaying its labour of division, it does not, however, simply show everything. It *confuses* divisions. The Groninger Museum, where we saw this picture, disrupts in a similar fashion: some of the paintings hang so high up on the wall that they are difficult to see. Walking around, you are never quite sure what is functional and what is decorative. The painting similarly works at displaying and hiding, laying bare and covering up. For a moment it holds together but immediately negates the illusion and no longer fits. It cannot be subsumed in a single narrative. Rather than allowing a summation after close and proper scrutiny, this painting requires continued exploration. This exploration leads to the discovery of an ambiguous relation which always, immediately, opens up a new exploration.

The Italian rules of projection have disappeared. However, the representational rules of Descriptive Assemblage don't work either. The painting does not solve the problem of how subject and object relate to one another, yet it is about subject/object divisions. It is a *discussion*, a deconstruction of these distinctions. This discussion is conducted by destabilizing, or reworking spatialization. The destabilization works, for example, by transgressing the frame of the painting, while at the same time the painting insists that the mice are a frame. The painting divides inside and outside, centre and periphery, and it does not. It constitutes a labour of division between subject and object, and it does not. In effect the painting is a meticulous performance and projection of *heterogeneity*. Heterogeneity, in the Lyotardian sense mentioned above, as related unassimilability. Some observations about heterogeneity as an effect of Deconstructive Excess:

We witness the depiction of *relations*. The objects in the painting are linked, or better, the objects are relational effects. This is a post-structuralist trope (though not unique to post-structuralism). Whatever its provenance, there is a shift away from a primary concern with objects and their relations in favour of a primary concern with relations and their (occasionally achieved) objects.[36]

This concern with relational effects is *ontologically unsettling*. Although it is possible to read the representational surface as an obscure depiction of the relations between recognizable objects, it can also be decoded as expressing ontological uncertainty. Or to put it differently, a labour of division is being performed, rather than a division of labour. This reversal reminds us that the effects of labour as division are insecure and could be otherwise.

We are in a world that combines the *necessary and the unassimilable*. The relations that are made don't add up. The cat (the painting) and the mice (its frame) are mutually dependent, as it were, stapled together. But there is no single way that we can *tell* of this link. First, there are several different inconsistent ways in which we might do so. Second, we ourselves are caught up in a related inconsistency. We are the subject-objects that lie beyond the frame, that view the picture from outside. Alternatively, we are the object-subjects in a frameless representation of which we form a part. Such pairings cannot be told together.[37] There is an excess which is developed within and through the painting.[38] For, as we have seen, the painting projects the subject inconsistently.

169

At one moment the subject looks at the centred cat, but in the next moment, the subject is caught up in the cat, it is projected to the periphery, among or beyond the mice. At that moment it is converted from the principle of order that it was a moment ago, to a principle of disorder. But then, as a form of mouse-like disorder, there is another shift. For that disorder is necessary to the order that made the subject in the first place. The subject continually shifts between order and disorder, from what is visible to what is invisible, from the centre to the periphery.[39]

Heterogeneity, in another way of putting it, is a representational effect which consists of multiple and *mutually exclusive narratives*. In telling those narratives we oscillate. One story is applicable within one domain, and another in another. But holding both of them together at the same time is not possible. The visual heterogeneity of Blanchard's representation shows precisely that impossibility: the impossibility of holding two mutually exclusive narratives together.[40]

If all narratives are part of the same surface then there is an important sense in which they have been homogenised. In a sense, at just the moment that the painting succeeds, it fails. At the moment we refuse to keep shifting we see a *failed* representation of necessary impossibility. Because to represent the unassimilable is to assimilate it, to render it, in one way or another, comformable. To represent heterogeneity is to colonize it, to make it comfortable.[41] In this sense, the Blanchard alludes back, or beyond, to that which cannot be imagined.

Ontological recovery: finite dreaming

Unlike the Uccello and the Vermeer, Blanchard's painting makes the relational work of representation explicit. The labour of division is no longer backgrounded to produce an ontological effect that seemingly resides in the order of things—which in retrospect becomes a description of what the Uccello and the Vermeer may have been up to. The painting resists producing a hidden ontology that comfortably grounds an epistemology (that may become naturalized). Instead the contingency of entities—and the labour of division in which they are generated and distributed—is made visible. But is this the only possible way? Is ontological foregrounding necessarily dependent on tension and incompleteness? Does it depend on the notion that representation is necessarily incomplete, the world necessarily in excess of the painting?

Our last picture is by Tim Leurah Tjapaltjarri, assisted by Clifford Possum Tjapaltjarri (Plate 4). Painted in 1980, it is entitled *Napperby Death Spirit Dreaming* (National Gallery of Victoria, Melbourne).[42] This is a huge painting, over twenty feet across. It is an artistic expression, but as such a function of an uneasy relationship between Aboriginal and white Australian culture (including an art market for Aboriginal paintings).[43] At the same time, it is a statement of political resistance, an exposition of the character of social and kin relations, a cosmological enactment, a geographical allocation, and (not least) an articulation of spiritual experience.

The painting is, precisely and explicitly, a *performance* of a right order of things. It enacts the reiteration of a pre-existing and proper order. In this order everything is related to everything else. The artist himself is also located within this order. It expresses itself, as it were, through the artist and his production. By virtue of its creation, the painting constitutes a further revelation and production of that order. To put it another way, it is an order which produces the world and the artist along with his painting.[44]

We are in the Australian desert, the Northern Territory. We are witnessing one of the performances—expressions, revelations, reiterations, re-negotiations—of an ordering that was determined at the beginning of the world. Usually, this ordering is translated into English as 'Dreamtime' or 'the Dreaming', though Helen Watson-Verran suggests that 'a more helpful name for this conceptual resource is the "epistemic imaginary" of Aboriginal knowledge systems' (Helen Watson-Verran, 1994:5).[45] The dreaming, or the epistemic imaginary, tells of Ancestral Beings that came out of the ground and moved across the world, by their actions creating people, animals, geographical and sacred features. Their movements and actions were foundational to the world and its inhabitants—they made everything. In particular, they made people-and-places-and-animals together, as a set of relations. These particular places, species, groups, generations, and moieties, were then and still are all bound up together. In this logic, it makes just as much sense to say that (for instance) the Anmatjera belong to the country of Napperby Station, as it does to put it the other way round. Or, it makes sense to say that a tribe belongs to, is related to, a particular animal.[46]

The world as a whole, was made at the time of the dreaming. This was the time the original stories were enacted. Nowadays a telling, or a ceremony, or a painting, is a re-narration of what is. The re-narration *finds* what is there, the world is revealed again. At the same time, the order of things is being re-asserted.

The fact that Ancestral Beings socialized the landscape and thus created its identity in that 'other time' does not mean . . . that the world is unchanging. The interrelated cosmos must be maintained by constant intervention—negotiation and renegotiation—by those responsible. There are no dualistic oppositions here, between good and bad, right and wrong, background and foreground. All elements of the world are constitutive of all other elements in the cosmos, through being related to them, and are in some sense responsible for them. (Helen Watson with the Yolngu community at Yirrkala, 1989:30)

The transcendent and responsible narratives of the dreaming allow us to make some sense of Tim Tjapaltjarri's painting.

The painting evokes the Death Spirit being as he travels the known earth of his homeland, revealed as a stylized map of the places where the Anmatjera lived, hunted, ate, fought and rested. The depiction of the spirit being as a human skeleton journeying along the central spiralling line dramatized his eternal presence in the landscape: not dead but supernatural. (Bardon, ndb:47)

The painting or *dreamscape* does not only provide an origin story, it is also a statement by the artist of his own (places in the) dreaming. His life trajectory is expressed as it is made by the dreaming. But some of what is told is not known to outsiders who do not have rights over, were not constituted in, the narratives of the various relevant dreamings. Some features in the painting may however be identified by outsiders with particular episodes in specific narratives. For instance, the artist tells that the dominant wavy line represents the journey of the Death Spirit being through (what is called by Westerners) the Napperby District at the time of the dreaming. The circles represent the resting places of the Spirit. The skeletal figure is, in part, a depiction of the figure of the Death Spirit. Many of the arcs represent windbreaks. Other motifs are projections of a boomerang or (in the case of the wavy lines) running water. Yet other features depict people eating meat. And although the dominant dreaming is that of the Death Spirit, the painting also depicts three further dreamings with which the artist had a special relation, and to which he had a particular responsibility: those of Old Man, the Yam, and the Sun and Moon who are lovers.

The painting is thus a gigantic re-presentation of this small area of central Australia, as well as a depiction of the dreamings of the artist. But since the artist is responsible for, belongs to, and is an expression of, the narratives of dreamtime, it is also a negotiation of (his location in) that ordering. Posed in territorial terms, it is thus a reaffirmation of the character of the tribal land, and it represents an angry political statement. A political statement which repudiates the white people's (mis)understanding of the land, its inhabitants and its physical and spiritual features.

> Tim often said to me that he did not really wish to know the white Australians, and the painting is his perception of his own tribal lands and spiritual destiny of the Napperby cattle-station areas. He appropriates Napperby to himself as his own Dreaming, and by implication takes it away from its white owners. This is one of the meanings of the paintings. (Bardon, ndb:46)

The observer, the world and its representation

This representation has little to do with Narrative Euclideanism—though it has everything to do with narrative. It has little to do with Descriptive Assemblage—though it has a good deal to do with description. And it has little to do with Deconstructive Excess—though it is quite explicitly about what is what, and how everything relates. Five observations:

Narrative is foundational. It distributes, it allocates. It forms links between the entities which it makes. This is the import of the dreaming. A dreaming is transcendental, it recreates itself in features and ceremonies in the present-day. This narrative is not centred on humans. 'Man' is not the measure.

Narrative is foundational of space. Space is an *expression* of narrative. The stories enacted in the dreaming, that are told and retold, *make* Aboriginal space. Space is a set of relations between places in a story, or between stories. Euclidean notions have no meaning in this cosmology. The idea that space might be experienced as a container or a patch waiting to be populated makes no sense at all. This is the political import of Tim Leurah Tjapaltjarri's representation. In this context, his painting is best understood as a statement of, or in, the ontological politics of spatiality. The world is not what you, the white men, believe it to be: an area with certain neutrally-topographical attributes. Space, land, social and kinship relations are all bound up together and made in narrative, a narrative that you do not (and partially cannot and may not) perceive.[47]

The distinction between object and subject is not really obvious. What we might imagine—coming from Uccello, Vermeer, or
Blanchard—as objects, act. *Objects have agency* in Aboriginal
narrative. There is no difficulty in imagining a tree or a rock as
an active agent.[48] The ancestral beings frequently converted
themselves into such objects. The narratives of dreamtime perform themselves in rocks, hills, rivers, or rainstorms, through
flora and fauna, through abstractions, and through persons and
their kinship relations. All are related, more or less distantly, by
the web of intersecting, partially overlapping, narratives.

Like objects, *subjects are narrative effects* caught up in, performing, and reflecting their roles in and responsibilities for those
narratives. The overlap, or rather, the irrelevance of the subject-
object distinction, is natural, given the character of the narratives
of Dreamtime. The skeletal figure in Tim Leurah Tjapaltjarri's
dreamscape illustrates this. The figure represents the Death Spirit
being. It also represents the artist's progress along the dreamline
of the Death Spirit, his own perception of his position, and his
premonition of his own death (Bardon, nd:46). The artist is
caught up in the painting. Other Aborigines are—to a greater or
lesser extent—similarly caught up in it. Only the non-Aboriginal
is outside this web.[49] We—the outsiders—are not, as it were, constituted as both subjects and objects in this depiction.[50]

Deconstructive Excess imagines the *creation* of incompleteness
by generating unassimilabilities. In this—high modernist—sense
it can be seen as a radicalization of the 'perspectival' constructivism we began exploring with Uccello. Alternatively, in a more
post-modern reading, the Blanchard renders the distinction
between completion and incompletion, or between finitude and
infinitude irrelevant. Ontological Recovery is different again. The
world is not incomplete, it is finite. It is a finite set of interweav-
ing narratives. There is no possibility of constructing something
new, another perspective. Somewhere, everything is already
known, has already been told. The world is complete within narrative. Least of all is the world unknown, because it is constituted
as a set of metaphors for linking, joining, and negotiating. While
most of the narratives are not known to all the individuals or
social groups (for they are owned by specific groups, while recip-
rocally, 'owning' those groups), the idea that the world is a finite
set of known metaphors makes perfect sense. A representation is
simply a revelation that extrudes itself in the form of specific
metaphors in specific places under specific circumstances. The

restless idea of construction—linked to the possibility that the world is of an indefinite incompleteness—is not available here.

After-words: paintings and politics

The interferences between different modes of making the world have created a kaleidoscope. The movements of the kaleidoscope have helped to de-naturalize the assumptions built into representation. They give us pause, making it easier to explore the character of those assumptions: the varying methods for constituting subjectivity and objectivity; the different ways in which the spatiality of the world is produced; and the diversity that is possible in the relationship between spatiality and narrative.

We have sought to resist the naturalizing epistemological account of representation that assumes that there is a common order of things. Or the notion that differences between representations can only be understood as some analogue of perspectives. Or that differences between representations can only be understood in terms of rules of method that more or less satisfactorily carry the burden of accurate or workable description.[51] The moving kaleidoscope of representational modes highlights the *ontological* character of representation. We have argued that representation not only describes, but also works upon the world that is described. Description is never innocent. The movements of the kaleidoscope have served to uncover the representational labour of division that generates the subjects, objects, their relations, and the worlds in which these exist.

We value the relatively safe haven these paintings have offered to explore such a precarious topic. Something can be said for an 'inappropriate' experimental site when the stakes are high. Not because the outcomes will be obscure or hidden, but because such a site may itself create a pause. It may arrest movement for a moment and thus make it easier to note the necessary detail.

Research like this tries to make a space for what we might, following Annemarie Mol, imagine as an *ontological politics*. An ontological politics asks how it is that the representational practices that make up worlds—and so the worlds made up in those practices—co-ordinate themselves. How it is that worlds go together, or don't.

How they *might* go together is what is at stake in this politics. It is a form of politics that works in the play between different places, seeking to slip between different worlds.[52] It is a form of politics that imagines that there always is such play. It imagines that representative allocation may be less standardized than, for instance, the hegemonic pretensions of Narrative Euclideanism might suggest. Accordingly, it moves away from a politics of perspectivalism (which asks how best to co-ordinate different views on the same world) towards more multiple worlds and views. It explores good ways of making partial connections, better connections, between many worlds. Between, we might suggest, the many worlds we all carry and perform.

Notes

1 We are grateful to: Anne Beaulieu, Bob Cooper, Mark Elam, Annemarie Mol, David Turnbull and Helen Watson-Verran for the support and inspiration that led to this paper.
2 See, for example, Wegener (1993) on the series of three paintings by Uccello on the battle of San Romano.
3 See, for instance, Gombrich (1989).
4 It notes, as historical specification, that Uccello was commissioned by the Medicis to paint celebratory accounts of one of their battles, to paint an adjunct to a human-centred, if not humanist, narrative. So the artist is located in a structure of patronage.
5 See the accounts offered, for instance, in Alpers (1989), Baxendall (1972), Blunt (1962), and Edgerton (1976). See also Alberti (1435–6/1966).
6 See Serres (1988) for an exploration of the motif of classical geometrical representation grounded in the (absence of the) point.
7 See Vasari (1568/1987).
8 The term 'drawing things together' comes from Latour (1990).
9 This is in part where Bruno Latour draws his notion of 'immutable mobile'. Note, however, that like Latour, we are not saying that the world 'is' a set of volumetric entities in a three-dimensional space. Rather we are saying that it is possible to build it that way under certain circumstances by using the representational performances of Narrative Euclideanism.
10 Marilyn Strathern, in her analysis of constructivism, talks of this set of assumptions as 'merological'. See Strathern (1991, 1992).
11 See Edgerton (1966:4) and Foster (1988).
12 See, for instance, Turnbull (1989), and for more general discussion Harvey (1990). We will have a collision with cartography—of a kind—in section 2.
13 We—the authors—are, of course, contemporary Westerners. Yet apparently we are able to note, to regret, to resist. Or, rather, we will do so. In this paper our object is to utilize other representations to forge a distance from Narrative Euclideanism. This distance does not provide a stable ground for organized resistance, but does provide a brief gap which we may pass through.
14 Mieke Bal (1991:216), writing more generally of realism, observes 'The problem with using a realistic mode of reading and looking exclusively is that it helps to pass off content as "natural" and thus fosters ideological manipulation. Yet realism has succeeded in becoming so "natural" a mode of reading that denying or ignoring its pervasiveness will not help.'

15 See, as examples, Norman Bryson (1990) on still life, and Philip Fisher (1991) on 'hand made space'.

16 The trope of 'invention' has its own problems, not the least of which is the often implied notion of an autonomous, creative, individual inventor. For our purposes here, invention amends the innocent and passive connotations of discovery.

17 Alpers makes a contrast with Italian painting and, though the Uccello is scarcely contemporary with the Vermeer, it serves to make the point.

18 On the inclusion of the spectator in the realm of the painting, and on the distinction between the world of man and the world of things see Barthes (1988) on Dutch painting.

19 See the work of Turnbull (1989) and Wood (1992).

20 See, for instance, Haraway (1989, 1991a).

21 Vermeer makes his own version of these fringe depictions in *The Art of Painting* (1666–1667, Kunsthistorisches Museum, Vienna).

22 These points are illustrated in *Jan Vredeman de Vries, Perspective*, published Leiden, 1604–5, plate 2.

23 See *Jan Vredeman de Vries, Perspective*, published Leiden, 1604–5, plate 28.

24 See, for instance, Bryson's discussion of the character of texture in Dutch representation, in the context of the tensions between the tactile and the development of long distance trade in luxury objects (Bryson, 1990:125 ff).

25 Alpers illustrates these points in a discussion of *David Bailly, Still Life*, 1651. This is at the Stedelijk Museum 'de Lakenhal', Leiden.

26 Norman Bryson in his *Vision and Planning* (1983), notes that the detail of the different surfaces depicted by Vermeer in, for instance, *The Art of Painting* varies from the fine-grained to the impressionistic. He treats this as a further commentary on the art of painting by a subject that displaces itself through different positions.

27 See Strathern (1991, 1992).

28 For a discussion of Blanchard's work, see the exhibition catalogue *Blanchard, Boisrond, Combas, Di Rosa* (1983).

29 We are not suggesting that other paintings are in no way ambiguous, that ambiguity is strictly a property of the mode of representation we call Deconstructive Excess. In this chapter, we are focussing most particularly on the differences *between* paintings, not on those *within*. The yardstick provided by looking at Uccello and Vermeer indicates the ambiguity of the Blanchard.

30 See Ehrenzweig (1993).

31 See Lyotard (1991).

32 This argument is developed by Robert Cooper (1986).

33 The observer becomes part of the picture, like, for instance, the viewer (or the adjacent pictures) in Jasper Johns' *Target* (Museum of Modern Art, Vienna, 1974). See Fisher (1991:77–80).

34 The Uccello and the Vermeer are comfortable (made so, seem so). But we have shown how this comfort is contingent, constructed. We have used an uncomfortable (post-structuralist) approach to render the naturalized comfort uncomfortable. For a discussion of discomfort and subjectivity, this time in the context of the paintings of Francis Bacon, see van Alphen (1992).

35 A matter of working on the surface of the canvas which goes back at least as far as Cézanne, and is arguably one of the dominant themes and preoccupations of painting for over a hundred years. See Fisher (1991).

36 Some of the implications of this shift are indeed explored in post-structuralism and those STS versions of the post-structuralist sensibility reflected in actor-network theory (Latour, 1988), feminism (Haraway, 1991b) and cross-cultural studies (Watson, 1990).

37 Telling impossible pairings simultaneously would be like painting a Uccello and a Vermeer on a single canvas. The simultaneous painting of impossible perspectives is achieved in the cubist work of Braque and Picasso.

38 There is always excess. Sometimes (Uccello, Vermeer) this distinction is not located within the representation, but between the representation and some other location.

39 The argument here mimics some aspects of Charis Cussins' (1996) work on identities in fertility treatments. And also that by Vicky Singleton (Singleton and Michael, 1993) on the UK cervical smear campaign. Both papers explore (necessary) oscillation between centering and decentering.

40 This argument is somewhat similar to Frederic Jameson's notion of 'cognitive mapping' (Jameson, 1991). In particular, his analysis of the Frank Gehry house makes the argument that this house is a device for thinking which conjoins two incompatible but mutually dependent forms of being: the First World and the Third World experience of global capitalism. In Jameson's way of thinking, the Blanchard painting might be treated as a form of cognitive mapping. (For further commentary on this, see Law (1997a).) Note, however, that Jameson appears, if ambivalently, to have made a prior decision about the order of things: that there is a beast called global capitalism that generates incoherences.

41 We are grateful to David Turnbull for a version of this argument. Applying it to the Gehry House described by Jameson, he has noted in discussion that if the house turns out to be comfortable to *live in* then the tension between the two narratives has been lost. They do, indeed, fit together.

42 These are the titles given to it respectively in Ryan (nd) and Sutton (1989). Titles for Aboriginal paintings are usually labels attached to them by whites after discussion with the artists.

43 The development of a market-related artistic tradition of Aboriginal painting is relatively recent, dating from the early 1970s, and appears, at least in central Australia, to have grown from a particular station, Papunya, under the impetus of art teacher Geoffrey Bardon. For more details of this extraordinary and savage story see Bardon (nda).

44 A cosmology in which agency performs itself through animals, aspects of the landscape, or spirit-like dreamings as well as through people sits uneasily with attributing special creative agency to the Aboriginal artist. Agency thus performs itself more or less ubiquitously as an expression of the order of things.

45 'It is', she continues, 'this epistemic imaginary, celebrated, venerated and providing possibilities for a rich intellectual life amongst all participants in Aboriginal community life, which enables the eternal struggle to reconcile the many local knowledges which constitute Aboriginal knowledge systems.'

46 The way the world—produced by and re-enacted in each account of the dreaming—belongs to the people—also made by that dreaming and re-enacted in each account—and vice-versa, has nothing to do with the feminist analysis of the camera as the proprietary male gaze onto the female body. This latter analysis examines the invasion by the camera of the woman's ownership of her body—the male gaze does not belong. The way world and viewer—to put in those terms—belong together does not invade ownership, but constitutes it. Of course, the limits of

this mutual belonging are tragic. The world originally dreamt, did not include the invading forces of the Western world. This invasion does resonate with the feminist analysis of the gaze.

47 Helen Watson-Verran notes that these different notions of spatiality and the way subjects are constituted generate profound misunderstandings between Aboriginal and Western negotiators over matters such as land rights. For a discussion of the difficulties and the historical asymmetries, see Watson-Verran (1994). For other discussion of the performed character of regional spatiality see Mol and Law (1994).

48 This notion of the active object resonates with the actor-network notion of the agency of non-humans (see, for instance, Callon, 1986). However, in Aboriginal cosmology, the act of non-human—or human—agent never brings anything new into the world. Actor-network theory appears to be framed by the assumption of restless change that is built into many current Euro-American practices.

49 Who the non-Aboriginal is, where 'outside the web' is, is not at all obvious. In this chapter, we have named non-Aborigines, Westerners, white people, white men, outsiders. Us and them. We, the authors, appear as the ultimate exception. While we are not constituted 'inside the web' we seem to describe the representation as if we were. We have initially approached this representation as an artistic expression. In this sense, it fits into our Western web. The representation as an artistic expression coincides with the representation as a political statement, as a re-enactment of the constitution of the world. The webs are not sealed off from one another. Nor are the links between them there to be discovered. The explanatory links that relate art with politics with ontology need to be forged carefully.

50 This means that before Aboriginals can deal systematically and consistently with a white person, they have to locate her in their kinship system by allocating parentage by adoption. In this way Helen Watson-Verran is located in the kinship relations of the Yolngu of North East Arnhemland (Watson-Verran, 1993).

51 Unlike texts, paintings are not typically understood in terms of accurate description, but rather in terms of artistic expression and aesthetic appreciation. It is a consequence of our textual bias—located as we are in STS which still tends toward textual connotations—that we have sought to argue against the naturalism of the former rather than the latter.

52 We begin to see the possible character of an ontological politics. This is the work being done by Helen Watson-Verran (1994) in her mediation between the Wik, an Aboriginal people of Cape York, and the pastoralists; by Annemarie Mol (1997; and Mesman, 1996) in her work on the relationships between medical practices (including representational practices); by Donna Haraway (1989, 1991b) in her motivated de-naturalising of metaphors for distinctions between subject and object; and by John Law (1996, 1997b) in his analysis of the collusive character of discourses which operate to generate, and simultaneously presuppose an ontologically stable 'virtual object' which is projected behind and beyond the surface of representation.

References

Alberti, L.B., (1435–6/1966) *On painting*, New Haven: Yale University Press.

Alpers, S., (1989) *The Art of Describing: Dutch Art in the Seventeenth Century*, London: Penguin.

Bal, M., (1991) *Reading Rembrandt: Beyond the Word-Image Opposition*, Cambridge: Cambridge University Press.

Bardon, G., (nda) 'The Gift that Time Gave: Papunya Early and Late, 1971–2 and 1980' in Ryan (nd), pp. 10–21.

Bardon, G., (ndb) 'The Great Painting, *Napperby Death Spirit Dreaming*, and Tim Leura Tjapaltjarri' in Ryan (nd), pp. 46–7.

Barthes, R., (1988) 'The World as Object' in Bryson (1988), pp. 106–15.

Baxandall, M., (1972) *Painting and Experience in Fifteenth-Century Italy*, Oxford: Oxford University Press.

Baxandall, M., (1985) *Patterns of Intention: on the Historical Explanation of Pictures*, London: Yale University Press.

Blanchard, Boisrond, Combas, Di Rosa (1983), Exhibition Catalogue, Groningen: Martinipers.

Blunt, A., (1962) *Artistic Theory in Italy, 1450–1600*, Oxford: Oxford University Press.

Bryson, N., (1983) *Vision and Painting: the Logic of the Gaze*, Basingstoke and London: Macmillan.

Bryson, N., (1988) *Calligram, Essays in New Art History from France*, Cambridge: Cambridge University Press.

Bryson, N., (1990) *Looking at the Overlooked: Four Essays on Still Life Painting*, London: Reaktion Books.

Callon, M., (1986) 'Some Elements of a Sociology of Translation: Domestication of the Scallops and the Fishermen of Saint Brieuc Bay' in Law (1986), pp. 196–233.

Chia, R., (ed.) (1997) *Into the Realm of Organisation: Essays for Robert Cooper*, London: Routledge, in the press.

Cooper, R., (1986) 'Organization/Disorganization', *Social Science Information*, 25, 299–335.

Cussins, C., (1996) 'Ontological Choreography: Agency through Objectification in Infertility Clinics', *Social Studies of Science*, 26, 575–610.

Edgerton, S.Y., (1976) *The Renaissance Rediscovery of Linear Perspective*, New York: Harper and Row.

Ehrenzweig, A., (1993) *The Hidden Order of Art: a Study in the Psychology of Artistic Imagination*, London: Weidenfeld.

Fisher, P., (1991) *Making and Effacing Art: Modern American Art in a Culture of Museums*, New York: Oxford University Press.

Foster, H., (ed.) (1988) *Vision and Visuality*, Seattle: Bay Press.

Gombrich, E.H., (1989) *The Story of Art*, fifteenth edition, London: Phaidon.

Haraway, D., (1989) *Primate Visions, Race and Nature in the World of Modern Science*, London: Routledge and Chapman Hall.

Haraway, D., (1991a) 'Situated Knowledges: the Science Question in Feminism and the Privilege of Partial Perspective' in Haraway (1991c), pp. 183–201.

Haraway, D., (1991b) 'The biopolitics of Postmodern Bodies: Constitutions of Self in Immune System Discourse' in Haraway (1991c), pp. 203–30.

Haraway, D., (1991c) *Simians, Cyborgs and Women: the Reinvention of Nature*, London: Free Association Books.

Harvey, D., (1989) *The Condition of Postmodernity: an Enquiry into the Origins of Cultural Change*, Oxford: Blackwell.

Jameson, F., (1991) *Postmodernism, or, the Cultural Logic of Late Capitalism*, London: Verso.

Latour, B., (1988) *The Pasteurization of France*, Cambridge, Mass.: Harvard.

Latour, B., (1990) 'Drawing Things Together' in Lynch and Woolgar (1990), pp. 19–68.

Law, J., (ed.) (1986) *Power, Action and Belief: a new Sociology of Knowledge? Sociological Review Monograph*, London: Routledge and Kegan Paul.

Law, J., (1991a) (1996) 'Organizing Accountabilities: Ontology and the Mode of Accounting' in Mouritsen and Munro (1996), pp. 283–306.

Law, J., (1997a) 'After Metanarrative: on Knowing in Tension' in Chia (1997).

Law, J., (1997b) *Aircraft Stories: Decentering the Object in Technoscience*, submitted.

Lynch, M. and Woolgar, S., (eds) (1990) *Representation in Scientific Practice*, Cambridge, Mass.: MIT Press.

Lyotard, J.-F., (1991) *The Inhuman*, Cambridge: Polity.

Mol, A., (1997) 'Missing Links, Making Links: the Performance of Some Artheroscleroses' in Mol and Berg (1997).

Mol, A. and Berg, M., (1997) *Differences in Medicine: Unravelling Practices, Techniques and Bodies*, Durham, NC: Duke University Press, in the press.

Mol, A. and Law, J., (1994) 'Regions, Networks and Fluids: Anaemia and Social Topology', *Social Studies of Science*, 24, 641–71.

Mol, A. and Mesman, J., (1996) 'Neonatal Food and the Politics of Theory: Some Questions of Method', *Social Studies of Science*, 26, 419–43.

Munro, R. and Mouritsen, J., (eds) (1996) *Accountability: Power, Ethos and the Technologies of Managing*, London: Chapman Hall.

Ryan, J., (nd) *Mythscapes: Aboriginal Art of the Desert from the National Gallery of Victoria*, Melbourne: National Gallery of Victoria.

Serres, M., (1988) 'Ambrosia and Gold' in Bryson (1988), pp. 116–30.

Singleton, V. and Michael, M., (1993) 'Actor-networks and Ambivalence: General Practitioners in the UK Cervical Screening Programme', *Social Studies of Science*, 23, 227–64.

Strathern, M., (1991) *Partial Connections*, Maryland: Savage, Rowman and Littlefield.

Strathern, M., (1992) *After Nature: English Kinship in the Late Twentieth Century*, Cambridge: Cambridge University Press.

Sutton, P., (ed.) (1989) *Dreamings: the Art of Aboriginal Australia*, Ringwood, Victoria and London: Penguin.

Turnbull, D., (1989) *Maps are Territories, Science is an Atlas* (with a contribution by Helen Watson with the Yolngu community at Yirrkala), Geelong, Victoria: Deakin University.

van Alphen, E., (1992) *Francis Bacon and the Loss of Self*, London: Reaktion Books.

Vasari, G., (1568/1987) 'A Selection' translated by George Bull, *Lives of the Artists, Volume 1*, London: Penguin.

Watson, H. with the Yolngu community at Yirrkala, (1989) 'Aboriginal-Australian Maps' in Turnbull (1989), pp. 28–36.

Watson, H., (1990) 'Investigating the Social Foundations of Mathematics: Natural Number in Culturally Diverse Forms of Life', *Social Studies of Science*, 20, 283–312.

Watson-Verran, H., (1993) 'Constructivism Clotting' paper presented to AAHPSSS Conference, La Trobe University, 9–13 July 1993.

Watson-Verran, H., (1994) 'Re-Imagining Land Title and Ownership: Working Disparate Knowledge Traditions Together' paper presented at the 'Working Disparate Knowledge Systems Together' Seminar, Deakin University, 26–7 November 1994.

Wegener, W.J. (1993) '"That the practice of arms is most excellent declare the statues of valiant men": the Luccan War and Florentine political ideology in paintings by Uccello and Castangno', *Renaissance Studies*, 7, 129–67.
Wood, D., (1992) with John Fels, *The Power of Maps*, London: Routledge.

In place of geometry: the materiality of place

Kevin Hetherington

Introduction

The Statue's Speech:
Unshakable human positivism: you never ask yourselves, you whose hair floats lightly on your heads, what your phantom witnesses on their plinths engraved with famous names think of your trickeries, positive or not. We, who speak with the sky, we, covered with dew, the mineral dancers feared by the nights, we, the tamers of breezes, the charmers of birds, the guardians of silence, beneath the mind's adorable chandelier that illuminates our irremediable attitudes, divine principles prisoners of our concrete liberty . . . (Aragon, 1987:169)

Perhaps statues have more to tell us about *place* than pilgrims, cameras more than tourists? At the very least, the story of a place cannot make sense without them. The questions I set out to consider, therefore, in this chapter are '*what is a place?*' and '*what do materials have to do with places?*' Another way of putting it is that my concern is with the labour of division that goes into the making of places and the ways in which geometries of objects and representations by subjects are folded into one another, by that labour, and the movements and stabilities they perform through difference.

Geographical tradition would have it that place, as opposed to space, is something subjective and meaningful. It has been tied with the issues of Being in the works of Heidegger and Bachelard, with belonging, with home, with community, collectivity as well as with existential issues of the self (see for example, Relph, 1976; Tuan, 1977; Keith and Pile, 1993; Massey, 1994; Urry, 1995). Place has been, and remains, fundamentally defined by humanist discourses. It is assumed that place is about agency, and that agency is invariably defined as human agency, even where places are seen to be contested and open to multiple interpretations—the current position advocated by many cultural geographers (for example Shields, 1991; Rose, 1993). It is this exclusive privilege given to the subjective and the human that I want to question in this chapter.

Space, by contrast, has tended to be associated with materials and their (often Euclidean) geometrical arrangements: the space between things, between the chair and the door, between the earth and the moon, between physical entities that do not in themselves mean anything. Turning a space into a place, giving it meaning, it has been assumed, is the act of human intervention. The way a room is arranged has meaning for me either in the present because of its relation to social conventions about how we recognize a space, or in memory, a space that I remember as part of my life, as some thing that becomes a place by association with events as well as spaces. We are led to believe that spaces become remembered landscapes and those landscapes are the substance of place. The chairs and pictures, the wallpaper and ornaments are all just seen as props that stand mute like Aragon's Statues waiting to become the texture of someone's Verstehen.

What, however, if we interrogate that muteness and let the objects speak of place? What if we let them move across that division between space and place? In doing so we have to leave behind both Euclidean geometry and hermeneutics and consider instead the issue of a more complex topology. The topological folding together of space and place leads to the creation of more complex geographies that allow us to see the spatiality upon which this division is usually performed (on social topologies see Deleuze, 1986; Mol and Law, 1994; Doel, 1996; Hetherington, 1997b). Contemporary geographical discourse only sees the difference between spaces and places and, in doing so, it has tended to make the material world disappear and to replace it instead with culture with all its symbolism and meaning (although see Thrift, 1996; Hinchliffe, 1996). My aim is to bring materiality back in and to see places as generated by the placing, arranging and naming the spatial ordering of materials and the system of difference that they perform. It is this threefold practice that constitutes a labour of division and the system of differences in which places are located as mobile effects. This does not mean that there is no space for the subject and subjective experiences and memories of a space; rather they become folded into the material world and each becomes imbricated in the agency of the other.

Mobile places

Imagine *place* as being like a ship. It is not something that stays in one location but moves about within networks of agents, human and non-human. Places move around in what has been described as arrangements or networks of heterogeneous materials (see Latour, 1988; Law, 1992, 1994) and can be seen as an ordering effect of those agents. To begin with, then, *place* is about relationships, it is about placing,

[I]f we think, after all, that the boat is a floating piece of space, a place without a place, that exists by itself, that is closed in on itself and at the same time is given over to the infinity of the sea and that, from port to port, from tack to tack, from brothel to brothel, it goes as far as the colonies in search of the most precious treasures they conceal in their gardens, you will understand why the boat has not only been for our civilization, from the 16th century until the present, the great instrument of economic development . . . but has been simultaneously the greatest reserve of the imagination. The ship is the *heterotopia* [other place] *par excellence*. In civilizations without boats, dreams dry up, espionage takes the place of adventure, and the police take the place of pirates. (Foucault, 1986:27)

This text, taken from Foucault's analysis of *heterotopia* (other places), continues his longstanding interest in the ship as a metaphor for the processes of social ordering. In *Madness and Civilization*, which discusses the links between ideas about the great confinement of the mad and the Enlightenment project of reason, Foucault's metaphorical use of the mythical 'Ship of Fools' offers us a vision of a place that is defined by its difference,

The madman's voyage is at once a rigorous division and an absolute passage. In one sense, it simply develops, across a half-real, half-imaginary geography, the madman's *liminal* position on the horizon of medieval concerns—a position symbolised and made real at the same time by the madman's privilege of being *confined* within the city *gates*: his exclusion must enclose him; if he cannot and must not have another *prison* than the *threshold* itself, he is kept at the point of passage. He is put in the interior of the exterior, and inversely. A highly symbolic position, which will doubtless remain until our own day, if we are willing to admit that what was formerly a visible fortress of order has now become the castle of our conscience. (1989a:11)

Places cross boundaries too, just like the mad. Indeed places are not what lies on either side of the boundary, they are constituted through boundary work. Foucault's reference to the 'Ship of Fools' traversing its way across the space of Renaissance Europe is seen as a metaphor, if a somewhat different one to that used by Brant in the 15th century and after him by Hieronymus Bosch, who were concerned in their images of the ship of fools with the folly of the pursuit of pleasure. For Foucault, the ship of fools is a marginal or boundary phenomenon that comes to represent social uncertainties and the problem of how to deal with them. It becomes an illustration of a type of confinement that shows the beginnings of a new labour of division between the normal and the insane (see Cooper, this volume). The presence of the fools is made apparent through the relation of the ship to its surroundings. Free to 'voyage' across Europe this prison space exists in a liminal state of passage; it has no fixity in the Renaissance ideas of incarceration, yet it is not a modern prison or asylum. It has a presence as a space, but is not a fixed space but defined as different through its relation to the space that is juxtaposed as it traverses. It is a source for representing new anxieties and certainties and a shift between different modes of ordering madness. This ship is ambiguous and difficult to understand because the signifying relationship between the mythical ship and the space that it enters is one of similitude—a juxtaposition of the incommensurate and the uncertain heterogeneity that this establishes (see also Foucault, 1989b).

Similitude involves the juxtaposition of things not usually found together, or which have no ordered meaning together and the ambiguity that they create in terms of representation. Similitude sets up a heterotopic space (Foucault, 1983, 1986; Soja, 1990, 1996; Hetherington, 1996, 1997a). Similitude is a form of *bricolage*, it signifies like a metonym rather than a metaphor; like that explored by Magritte in his paintings. In similitude meaning is dislocated and then relocated, skating across a surface through a series of deferrals that are established between signifier and signified. This shift from modes of representing similitude is important to the understanding of place. As Harkness suggests,

> Resemblance, says Foucault, 'presumes a primary reference that prescribes and classes' copies on the basis of the rigor of the mimetic relation to itself. Resemblance serves and is dominated by representation. With similitude, on the other hand, the reference 'anchor' is gone. Things are cast adrift, more or less like one

another without any of them being able to claim the privileged status or 'model' for the rest. Hierarchy gives way to a series of exclusively lateral relations. (1983:9–10)

What I am suggesting, following Foucault's arguments about similitude, is that if we stop thinking about places just in terms of human subjectivity and the way it narrates identities such as the identities of spaces, then we no longer have to look at place as fixed by subjectivity. Place is the effect of similitude, a non-representation that mobilized through the placing of things in complex relation to one another and the agency/power effects that are performed by those arrangements. Places circulate through material placings, through the folding together of spaces and things and the relations of difference established by those folds. They are brought into being through the significations that emanate from those material arrangements and foldings (see Hetherington, 1997b). Subjectivity is not something that stands outside this process, it is constituted within this folding of spaces and things. Sometimes such foldings are visible, at other times they disappear only to re-appear somewhere else. They can move from being material to textual to aesthetic to cognitive and back with ease. Places are not fixed by the geometry of space but are free to move across the boundaries of geometry into some elsewhere which lies beyond the limitations of subjective ways of representing objects and their spatial distribution. Places are always unfinished, deferred and lacking a unity or order established through representation. They make no sense in themselves, rather they establish a system of differences that requires an ordering. In most instances, however, that is not the end. This is just one part of the picture: placing heterogeneous things together. Another part of the picture is the ordering process that goes in to the making sense of that similitude (see Levi-Strauss, 1966). Places are not naturally inscribed either in the minds of humans nor in the material world. Places are ways of making sense of these heterogeneous placings and their spatial, temporal and material arrangements. That ordering process, however, is not just subjective but derives from the labour of division associated with the difference of placing, what Law describes as distributional effects (1997) established within material networks.

My first point then in answering the question *what is a place?* is to argue that we should think about places that derive from the differences established by similitude and the ways in which it generates modes of semiotic ordering. Rather than taking a place as a site

187

that stands for something, that has intrinsic or mythic meaning because of its supposed fixity in space, we should think of places as relational, as existing in similitude: places as *being in the process of being placed in relation to* rather than being there.

Another ship helps us further in this exploration of place. This time not a ship filled with the mad but with soldiers and marine technology; a Portuguese Man O' War (Law, 1986). Law's discussion of how the Portuguese managed to exert social control over considerable distances addresses directly the whole question of non-human agency and opens up the possibility of a discussion of the material constitution of places (1986). Networks of agents, made up of three principal groups, documents, devices and (drilled) people allowed the Portuguese to practise long-distance control over the Indian Ocean and surrounding lands during the 16th century without the need for extensive garrisoned armies in the colonized countries. As well as the fighting ships themselves, other sources of agency within the heterogeneous network included maps and charts (documents), navigation instruments and the technologies associated with the long-distance travel of the ships (devices), as well as disciplined fighting men (people). For Law, this combination of heterogeneous elements into a network that extends across time and space, of which the boat which provided mobility over space was crucial. It allowed those 'in one place' (Portugal) to effect power over those 'in another' (India) (1986). The only thing we might take issue with here in Law's account is that places are left fixed in this story. While this approach allows us to look at agency in terms of materials and networks, it tends to leave the question of the places involved as already established prior to this network of heterogeneous agents. The issue of placing in relation to heterogeneous networks has been left to be explored. Portugal is here and India is there and the one can dominate the other because of its better use of the agency generated by the documents, devices and people at its command. But is this true? We might say that Portugal only exists as a place, or is re-configured as a place, because of the placing that derives from the mobile effects of the agency within the heterogeneous network of materials that it is able to benefit from. Similarly India is (re)configured as a place by this network, as is the ship itself, the sea it sails on, indeed, and perhaps most importantly over the long duration, the world is made as a place by the explorers, conquerors and merchants who were in the best position to translate the agency and power effects distributed by the materials that made up the network of sea travel.

Places and spaces can become detached and re-attached through mobile arrangements constituted by human and non-human agents and the semiotic representations that they heterogeneously generate as effects of their agency. They exist in a condition of similitude within heterogeneous networks. They make sense when those materials are selectively drawn together into an assemblage, or homology (Levi-Strauss, 1966). Places involve arranging or ordering the *bricolage* of heterogeneous placings into a system of differences (see Shields, 1991). There is another concept from this actor-network approach that is useful in this discussion of place, namely what Latour has described as immutable mobiles (1990). In his account of the effectiveness of truth claims in science, and of the dominance of scientific knowledge over other forms, Latour suggests that knowledge is made effective by being made both immutable and mobile. The issue is one of representation. Data of all kinds is collected and then turned into scientific representations: academic papers, charts, graphs, tables and so on. These are immutable, they have the appearance of a solid fact, and yet they are mobile, they can be moved around and reproduced in the same form in other spaces, so that others can see them and judge them for themselves many thousands of miles from their point of production. In other words, immutable mobiles have the capacity of fixing knowledge and yet also allowing it to travel and be disseminated well beyond its spatial point of origin. If the concept of an immutable mobile can be applied to knowledge about a scientific experiment it can be applied to other forms of knowledge as well: in this instance knowledge of space, and what we call a place (see Hetherington, 1997c). Places are assembled through immutable mobiles too: maps, photographs, paintings, televised images, textual descriptions, poems and so on. These representations assemble and transform the similitude of the materiality of space into the ordered arrangement of a place. They arrange, order, include and exclude, they *make knowable* a space to everyone who might choose to look at these representations and also make it possible to compare it with another space. The subjective world of memory, image, dream and fantasy, so often associated with place, operates by assembling materials into representations and using those representations to establish the difference between one place and the next. Those representations contain truth claims (not necessarily scientific) about a space. They perform place myths as places (Shields, 1991).

If the first of these mobile places we call ships tells us that place is about the *bricolage* or similitude of placing, then the second tells us that placing also involves assembling and arranging into knowable and reproducible representations and the location of those representations in relation to others. Arranging establishes categories of identity and non-identity. It suggests too that some are better located to make use of that arrangement than others, it is they who make best use of their material allies to help them define a place. Some spaces become obligatory points of passage through which places are ordered by the agents associated with those spaces (Latour, 1988, 1990). In both cases place is about ordering. Similitude generates a distribution that makes no immediate sense, it derives from the heterogeneous placing of materials in relation to one another. Arranging is a way of making sense, of giving order, of establishing division and of allowing placings to become known through representation. This is what immutable mobiles do. But that too is only part of the picture. Place, of course, is also about naming and that is an equally important part of this ordering process that constitutes a place and its differences from another.

We can now look at a third ship, this time one imagined by Thomas More sailing towards the imaginary island of Utopia (1985), more specifically a ship interpreted by Louis Marin in his reading of More's *Utopia* (1984, 1992). In a paper written shortly before his death, Marin explored, through the example of America, the ambiguities in the concept of utopia (1992). For Marin it is the frontier and the horizon that are the key spaces that mark out utopia as they are seen from the arriving ship:

> The limitless horizon is one of the main characteristics of the romantic landscape, an indefinite extent related to the display of a transcendence at this extremity where it seems possible to have a glimpse of the other side of the sky, a 'beyond space' encountered through the poetic and rhetorical figure of the twilight, in terms of which a bridge seems to be established between the visible and the invisible. (1992:407)

He goes on:

> In the case of the island of Utopia, the frontier is the infinity of the ocean, its border, a boundless space. Utopia is a limitless place because the island of Utopia is the figure of the limit and of the distance, the drifting of frontiers within the 'gap' between opposite terms, neither this one nor that one. (1992:412)

Places are named through a process of spatial play, a spatialization known as utopics (Marin, 1984). Utopics are associated with the translation of values into spatial practice. This practice takes place in a hiatus, a gap that Marin calls *the neutral* that emerges from the conditions of *undecidability* that lie behind representations of space (1984). This gap is a space between, a space of deferral. Drawing on Derrida's notion of différance (1976), whereby the meanings of texts are not seen to be fixed but endlessly deferred, Marin goes back to Thomas More's 16th-century writing on Utopia to derive his concept of utopics (see More, 1985). More called his imaginary island Utopia but this was based on a pun, u-topia means both *ou-topia*, no-place and *eu-topia*, good place. For Marin, the tension between these two meanings sets up the play of différance that constitute the spatiality of utopics (1984; see also Hetherington, 1997a: chapter 4). The movement between a nowhere and an imagined perfect place and *vice versa* takes place across a space of uncertainty, ambivalence and undecidability. Utopia is always not yet there but it is not here either. It is through this mobility and the attachment of a name to it that the difference between the arrangements of here and those of there are established.

The question for Marin is, in effect, how does one name a condition of similitude? Part of the process, making it known, involves the use of immutable mobiles but their use involves the imputation of value to the place being represented through a name. Utopia is a boundless space of connections, the endless horizon of possibilities that offers a glimpse of the 'other side of the sky'. As a place it is made up of a space into which social relations are extended, beyond their own limits, into a gap that is betwixt and between, unlocatable, unrepresentable and impossible. A space of integration and disintegration, of combination, resistance and disorder. It is a space of difference. It is also a space of an endless striving for an imaginary beyond in which all of that uncertainty will be resolved and a form of closure achieved. Of course, not all places are called utopia, but there is a utopic behind every place (alternatively, perhaps, a dystopic behind some as well). Naming is also about valuing and comparing. Arranging is a selective process that includes and excludes. In doing so it allows some to name, to make known, a place as meaning something in particular: my home, the place I was born, a prison, a school, a scientific laboratory. The name of each of these places derives from an ordering that is given by a name that carries with it a utopic, a name implies some sort of meaning to what the place is about, what its purpose is and what it stands for and how that contrasts with places that are not of this kind.

Places then, are materially constituted through an ordering process that involves an ongoing and recursive process that has three parts: i) the placing of materials within a network, ii) arranging those placings so that they can be known and represented through immutable mobiles and iii) naming those arrangements and through that name trying to allow their mobility and deferral to settle down. This threefold process, then, is a labour of division in which place as a mobile arrangement is given stability through difference. What is placed, how those placings are arranged at the type of name that comes to be attached to such arrangement, labours to divide one place from another through a process of inclusion and exclusion.

A space for the subject?

So far I have argued that *place* is a contingent effect of the processes of placing, ordering and naming that emerge from the actions of heterogeneous materials within a given network and the system of differences that are generated to give stability to such a mobile process. I want to develop this argument a bit further by way of another illustration, one that goes right to the heart of the humanist discourse of place, that of the idea of home.

There's no place like home. Home in western cultures is the quintessential basis for the idea of place as individually and socially meaningful. Home implies not only a particular familiar site in which we dwell and live out our everyday lives, it also implies more broadly a sense of belonging, security and identity that adds to our own understanding of ourselves. Belonging is its utopic. The very idea of a centred subject—essential and unique within every individual—implies this sense of belonging and nurturing to be found in the utopic that is given the name of home. Home is where we can be ourselves, our own little back-stage regions where we can mooch about in old slippers. Of course cultural geographers would rightly point out that this vision of home is culturally and historically specific, often class-based and gendered. *He* may mooch about in his slippers but it is often left to *her* to clean up after him. Her experience of the same home may well be quite different to his even if they share in the task of home making. But what about those other heterogeneous materials—carpets, doors, fridges, clutter, the dog, beds and so on? It is not just that we humans make a place, often in different ways because of our different locations in social relationships; place has to be considered as emerging from the placing, arranging and naming that occur in a heterogeneously constituted network and not from my subjectivity or hers. We are interpellated by such a process rather than being its instigators.

A second issue that arises from this perspective on the place of home is that of memory. It is one thing to say that places are socially and technically constructed and that through such a process they are continually being made; but one also has to recognize that a place is often thought of as something that endures and as a consequence has a past. Places are things we come back to after having been away and even if they do change physically they still endure in our memories of them. Human beings are able to remember the past and their understanding of that past is often profoundly linked to the idea not only of home but of place more generally (see Heidegger, 1978). Our sense of identity is generally seen to be tied up not only with who we see ourselves as being now and what we want to become but perhaps most significantly of what we have been. The places where we have been are an important part in the narrations of self that we make. To what extent, therefore, can this also be seen as an effect materials?

The idea of a place as meaningful is one thing, that there is a continuity of meaning that stretches over time is another important factor in the constitution of the idea of place. I remember this place when I was a child. She lived there all her life. Heritage, tradition and belonging—social and personal—that is what places are usually thought to be about. In this too we have to consider not just the thinking, remembering subject but a heterogeneous materiality that is the fabric of such memory. While a table or a painting on the living room wall cannot think and remember its past, it is impossible to conceive of a place and the memory of places without these materials. When Mrs Smith looks at the photograph of 'the two of them' together at Margate in 1963, Bert comes alive again, as if he were still with her in the house, in the home they made together, even though he has been dead now these past five years. In such a case materials are mobilised through some immutable form in this case a photograph. Photographs are placed, those placings are ordered and the representations generated by those orderings are used to allow values to emerge from the names that have been associated with the orderings. Places move in time as well as in space. There is human agency but there are other forms of agency too, without which places cannot be.

Something of this materiality of place and its relationship to memory was captured by Bachelard in his *Poetics of Space* (1969). While his work remains firmly entrenched within a humanist approach to place, it can be read against the grain to provide us with a further part of the picture by which we might come to analyse place. The poetics of space can be seen as a form of utopics, it is a means of naming our own personal assemblages and the networks through which we have moved.

Bachelard adopts a highly poetic style that breaks with conventional scientific modes of writing. His break, in terms of his writing on space, involves a discussion of the significance of the groundlessness of the poetic image; his philosophy of space provides us with a phenomenological reception of the reverie enclosed in groundless poetic images; images of places we might add often conceived in terms of their materiality. The space with which Bachelard is primarily concerned is that of the imagination and day-dreams. In a manner not dissimilar to Proust or Walter Benjamin, and very similar to Surrealists like Aragon (1987), the reception of the poetic image for Bachelard, constitutes a means by which the past can be recovered in memory and remain a source of novelty and new ways of seeing,

> The poetic image is not subject to an inner thrust. It is not an echo of the past. On the contrary: through the brilliance of an image, the distant past resounds with echoes, and it is hard to know at what depth these echoes will reverberate and die away. Because of its novelty and its action, the poetic image has an entity and a dynamism of its own; it is referable to a direct ontology. (Bachelard 1969:xii)

Memories constitute places anew; they add temporal mobility. Bachelard's aim is to seek out the 'reverberations' of Being in the poetic image. The problem that Bachelard sets out to analyse is the intersubjectivity of the poetic image and in that, the communicability of a shared feeling of wonder and reverie that places hold. It is in this reverberation of the poetic image that Bachelard believes he will discover the basis of all expressions of intersubjectivity. What he shows, perhaps unwittingly, is that in this intersubjectivity, the construction of place is impossible to conceive without taking into account the translating effects of the material actants involved. In taking the poetic image as the basis of communication and intersubjective experience, Bachelard focuses on two of its constitutive aspects, its fragmentary nature and its intimacy. The poetic image, for Bachelard, has no ontological ground, it begins from the standpoint of not knowing and aims at total revelation. It exists within Marin's gap between the no-place and the good-place (1984). In this respect, just as Bachelard attempts to free the poetic image from the structure and rules of the poem, so too, he aims to philosophize from the standpoint of the imagination freed from constraints.

Bachelard's approach to the uncovering of the Being of the poetic image is described as topo-analysis: '[. . .] the systematic psychological study of the sites of our intimate lives' (1969:8). In this respect, Bachelard considers the images of 'felicitous space' (1969:xxxi), loved spaces; a topophilia of undisclosed intimacy, that people make meaningful but which also make them 'meaningful' as subjects.

Bachelard's work on the poetics of space looks, by way of poetic images, at these intimate spaces that we value, or imagine ourselves inhabiting: houses; nests; shells; as in the intimacy associated with the miniature and interior, such as in corners, chests of drawers, and wardrobes. His concern with space is that of everyday space and the location of Being in the familiar. In contrast to many writers on everyday life (see Lefebvre, 1971), Bachelard sees in the poetics of such spaces as the house not simply a routine banality, but the source of an opening up of the imagination and the ability to communicate this to others. These everyday felicitous spaces are represented most significantly in the realms of day-dream and memory.

For Bachelard, home is the ultimate 'inside space' (1969:3), it is the primary space of intimacy, shelter, continuity and of the day-dream. The day-dream, for Bachelard, is where most of us encounter our own poetic images; home, itself a day-dream, is brought forward from the past in memory,

> The values that belong to daydreaming mark humanity in its depths. Daydreaming even has a privilege of autovalorization. It derives direct pleasure from its own being. Therefore, the places in which we have experienced daydreaming reconstitute themselves in a new daydream, and it is because our memories of former dwelling-places are relived as daydreams that the dwelling-places of the past remain in us for all time. (1969:6)

Space in this account is not simply an abstract set of relations between substances, nor a container of actions, but is encountered through the relationship that materials have to one another over time. Those relationships are brought to hand through memory and represented as the source of a sense of place. One cannot imagine memory without materiality and its semiotics. The role of memory and day-dream, and of the communicability of memories to others in particular, is said to encapsulate the spatialized moment of time. Place, for Bachelard, is embodied not simply in memory but, more specifically, in the recovery from the memory of a sense of belonging. And that belonging is generated most clearly through the materiality of the place in question and the means of representing it to others. The smell of the sheets in the cupboard, the slope of the cellar steps, the patch of paint picked off the edge of the windowsill in a moment of childish boredom, all become the material substance through which memories are constituted. Memory takes hold of similitude and orders it into representations. 'My home was here, everywhere else was in some way next door or the nth door beyond that.' Sometimes these representations remain personal, at other times they are communicated through representations to others. To dwell, in the Bachelardian sense, is, through daydream and memory, to bring back from the past that which has been forgotten and live within the reverberations of its remembered intimacy.

Place is also, for Bachelard, the remembering of time. Time becomes the memory trace of a place (Harvey, 1989:218). The importance of the family photograph is a good example of this. The photograph, as a snapshot, is similar to the poetic image in that it represents a place as time remembered, such that it has an after-life and a mobility outside of the immanence of its becoming. Viewing snapshots from one's intimate life, of loved ones in particular, either when young or after they are long dead, is an example of the process of the sensuous recovery of the intimacy of the Other through the remembering of places (heterogeneous material assemblages) where one has been. That memory of place is generated by the photograph as an immutable mobile, which orders the placing of certain things, and allows that arrangement to be named. Such representations generate performances of remembering and forgetting. The significance of the photographs in the family album lies in their ability to reveal anew to the present a fondly remembered person, for example, through the recovery of an intimate memory, out of the place where the person whom one loved has been and left an enduring trace of themselves in the world. The pettiness and banalities of everyday life are forgotten by the photograph allowing it to selectively represent the past and for that representation to generate a utopics of the place remembered.

While one has to circumnavigate a way around the humanist subject in Bachelard's perspective on place generating these memories and their representations, he reveals, almost in spite of himself, the importance of the materiality of place in the processes of remembering and the materiality of its representation and difference. Materials are the texture of our memories and it is through their effects that places come to be. These materials, whether they be photographs, the materials represented in the photographs, antiques handed down within the family from one generation to the next, perhaps a piece of music playing in the background or parts of a house, are the means through which places like home are constituted. Not only are they a product of the past, themselves encoded with social memory in their production and consumption, with the skill and tastes or lack of them of a time gone by, but they perform that past through their existence in the present and allow material representations to become memories.

Conclusion

Places, even those associated with the most intimate and personal memories, are not produced by acts of pure volition but are the effects of arrangements of spaces, times, things, people and events in materialities from which a naming process can be performed and difference established in that name and the values associated with it. Those representations can be produced as memories or they can be communicated to others through some material form that is both immutable and mobile. In either case, a place as somewhere lived or somewhere remembered involves the use of representation that tries to make sense of the placing of things. Spaces, or the representation of those spaces, are semiotic in character, placing signs, arranging those signs into some form of ordering and naming those arrangements as signifieds. Places are the effect of the folding of spaces, times and materials together into complex topological arrangements that perform a multitude of differences.

The labour of division that goes into the processes of placing, arranging a naming a bit of space in relation to others is a labour that constitutes a mobile arrangement and gives it stability through difference. In that sense the idea of place is also an idea of difference. It is a process that is both inclusive and exclusive. Places are not just attached to space, they are diasporic, they travel with us and with the materials through which they are articulated. They move through representations (spaces) and they move through memories (time). Like the ship they are not fixed, they are not anchored, but they mobilize difference and are given temporary stability through their difference. Ships tack. Their course is made through a series of movements and relative stabilities.

References

Aragon, L., (1987) *Paris Peasant*, London: Picador.
Bachelard, G., (1969) *The Poetics of Space*, Boston: Beacon Press.
Deleuze, G., (1986) *Foucault*, London: Athlone Press.
Derrida, J., (1976) *Of Grammatology*, Baltimore: Johns Hopkins University Press.
Doel, M., (1996) 'A Hundred Thousand Lines of Flight: a Machinic Introduction to the Nomad Thought and Scrumpled Geography of Gilles Deleuze and Felix Guattari', *Environment and Planning D: Society and Space*, Vol. 14(4):421–39.
Foucault, M., (1983) *This is Not a Pipe*, Berkeley: University of California Press.
Foucault, M., (1986) 'Of Other Spaces', *Diacritics*, 16(1):22–7.
Foucault, M., (1989a) *Madness and Civilization*, London: Tavistock.
Foucault, M., (1989b) *The Order of Things*, London: Tavistock/Routledge.
Harkness, J., (1983) 'Translator's Introduction in M. Foucault, *This is not a Pipe*, J. Harkness (ed.), Berkeley: University of California Press, pp. 1–12.
Harvey, D., (1989) *The Condition of Postmodernity: an Enquiry into the Origins of Cultural Change*, Oxford: Basil Blackwell.
Heidegger, M., (1978) 'Building, Dwelling, Thinking' in D. Krell (ed.) *Martin Heidegger: Basic Writings*, London: Routledge and Kegan Paul, pp. 319–39.
Hetherington, K., (1996) 'Identity Formation, Space and Social Centrality', *Theory, Culture and Society*, Vol. 13(4):33–52.
Hetherington, K., (1997a) *The Badlands of Modernity: Heterotopia and Social Ordering*, London: Routledge.
Hetherington, K., (1997b) 'Museum Topology and the Will to Connect', *Journal of Material Culture*, Vol. 2(2):199–218.
Hetherington, K., (1997c) 'Representing the Potteries 1800–1686: Place Myths and Immutable Mobiles'. Mimeograph.
Hinchliffe, S., (1996) 'Technology, Power and Space: the Means and Ends of Geographies of Technology', *Environment and Planning D: Society and Space*, vol. 14(6):659–82.
Keith, M. and Pile, S., (eds) (1993) *Place and the Politics of Identity*, London: Routledge.
Latour, B., (1988) *The Pasteurization of France*, Cambridge, Mass.: Harvard University Press.
Latour, B., (1990) 'Drawing Things Together' in S. Woolgar and M. Lynch (eds) *Representations in Science*, Cambridge, Mass.: MIT Press, pp. 18–60.
Law, J., (1986) 'On the Methods of Long-Distance Control: Vessels, Navigation and the Portuguese Route to India' in J. Law (ed.) *Power, Action and Belief*, London: Routledge and Kegan Paul, Sociological Review Monograph 32, pp. 234–63.
Law, J., (1992) 'Notes on the Theory of the Actor-Network: Ordering, Strategy, and Heterogeneity', *Systems Practice*, Vol. 5(4):379–93.
Law, J., (1994) *Organizing Modernity*, Oxford: Blackwell.

Law, J., (1997) *Aircraft Stories: Technoscience and the Death of the Object*, forth-coming.

Lefebvre, H., (1971) *Everyday Life in the Modern World*, London: Allen Lane/Penguin.

Levi-Strauss, C., (1966) *The Savage Mind*, London: Weidenfeld and Nicolson.

Marin, L., (1984) *Utopics: Spatial Play*, London: Macmillan.

Marin, L., (1992) 'Frontiers of Utopia: Past and Present', *Critical Inquiry*, Vol. 19(3):397–420.

Massey, D., (1994) *Space, Place and Gender*, Oxford: Polity Press.

Mol, A. and Law, J., (1994) 'Regions, Networks and Fluids: Anaemia and Social Topology', *Social Studies of Science*, 24:641–71.

More, T., (1985) *Utopia*, London: J.M. Dent.

Relph, E., (1976) *Place and Placelessness*, London: Pion.

Rose, G., (1993) *Feminism and Geography*, Oxford: Polity.

Shields, R., (1991) *Places on the Margin: Alternative Geographies of Modernity*, London: Routledge.

Soja, E., (1990) 'Heterotopologies: A Remembrance of Other Spaces in Citadel-LA', *Strategies*, 3:6–39.

Soja, E., 91996) *Thirdspace*, Oxford: Blackwell.

Tuan, Y.-F., (1977) *Space and Place: the Perspective of Experience*, Minneapolis: University of Minnesota Press.

Thrift, N., (1996) *Spatial Formations*, London: Sage.

Urry, J., (1995), *Consuming Places*, London: Routledge.

Home-made space and the will to disconnect

Steve Hinchliffe

Introduction—performing homes

At the time of writing there's an advert doing the rounds. Made for cinema audiences, the advert is for a brand of expensive ice-cream, a product which emerged in the heady days of the late 1980s and whose name has become a (most probably temporary) metonym for upwardly mobile Euro-American style, youthful success and sexual desire. Perhaps the most striking attribute of the film is that it is shot using a heat-sensitive camera so that the warm bodies in the scene are depicted as glowing yellows and reds, whilst the colder bodies are identifiable through their blue colour. The film starts with a young male and female couple sharing the as yet unrevealed product in a sensuous act combining music, intimacy and eating. These warm (red) human bodies are in a warm, relaxed atmosphere (conveyed by the heat sensitive camera and the retro-style romantic music) and the cool product stands out as a blue play-thing which completes the scene of seduction. The paradigmatic arrangement of the product, youthfulness, fashion, romance and affluence is emphasized by the panning out of the camera to show the flat downstairs. Here the scene is more blue than red. An elderly couple sit in front of the one red body in the room—a small one-bar electric fire which is evidently having little or no effect on the temperature of the room. The relationship between the people below and the people above is suddenly made explicit through an exchange of words, gestures and glances (even though the separated couples cannot see each other). The young couple upstairs momentarily turn the music down as the elderly man bangs the ceiling with a broom (presumably because the music emanating from upstairs is too loud and not to the taste of the 'out-of-style' residents of the cold flat). As the camera returns to the comfort of upstairs, the couple briefly bring a halt to their play. Momentarily disturbed, they look down and then let out a kind of laughter that you might associate with naughty children. The laughter is reminiscent of the kind that children make when they have been caught doing something wrong. But it is not so much an embarrassed laugh as one that regards the person who has caught them as powerless to do anything and holding onto a set of beliefs and norms that are out-of-date, prudish and comical. The music is returned to its previous level and the couple continue to enjoy their warm flat and re-engage in their sophisticated consumption. Miserable, the couple downstairs remain in the blue. One message of the advertisement is that to buy into this product is to buy into a lifestyle that will set you apart from those below. You will become an 'insider' and won't be left in the cold.

The division between inside and outside, played out here through the metonym of upstairs and downstairs, is clearly precarious. Perhaps there wouldn't be any point in advertising if we, in this case the audience, couldn't aspire to moving upstairs. For those who would consider themselves 'there', advertising plays on the fear that we might give the impression that we live like those downstairs. But even those that feel as if they're upstairs have to suffer disturbances to the apparent solidity of their dwelling. The abject poverty downstairs, or the other abject things that hover on the borders of the subjects' identity (Kristeva, 1982; Sibley, 1995), are permanent threats. Permanent, because rather than just being things-in-themselves, these categories are also relational. For those aspiring to be upstairs there must always be room for a downstairs. The ambivalence lies in the desire to expel that which is downstairs and in the powerlessness to achieve expulsion without suffering a collapse of the living room floor.

The sympathies in this account of the advertisement could easily be reversed—I could have sided with the ice-cream couple and painted the people downstairs as unnecessarily interfering. Perhaps if I had noticed a picture of the Queen on the wall or some other signifiers of 'Alf Garnet' life-style, I could have consigned downstairs to a petty-minded, intolerant representation of old England. A regime of little Englanders that the foreign-sounding ice-cream product signals is ending. Here, the downstairs residents project all that they fear and desire onto the upstairs. So, despite the on film laughter of the upstairs couple, the miserable couple downstairs may have the next laugh. Opening the post tomorrow, the residents upstairs may find that their tenancy agreement has been terminated by the owners of the property, who live downstairs. It is their turn to be thrown out, to lose their insider status. The ice-cream aided night of fun turns sour.

Whatever the scenario, there is a good deal of potential traffic between these two rooms. At least three related issues can be drawn out from this imagining of what's in the advert. I will list these below as they help to inform the argument that I want to develop in this chapter.

1. First, a re-statement. Outsiders are always and already part and parcel of insiders, and it couldn't be otherwise. So the upstairs is built upon a fear of what is simultaneously constructed as downstairs, or vice versa. This is one way of suggesting that rooms that seem so separate can also be coexistent, overlapping and mutually constitutive. It is also one way of suggesting that labours of division are complex and multiple. In particular, the divisions between upstairs and downstairs are spatially and temporally complex matters where boundaries can appear and disappear, movements can change direction and transformations can be subtle as well as disruptive.

2. Second, there are inequalities in these interrelationships, but these inequalities are also far from fixed. In the first description of the advert, the insiders and the outsiders are ambivalent categories, but the insiders seem to be getting the best deal. They are the ones who appear to be able to do all the definition work. It is their labour of division which seems to be working better than the one being produced downstairs. The upstairs arrangement, or 'collective', loudly presents itself as young, playful and prosperous, and at the same time performs representations of those downstairs as old, rigid and miserable.

3. Third, in performing its own drama, upstairs also manages to set a script for those downstairs who can't hear their own thoughts. In this version, upstairs performs downstairs. Even so, and as I have suggested, the boot may well be on the other foot, and the script may be changed, although it will never be as simple as everyone and everything following the same script. There will be manoeuvres, inflections and re-inscriptions as part of the performances.

In this chapter I want to consider the processes of ordering home spaces in the face of continuous disturbances. But rather than focus upon the image of human subjects doing all the work of this ordering, or setting things in motion, I want to think through the multiple materialities of ordering homes (see also Hetherington, 1997a). By doing so, I will drawn attention to the political, or distributive, aspects of making spaces and consider the possibilities for changing some of those arrangements. In particular, I will focus upon the possibilities afforded by considering the discursive arrangements of 'nature' in relation to home-making. By discursive arrangements I hope to emphasize that I am neither referring to a 'purely' linguistic construction nor to a reducible material entity, but rather to a co-construction of semiotic-materialities (see Latour, 1993, on purification, Lenoir, 1994, and Law and Mol, 1995 on the theory metaphor if material semiotics). I will expand on the possibilities of this project by referring to empirical work on household consumption that I carried out on a housing estate in Denmark.

I have organized the account along the following lines. Starting with a brief discussion of the term nature, the first two sections provide some detail on co-existing spatializations of home/nature relations. A characteristic quality of the first of these spatializations is marked by attempts to remove nature beyond the walls of the home. In contrast, the second spatialization is characterized by an attempt to re-embed human-nature relations by tracing the connections between the two 'realms' of thought and practice. By demonstrating how these two spatializations are unhelpfully pitted against one another in a dispute over the most appropriate way of organizing consumption on a housing estate, and by seeking to destabilize their supposed solidity, the chapter suggests the possibilities for other spatializations which can evoke some of the complexity and multiplicity that I introduced in the opening discussion. In this sense, the chapter is an attempt to think behind some of the binaries that are invoked to characterize spatialities, commodities and cultures and natures.

Orificial ordering—the making of discrete homes

Shane Phelan (1993) provides a suggestive reading of the multiple effects which the term nature can perform. She provides four 'meanings' of the term: nature as origin, as limit, as lawgiver and as process. The first of these, nature as origin, has at least two usages. Nature is both a 'source of authenticity' and 'the primitive, the incomplete'. As a limit, the term nature is employed to halt debate, to designate a fixed state of affairs and to privilege the world and word as given. As a lawgiver, nature is a goal, a state of affairs to which things aspire. Before I mention the last of Phelan's natures, it is worth noting that each of these three 'foundational' natures are ordering devices, performing where possible, labours of division, and in this sense all 'share the quest for clarity, for certainty, that dogs Western thought' (Phelan, 1993:46). In some ways, they can be said to be part of a performance of 'ontological security'. They are also co-existent in many ordering practices. Phelan's fourth meaning is closer to a dialectical reading (see also Harvey, 1996), turning nature into a process, a 'second nature', a displacement. As this chapter is, in part, about the possibilities for disturbing foundational natures with more open natures, I will return to these in more detail in the final section of the chapter. For the moment I want to dwell on the roles of some of the foundational natures in the arrangement of home-making.

Nature as origin is perhaps the most productive of meanings in the arrangements of ideal homes. As already mentioned there are at least two forms that this narrative of beginnings can take. Origins can 'call us home' (Phelan, 1993:45) and, through consuming acts, bestow authenticity on home life. I will have more to say about this organicism later on. The second originary discourse, and the one that I will focus on in this section, is in contradistinction to this wholeness. As an origin, nature is also a less than satisfactory condition. It is a lack, 'requires supplementation' (*ibid.*) and labours a division which in turn privileges becoming 'human' over 'nonhuman', mind over body, male over female and so on.

As a narrative device, the image of a primordial nature fixes space and time to produce seemingly concrete cartographies of individual, household and state, all of which gain strength through their abilities to order waste and arrange geographies of exclusion (Sibley, 1995). Human individuals become, at least in part, delineated by a degree of closure, producing the ascetic body and opposing this to the grotesque, leaking body (Stallybrass and White, 1986; Anderson, 1995). Furthermore, a pure self becomes possible through a despising of bodily residues, and 'faeces, urine, sweat, scurf . . . become symbols of defilement' (Sibley, 1995:127). Ideal homes are an extension and condition for a division of labour. In this version of household geography, the lavatory and the household plug form typical arrangements which convey 'nature' to an elsewhere in the past. Meanwhile, Anderson's paraphrasing of Laporte's observation that 'the rise of a strong state led to the privatizing and constrained circulation of smell-producing excrement' (1995:642) can be inverted to suggest that a strong state was an effect of the ordering of waste. Indeed, it is surely possible to suggest that the cartographies of individual, household and state are the effects of ordering practices rather than transcendent starting points (see also Whatmore, 1997). In Mol and Law's (1994:650) terms, the entrenchment of these cartographies mark inter-topological effects, a folding together of regional and network topologies. I will come back to this formulation a number of times in this chapter.

Focusing upon the ideal home in particular, it is fairly straightforward to link this narrative of improvement and supplementation to the material arrangements of the household. Advertisers love to play on this ever present threat of the return to a condition of lack by producing representations of household surfaces 'brownwashed with a thin film of germs' (Anderson, 1995:641). The imagery of the kitchen in particular as a laboratory, white-washed, delibinized, a place of somatic control, matches that of the bathroom (although, as I will mention again later on, these can also form back stage places, where binges amongst other things are possibilities). The square tiles and wipe clean surfaces are indicative of an abstractness of space—a formal, calculative and quantitative space. Perhaps it is possible to go further and mention the regulation of exchanges between home spaces and their surroundings. In particular the installation of meters to regulate exchanges through the media of measurement, inscription and money might be significant contributors to this arrangement of homeliness. This might also be about the creation of scopic regimes (Jay, 1992), the making invisible of those very labours that perform the divisions to which I have alluded. As in the examples of a blocked drain or a 'plague' of ants in a kitchen, homeliness may well be disrupted by leakages to such a regime. The gendering of this division may also be central to this scopic regime. One image of home is as a place for passive consumption, a place where order prevails and time can stand still. In this arrangement, a good deal of the housework should be invisible (inside of office hours when the 'masters of the house' are out—and when they come home, their workplaces are reproduced to appear clean for the next morning).

There is a peculiar spatialization at work in this version of homeliness. In terms of topological metaphors, this is a regionalization. In the region called the home there is a suppression of difference within the space so defined. This is a bounded space, a neat space where overlaps are frowned upon. But, as Mol and Law (1994) suggest, this is but one performance of a spatial type, and 'the social does not exist as a single spatial type' (1994:645). In contrast to the examples where home-making activities are made invisible, and are consigned to other time-spaces, there are home-making actions which are made visible. Nature as origin can, as I have already mentioned, be something of a 'calling home'. For example, people build fires and light candles, even when they have central heating and electric lights. Indeed, there are moments when these performances of space and natures are brought together. At the very moment when 'all known germs are killed—dead', the germicide is executed with a flourish of 'fresh pine' or 'spring meadow'. Similarly, household plants are arranged in homes to purify the air. It is to these disturbances of the regional space and the orificial economy of the home that I will now turn.

Bearing the connections

There are at least two ways of opening up the regional space of the home. One is to employ a network metaphor, the second is to conjure with some ideas, or topologies, where the language is less fixed (Doel, 1996; Mol and Law, 1994). In this section of the paper, I will be mainly focusing upon a network topological metaphor (see Mol and Law, 1994) and will be concerned to show how, taken together, regional and network topologies form a familiar binary which inhabits much spatio-temporal thinking (see Harvey, 1990 and 1996). Throughout this and later sections, I will also be working at empirical material on the arrangements of household consumption in order to suggest the pervasiveness of the modes of spatialization to which I refer. The empirical work forms part of a case study of a housing estate called Hyldebjerg in a town called Hvalsø, Denmark. Here, starting in the early 1990s, a number of environmental campaigners tried to promote a project to change the form in which the estate bought and used energy services. In brief, the campaigners wanted to convert the estate from electricity based heating to a district heating scheme. In following the conversations that took place in residents' meetings and in interviews, I will suggest that the scheme drew upon a number of spatializations of consumption and home-making. I will also suggest that, at times, these spatializations were unhelpfully pitted against one another to produce a political stalemate.

There is a qualification needed here. In adopting the term network to describe a way of performing space in Hvalsø I am no doubt taking a few liberties with that term. When I talk about electricity and district heat networks, the 'network' that I use may seem far too literal for it to communicate the nuances that are implied by the term in actor-network theory. In part this is a result of using the term to refer to a set of arguments raised by environmental campaigners which tended to focus on particular aspects of these networks. Therefore, it is worth re-stating that the term network derives its valence from Greimasian semiotics (Lenoir, 1994; Mol and Law, 1994) to suggest the ways in which meanings and other relations (including power effects) are co-constructed out of the arrangement of network elements.[1] Mol and Law (1994:649) provide a neat account of the network metaphor:

> A network is a series of elements with well defined relations between them. The metaphor comes from semiotics where it is used to apply to language. But the elements of a network do not need to be words, and the relations between them don't necessarily have to do with the question of giving each other meaning. Network elements may be machines or gestures . . .

As Mol and Law suggest, a network topology judges distances in non-metric ways. Proximity, in network terms, is a condition of similarity. Thus, '[p]laces with a similar set of elements and similar relations between them are close to one another, and those with different elements are far apart' (*ibid.*). So the network of wires and pipelines is also a network of measurement (for example, Kwh), monetary exchanges, shared meanings and energy conversions. In this particular sense, homes are proximal to power stations and other 'elements' of the network. The proximity is not just a result of the materials and energies that 'flow' from one site to another, it also includes the distribution of agency across the network which can account for the various material shifts, and the shared understandings of the means and ends of the relations that are co-constituted within the network. Akrich's study of the electrification of households in the Ivory Coast is exemplary in detailing the ways in which an electricity system grew along with the State, more definite property relations and fixed exchange systems (see Akrich, 1992). As I have hinted, in the case of Hvalsø, the network metaphor took on a particular set of meanings, informed by materialist and ecological thinking. Nevertheless, in terms of the spatialities invoked, it captures something of the arguments that were made. I will now provide some background on this study and say some more about the performance of networks as I go.

The households studied were arranged into an estate called Hyldebjerg, and were built in the early 1970s. At the time of their design and construction, electricity was regarded as the most suitable and flexible form of energy for space and water heating. In this sense the houses were built towards the tail-end of a relatively long period of triumphalism in the electricity supply industries in Denmark and in many other countries (see Luckin, 1990; Nye, 1990; Ross, 1995; Thrift, 1994; Throgmorton, 1996). At this time, and partly as a result of oil price hikes, the Danish government and the electricity companies were starting to take nuclear power seriously. The all-electric houses were regarded as the most flexible means of keeping pace with any changes that might occur in the future supply of energy in Denmark. In the early 1990s, after there had been a referendum vote against the construction of nuclear power stations on Danish soil, the Danish Government made it more or less illegal to construct houses with electricity as the main form of energy for heating purposes. Instead, households should be connected to district heating systems and natural or bio-gas pipelines (Danish Ministry of Energy, 1990). Whilst the rationale for this move was undoubtedly a result of the Danish government's financial investment in these forms of energy supply, the energy planners' rhetoric was also infused with technicist-environmentalist arguments. The extra energy conversions necessary to deliver electric heat energy to households made electricity less efficient and more 'environmentally damaging' than other forms of provision (*ibid.*, IEA, 1991).

Within walking distance of the Hyldebjerg estate there was a district heat station with excess capacity, and some residents on the estate were looking into the prospect of connecting the estate to the district heating network as a way of saving money and reducing the environmental impacts of their consumption activities. In order to do this, they needed to mobilise the other residents on the estate because the change over to district heating would only be cost-effective for the heating company if all the residents opted for change. Meanwhile, given the relatively large initial financial costs involved in connecting up, a concerted effort would be needed by as many residents as possible to lobby local and national government, and energy suppliers and distributors, in order to secure some financial assistance for the project. The problem for those acting as the protagonists of this campaign was that most of the residents were happy with electric heating, it did the job. This expression of satisfaction was the cause of exasperation to the residents who wanted to change things.

Here are some examples of that satisfaction in the form of excerpts from interviews that I staged on the estate in late 1992 (after the proposal had been rejected by the residents' committee). They are worth focusing on because they can be linked to the discussion of spatialities that is being drawn upon in the paper.

Karen had moved from an old farm house into the relatively 'modern' house on Hyldebjerg. She missed aspects of the old house but:

> Karen: 'I was rather happy to move to the house in Hyldebjerg (. . .) it (the house) was clean and in some ways it was easy to handle. This electrical heating is very fast . . . '

Henrik liked electricity because it was controllable and he could use it without having to worry about what other people did (this was not the case, he said, with collective heating systems).

> Henrik: 'I like electricity, and for several reasons really—erm, because when I turn it off it doesn't cost me money, and it always cost me with the central [district] heating (. . .) That was the impression that I had, even though we turned the heat all the way down, I still had to pay.'

Kirsten liked electricity because it was 'easy'.

> Kirsten: 'I think it's very easy to use electricity (. . .), because, I remember when I lived in a house with central [district] heating, when you turned it on in the autumn there was always something wrong with the radiators or something. [Electricity heating] is very easy, either the radiators come on or they don't . . . and then you buy a new one (laughs). [With electricity] you turn it on, put it on the right temperature and you don't have to be bothered.'

Cleanliness, ease, speed, individual billing, not having to be bothered—all of these relate to a performance of bounded, regional spaces. More than that, they also refer to a network which provides the conditions of possibility (Mol and Law, 1994) for the regional space of the home and the individual. This immediately opens up the possibility of challenging Karen, Henrik and Jens with a 'yes, but . . . '. Which is exactly what the protagonists for change did. Suggesting that residents viewed their homes as separate to and distant from the outside world, the campaigners presented a relational space, where homes were proximal to nuclear power stations in Sweden and to coal power stations in Denmark. In this topology, homes were also linked along a chain to general circulation models, government and university laboratories, chemical abstractions signifying pollutants, depletions of resource stocks and through all of these to issues of human welfare and environmental change in places which, from the regional topology, might have seemed distant. In letters and other documents, the campaigners suggested the need for 'consciousness-raising' activities in order to promote their project. Indeed, this project was partly based upon a making visible of the connections which made home spaces possible. In this, the Hyldebjerg information campaign shared several features with other 'environmental' and consumer campaigns (see Hinchliffe, 1996 on energy in the UK, and Cook and Crang, 1996, on food consumption).

Here, as in other campaigns, the protagonists argued for a different (and, in their terms a better or more comprehensive) view of the world. A view that, following the albeit ironic terminology of Cook and Crang (1996:146), 'show[s] the veil of fetishism for what it is—a mask of myths and smokescreens—and lay[s] bare the real histories and geographies of connection in which commodity production and consumption are implicated'. It would be wrong to suggest that such challenges are wasted effort and it is surely right that under some circumstances tracing connections, and privileging the network topologies is a valuable means of addressing inequalities of various kinds. But, and as the resistance of the Hyldebjerg residents suggests, there are limits to this strategy. Indeed, Cook and Crang (1996:146–7) suggest that 'thickening the connections runs the danger of evacuating the realm of consumption altogether'. Meanwhile, in asserting that the network view is the 'real' view, an unhelpful opposition is set up between competing epistemologies, between so-called expert knowledge and popular geographies (*ibid.*, see also Crang, 1996). In setting up this opposition, and casting it in terms of competing moralities, regional and network topologies are reified and fixed. So too are the materials. In these battles over epistemology, the order of things is largely assumed to be pregiven and static. For the protagonists in Hyldebjerg, connecting homes to a chain of consumption is performed in such a way that fixes the sequence and shape of the members of the chain. 'Nature', for example, takes shape as a set of manageable abstractions. But in Hyldebjerg the residents failed to see themselves in either of these spatial arrangements or fully to recognize nature as it was being represented by the campaigners:

Lene: 'I think that when people say: "Well, we are very energy
conscious—we think a lot about that and it's because we want to

save nature and so on, and we care about how much energy we use (. . .)"—now and then, it's something they boast about. But, they might as well think of the little people who also think about their own economy, there's nothing bad about that. (. . .) I don't think that nature is unimportant but I think that many people who say that they are only doing that for the sake of nature, they think they are a little better than the rest (. . .) they act like priests.'

The binary should now be taking some shape. According to the campaigners, most of the residents thought regionally about homes. They accepted the commodity fetishism which masks the origins of the product. On the other hand, many of the residents thought that the campaigners were dupes of a different kind. They were so busy thinking about connections to other times and places that they forgot to think about where they were—the region that they shared with the other people on the estate. Hyldebjerg was being performed as two spatio-temporalities. The experiential 'lifeworld' of the residents was set against the 'abstract "rationalized"' spatio-temporalities attributed to modernity or capitalism' (Harvey, 1996:233). As Harvey suggests, this duality is implied in Marx's analysis of the fetishism of commodities (*ibid.*, p. 234). The latter may take a number of forms. An example would be Cook and Crang's (1996) double commodity fetish which is used to suggest the ways in which commodities are divorced for and by consumers from the social relations of their production, and simultaneously mythologized and aestheticized as the people, places and materials become touristic constructions (Lash and Urry, 1994). Whatever the form, the fetish suggests its incompleteness, and that a 'full story of social reproduction through commodity production and exchange' (Harvey, 1996: 233) can be told.

I have argued that this epistemological battle was unhelpful. Not only did it label most of the people as ignorant (as do many of the academic writings on the public understanding of science or on 'lay perspectives on environmental change'), it also posited the world as pre-given. And, like the perspectivalist representations of Renaissance Italy, it depicted a world containing objects, like nature, 'which have continuities. They pass through time revealing substantial geometrical stability—or differences that are explicable in terms of object-interactions, collisions, etc.' (Law and Benschop, 1997: 158). As these and the other authors cited suggest, this polarization of worlds and spaces might not be the only way of performing.

There may be ways of working with, rather than against, the fetish (Cook and Crang, 1996; Taussig, 1992).

Moving spaces

I now want to think about what happens to the question of consumption and space on Hyldebjerg if the language and materials are allowed more room for manoeuvre, and the so-called objects, like nature, are no longer seen as fixed entities.

If space is performed in several ways, then there are other possibilities which may coexist with regional and network topologies. There may be spaces which defy the solidity and the bounded features of the region, and confound the structure and formalism of the network. One way of imagining and working with these possibilities is to focus on social objects or things and watch for their ability to slip through the categories of space that have been described so far in this paper. Harvey (1996) provides a suggestive example of money behaving in this way and opening up a multiplicity of spatiotemporalities. In doing so, and in folding these spatialities together, regions may look less homogeneous than we might have wanted to believe. Objects might be shown to fold what have formerly been regarded as strongly bounded spaces (Hetherington, 1997b). Likewise, elements within the space of networks might undergo complex transformations which might not involve the disruption of semiotic orderings, or the collapse of social worlds. I take it that this formulation captures something of Law and Mol's interest in multiple materialities (Law and Mol, 1995) and in fluid spaces (Mol and Law, 1994). In these analyses, the possibility is opened up that extending practices across time and space is not always about generating immutable mobiles, objects which hold their shape as they move from one place or context to another (see Latour, 1990). Rather, there may be changes and these changes can occur without there being a collapse of the social worlds that the mutable objects help to consolidate. Holding the social together may be about variation as well as being about constructing networks. Thus,

> There are social objects which exist in, draw upon and recursively form fluid spaces that are defined by liquid continuity. (Mol and Law, 1994:659)

These are far from free-floating, frictionless objects and spaces. There is a stickiness here that is not altogether captured by homogeneity and boundaries, nor is it endowed by syntactical ordering.

Fluid spaces may share something with Doel's 'scrumpled geography'. A geography 'composed of intervals, joints and folds, whose immanence and consistency thwarts and displaces the more familiar, arboreal, and sedentary prose of "is" and "is not"' (1996:435). Here, nature is produced in a multiplicity of ways which can fold the regional and network topologies invoked by the campaigners on Hyldebjerg. There, nature did not move across a network, unchanged and unchanging. Nor was it something that residents always sought to exclude from their lives in simple acts of purification. Rather, 'it' was a complex 'thing' that flowed across and between these spatio-temporalities. Here is a possible illustration of how analysis can move with this movement.

I have already mentioned the ways in which the regional spaces of the home can be disturbed by, amongst other things, binges and fires. With reference to the latter, there was an *apparent* anachronism in the houses that I visited. Some of these houses in Hyldebjerg had solid fuel burners, stoves or fireplaces, which had been installed at great expense and which took up a considerable amount of space in the home (two reasons which were cited for not wanting to install district heating). Here are some of the residents talking about '*hyggelig*', a Danish term which translates (somewhat uneasily) as homeliness.

> Suzanne: 'I shouldn't do it, but I like the way, just lighting the fire, I like that. (. . .) Something about being back to nature—something, it's very cosy.'

> Henrik: 'I don't know if the fire's a good idea or not, but if you want it. It's cosy though.'

The all electric homes were often augmented in this way. And the ways in which people talked about their fire-places made me think that they were cherished objects. Their 'use', which was relatively infrequent, also suggested that the warmth they produced was only partially related to the heat of the flames (see Øllgaard, 1991:188). Another resident, Per, told me that the fire-place was something to do with security. If there was a power cut, his family would still be warm. It was also part of a weekend and holiday ritual which included the collection and preparation of wood, the cleaning of the grate, the building, lighting and maintenance of the fire. It performed a slower pace of time and, for Per, it was part of the performance of a family and a degree of independence. Like the barbecue, it also performed masculinity.

Before I press the example further, the question of whether this is simply another network operation which enables the regional home space to be maintained needs to be posed. Isn't it the case that Per is referring to a back-up network that could be 'switched on' when other networks went wrong? Isn't this just a smaller network than the one that was labelled the electricity network? One that involves less actants and therefore one that may not be as extensive as others, but one that can be relied upon if the others sometimes become unwieldy on account of their size and widespread distribution of discretion (Law, 1991)? As Mol and Law (1994:655) suggest, networks do 'co-exist and they may interweave with one another'. This is a possibility, but analyses of this sort would find it difficult to account for the multiple uses of stoves and fire-places on Hyldebjerg. Perhaps it is more telling to suggest that these are very different networks and they produce different effects to their larger counterparts. This is also a possibility. So, there is a 'nature' material-semiotic network. The walk in the nearby woodland, the patient collecting of wood, the lighting of the fire and the sitting around the hearth all perform a network that can be called nature. And this nature is close to some of the foundational natures that I mentioned earlier. A sense of origin, destiny and order prevail in accounts like these. Clearly, in this version, there is a region called nature too. The weekend, the holiday and the activities that make up the production of the glowing hearth are bounded. They are different from the rest of the week and from the other time-spaces of work and school, where/when there are fewer possibilities to engage in extending the nature network. This is one way of agreeing with the prognoses of the campaigners. Residents on Hyldebjerg were engaged in a double commodity fetish—ignoring the reality of the weekly consumption, yet mythologizing nature in their leisure time-space. Such a prognosis calls for enlightened campaigns.

But there is another possibility, one that doesn't necessarily invalidate the others, but may in itself offer other ways of thinking about the production of nature on Hyldebjerg, and may even start to offer escape routes from the epistemological battleground. What if the fire-places were thought of as interfering with the narrative of progress which helped to inform the design and construction of the all electric houses on Hyldebjerg? What if they were seen as a set of practices whereby divisions, which marked out the borders of the home, were simultaneously reinforced and disturbed? Like the pet cat (Sibley and Griffiths, 1997), might not these practices talk of multiple spatializations which start to dissolve some of the object markers of differences between insiders and outsiders? The smells, dust and dirt of the fire (and for that matter the cat) are at once homely and un-homely.

Conclusions

If one of the aims of analysis is to think through the multiple ways in which social worlds are maintained and through this to imagine possible routes for change, then this chapter has two things to say. First, the means of achieving solidity are multiple. There is more to solidity than setting up boundaries and constructing rigid networks. Second, attempts to produce change by pitting regional and network effects against one another can simply re-entrench a division in spatio-temporal practice.

On the issue of solidity, and in the terms of this chapter, home-making was not simply about the performance of a regional topology, where difference was suppressed through a network topology holding itself together. In the version of homeliness discussed, the materials and practices were less bounded than might be expected. The reading of the ice-cream advert was one way of emphasizing that home-making is sometimes a fraught process. Importantly, 'home does not pre-exist' (Deleuze and Guattari, 1987:311). 'It' is neither origin nor destiny. In the relational cartographies that I opened with, homes are made. But that is not the end of the story. The idea of 'drawing a circle around an uncertain and fragile centre' (*ibid.*, see also Morris, 1996:386) evokes the continuing labour of division. Meanwhile, the movements that are involved or en-folded in home-making and in nature-making are suggestive of other spaces. As Morris (1992, 1996) hints, the circle is not sealed-in. Rather it provides a space for movement, for venturing forth. And, this space might not be best conceived of as another region, subject to another set of binding rules. What Mol and Law's (1994) writing on multiple topologies can suggest is that this space of the circle may work in ways that sometimes looks like a region, sometimes a network, sometimes a fluid, and sometimes all three. The account of homeliness and home-making in Hvalsø illustrates some of this production of cohesiveness which does not always conform to the performance of regional space. The fires and natures that were being produced on the estate were not always comfortably accommodated within formal networks, or rigid chains of components. To be sure, *hyggelig*, cosiness and comfort drew upon regional and network topologies, but not exclusively so. It was not simply a matter of a geography of exclusion, or a geography of connection along a determinate pathway or route, within which elements remained stable or retained their shape. This possibility for working with complex spaces, materialities and the interferences that can be produced within and between them brings me to my second point of conclusion.

The possibility for continuous variability and for complex differentiations of spaces and materialities makes a perspectivalist approach to nature-politics difficult to sustain. Indeed, all this movement suggests that tensions and overlaps, zones of mixed orders (Star, 1991), may mark more promising routes for nature (and other forms of) politics than those which disregard the complexities of boundaries and the practical character of living-spaces. Otherwise, there is a risk of making the divisions seem even more entrenched than they need to be. I have illustrated this tendency at length in the example of the campaign on Hyldebjerg. I have suggested that the epistemological battleground that emerged from the language and spatialization of the fetish only managed, in this instance, to re-inscribe social, material and political differences. Similarly, if we no longer regard natures and homes as static enclosures with pre-given foundations, fixed origins or destinations; and if concepts like these are placed on the move,[2] then nature-politics must move too. In Haraway's (1991:154) terms, this politics is not about recalling origins, or 'an imagined organic body to integrate our resistance', nor is it about 'sorting consciousness into categories of "clear-sighted critique grounding a solid political epistemology" versus "manipulated false consciousness"' (*ibid.*, p. 173). To do so would, as I have argued, serve only to imagine fixity where there might also be movement. I have suggested that Mol and Law's (1994) treatment of spatialities and materialities provides suggestive routes for thinking through the possibilities that these movements might embrace. In so doing I have sought to think through ways in which nature-politics can head off the tendency to further entrench the battlelines and cartographies of cultures and natures and heres and theres.

Acknowledgements

Thanks to the editors for their helpful suggestions on earlier drafts of this paper. Thanks also to John Bale and Simon Naylor for their encouragement and criticisms. The remaining errors and limitations are all mine.

Notes

1 'Element' is merely a convenient stopping term which shouldn't invoke the idea that there are pre-existing building blocks or materials that are not themselves co-constituted in this and other networks, see Akrich and Latour, 1992.
2 For further thoughts on this kind of move, see Munro, forthcoming.

References

Akrich, M., (1992) 'The De-scription of technical objects', pp. 205–24 in W. Bijker and J. Law (eds) *Shaping technology/Building Society: Studies in sociotechnological change*, Cambridge, Mass.: MIT Press.

Akrich, M. and Latour, B., (1992) 'A summary of a convenient vocabulary for the semiotics of human and nonhuman assemblies' pp. 259–64 in W. Bijker and J. Law (eds) *Shaping technology/Building Society: Studies in sociotechnological change*, Cambridge, Mass.: MIT Press.

Anderson, W., (1995) 'Excremental Colonialism: Public Health and the Poetics of Pollution', *Critical Inquiry*, 21:640–69.

Benschop, R. and Law, J., (1997) 'Representation, distribution and ontological politics, pp. 158–182 in K. Hetherington and R. Munro (eds) *Ideas of difference: social spaces and the labour of division*, Oxford: Blackwell.

Cook, I. and Crang, P., (1996) 'The world on a plate: culinary culture, displacement and geographical knowledges', *Journal of Material Culture*, 1(2):131–53.

Crang, P., (1996) 'Popular Geographies', *Environment and Planning D: Society and Space*, 14:631–3.

Danish Ministry of Energy, (1990) *Energy 2000*, Copenhagen.

Deleuze, G. and Guattari, F., (1987) *A Thousand Plateaus: Capitalism and Schizophrenia*, London: Athlone Press.

Doel, M., (1996) 'A hundred thousand lines of flight: a machinic introduction to the nomad thought and scrumpled geography of Gilles Deleuze and Felix Guattari', *Environment and Planning D: Society and Space*, 14:421–39.

Haraway, D., (1991) *Simians, Cyborgs and Woman: The Reinvention of Nature*, New York: Routledge.

Haraway, D. and Harvey, D., (1995) 'Nature, politics and possibilities: a debate and discussion with David Harvey and Donna Haraway', *Environment and Planning D: Society and Space*, 13:507–27.

Harvey, D., (1990) 'Between space and time; reflections of the geographical imagination', *Annals of the Association of American Geographers*, 80:418–34.

Harvey, D., (1996) *Justice, nature and the geography of difference*, Oxford: Blackwell.

Hetherington, K., (1997a) 'In place of geometry: the materiality of place' pp. 183–199 in K. Hetheringon and R. Munro (eds) *Ideas of difference: social spaces and the labour of division*, Oxford: Blackwell.

Hetherington, K., (1997b) 'Museum topology and the will to connect', *Journal of Material Culture*. Vol 2 (2): 199–218

Hinchliffe, S., (1996) 'Helping the earth begins at home: the social construction of socio-environmental responsibilities', *Global Environmental Change: Human and Policy Dimensions*, Vol. 6, No. 1, pp. 53–62.

IEA, (1991) *Energy Policies of the IEA Countries: 1990 review*, Paris: OECD.

Jay, M., (1992) 'Scopic regimes of modernity' pp. 178–95 in S. Lash and J. Friedman (eds) *Modernity and Identity*, Oxford: Blackwell.

Kristeva, J., (1982) *Powers of Horror*, New York: Columbia University Press.

Lash, S. and Urry, J., (1994) *Economies of signs and space*, London: Sage.

Latour, B., (1990) 'Drawing things together' pp. 19–68 in M. Lynch and S. Woolgar (eds) *Representation in scientific practice*, Cambridge, Mass.: MIT Press.

Latour, B., (1993) *We have never been modern*, London: Harvester Wheatsheaf.

Law, J., (1991) 'Power, discretion and strategy' pp. 165–91 in J. Law (ed.) *A Sociology of Monsters: Essays on Power, Technology and Domination*, London: Routledge.

Law, J. and Mol, A., (1995) 'Notes on materiality and sociality', *The Sociological Review*, 43(2), 274–94.

Lenoir, T., (1994) 'Was the last turn the right turn? The semiotic turn and A.J. Greimas', *Configurations*, 1:119–36.

Luckin, B., (1990) *Questions of power: electricity and environment in inter-war Britain*, Manchester: Manchester University Press.

Mol, A. and Law, J., (1994) 'Regions, networks and fluids: anaemia and social topology', *Social Studies of Science*, 24:641–71.

Morris, M., (1992) 'On the beach' in L. Grossberg, C. Nelson and P. Treichler, *Cultural Studies*, London: Routledge, pp. 450–78.

Morris, M., (1996) 'Crazy talk is not enough', *Environment and Planning D: Society and Space*, 14:384–94.

Munro, R., (forthcoming) 'Belonging on the move: market rhetoric and the future as an obligatory passage' mimeograph.

Nye, D., (1990) *Electrifying America: Social meanings of a new technology, 1880–1940*, Cambridge, Mass.: MIT Press.

Phelan, S., (1994) 'Intimate distance: the dislocation of nature in modernity' pp. 44–64 in J. Bennet and W. Chaloupka (eds) *In the nature of things: language politics and the environment*, Minneapolis: University of Minnesota Press.

Ross, K., (1995) *Fast Cars and Clean Bodies: Decolonization and the reordering of French Culture*, Cambridge, Mass.: MIT Press.

Sibley, D., (1995) *Geographies of exclusion*, London: Routledge.

Sibley, D. and Griffiths, H., 91997) 'Feral cats in the built environment: domestication, tolerance and control', Paper presented at the Annual Conference of the Institute of British Geographers/Royal Geographical Society (January) Exeter.

Stallybrass, P. and White, A., (1986) *The Politics and Poetics of transgression*, London: Methuen.

Star, S.L., (1991) 'Power, technologies and the phenomenology of conventions: on being allergic to onions' pp. 26–56 in J. Law (ed.) *A sociology of monsters: essays on power, technology and domination*, London: Routledge.

Taussig, M., (1992) *The Nervous System*, London: Routledge.

Thrift, N., (1994) 'Inhuman geographies: Landscapes of speed, light and power' pp. 191–248 in P. Cloke, M. Doel, D. Matless, M. Phillips and N. Thrift (eds) *Writing the rural: five cultural geographies*, London: Paul Chapman Publishing.

Throgmorton, J., (1996) *Planning as persuasive story-telling: The rhetorical construction of Chicago's electric future*, Chicago: University of Chicago Press.

Whatmore, S., (1997) 'Dissecting the autonomous self; hybrid cartographers for a relational ethics', *Environment and Planning D: Society and Space*, 15:37–53.

Øllgaard, G., (1991) 'Consumption as an act of *Bricolage*' pp. 185–93 in D. Nye and C. Pedersen (1991) *Consumption and American Culture*, Amsterdam, VU University Press.

Section IV
Deferring division

Introduction

In questioning the metaphors of spatiality, the previous three chapters can be thought of as problematizing received notions of mobility. That is, they juxtapose the advantages of travelling 'through' different social spaces with an attention to the precise labour of division entailed in any particular engagement. In their problematizing of existing notions of time, the next three chapters might seem more concerned to explicate a notion of *motility*, the facility to bring the material of social spaces near or far and make matters appear present or absent. Each chapter, in its different way, juxtaposes the effects that flow from movement 'across' social spaces against the capacity for *deferral*—a withdrawal from divisions.

Ostensibly Heather Höpfl's chapter examines Ionesco's play *The Chairs*, but the central concern of the chapter is 'with the gathering or swelling which precedes division and separation'. For Höpfl, the site of production where the labour of division is performed is the 'site at which proliferation' occurs and the 'paralysis of dependency' is experienced. As in Brown's chapter, when there is a moment in which the reader begins to feel that they cannot take yet anther event—at least not before Brown has staged his return to the concept of the labour of division—there is a problem in the disposal of detail. In its interest in making us experience the 'swelling' before rupture, Höpfl's chapter is even more unrelenting than Brown's. Noting that Ionesco's plays carry a common theme of the 'fear of proliferation, of overwhelming growth, of overpowering size and oppressive intervals of time, of compulsive production and reproduction', Höpfl's writing mimics Ionesco's 'intensification, acceleration, accumulation, proliferation'.

The point of departure for the chapter is announced in the title, where the Latin root of the word division (*dividere*) is related to the idea of 'widow' through its Sanskrit word (*vidhava*), meaning bereft of a husband. The loss of its complement (in Strathern's meaning), forecloses on completeness. Except here, the iterations do not add, so much as they *multiply*. Every division effects a multiplication, so that the loss marks melancholia, blackness, bile, a blind-ing that is on its way to hysteria. In taking forward the theme of oppressive banality from his first play *The Bald Prima Donna*, Ionesco gives considerable emphasis in *The Chairs*, his third play, to the notion of proliferation and the notion of being overwhelmed. According to Ionesco, the theme of the play is 'nothingness'. Gradually the stage is filled with chairs for guests who arrive, but are never seen or heard, although the stage instructions call for the sounds of a room filling up with people and the old couple, who have invited them, are frenetic in their attempts to accommodate the many guests. The device is to make the 'invisible elements' more and more 'clearly present' until the 'unreal elements speak and move . . . the nothing-ness can be heard, is made concrete'. Indeed, the structure and the substance of the play are brought together like a baroque edifice, expressing an overabundance of 'elaboration, intricacy, caprice, whimsy, stylisation, indulgence, exaggeration'.

Addressing the absurdity of production, in both its sense of pro-liferation and performance, *The Chairs* confronts the consumption of the site of production at the point of being in which, in Sartre's phrase 'nothingness enters the world'. Of course, profundity, via authority and authorship, is one way to repress the ever-present banality. And division—separating what is important from what is not—is clearly a principal way of achieving this repression. But, as Höpfl has already shown in ways that recall Strathern's gibe about Euro-Americans being in an 'adding culture', division is no help. For, when bereft, division locks us into still further cycles of need-ing ever more divisions. Ionesco suggests that the final defence against proliferating meanings and colonizing materiality is 'defiant silence'. But as Dale has remarked in her chapter, which academic is going to choose that? It is fitting therefore that Höpfl ends her chapter by drawing a parallel between *The Chairs* and the 'cacoph-ony' of so-called postmodernists, with all their 'fetishisms of local-ity, place or social grouping'.

The fetishisms of 'locality, place and social grouping' are all familiar material to Ruud Hendriks, as he makes clear in the sub-title to his chapter, 'temporal ordering in a ward for autistic youths'. There are social groupings, residents and counsellors, and the place in which this division is enacted is a ward for mentally handicapped autistic youths. The problem which Hendriks addresses is not this grouping of the social, or the problem of space, but the fact that the symbolic concepts of time seem incomprehensible to some of the residents. They do not seem to know what 'waiting' or 'tomorrow' means. Indeed, in so far as they have difficulty in stopping, or putting off any activity within which they are engaged, they seem to get stuck inside the social spaces (or events?) which they enter, whether this is eating a sandwich, or making the bed.

When it comes to interpreting the behaviour of someone like Peter, a 'big guy' who we first meet eating sandwiches, counsellors are seen by Hendriks as 'groping in the dark'. Cast in the role of carers, it is the counsellors who are blind. So Hendriks' study of autistics is not an attempt to understand the Other, by creating some 'monstrous ways of representing them', or by supposing autistics to be some 'damaged version' of himself. In his ethnography, he is acknowledging the idea that the autistics and the counsellors appear 'equally alien' to each other. Yes, in line with interpretive sociology, he will draw on the stories of the residents and counsellors. But, rather than attempt to translate the 'words' of the autistic, which are few, across to the narratives of the counsellors, which are many, Hendriks takes as his principal 'informants' the material objects, such as benches and gates, that 'seem to play a crucial role in the temporal ordering of life in the ward'. These are the main actors that he 'follows' and then *magnifies* in order to gain a distance from 'familiar, non-autistic frames of reference'.

Stripped of the speed of speech to get over their messages and make ward life 'tick', counsellors introduce an unadorned, non-linguistic way of ordering. The first actor we meet in this regard is an egg-timer. When Peter has finished a sandwich, he takes the egg-timer and hands it to the counsellor who sets it for ten minutes. Peter—who the counsellors say has no concept of waiting—now waits in 'perfect patience' until it rings before continuing his meal. Through such material translations as the egg-timer, the black box of temporal order becomes more transparent and life on the ward becomes what the counsellors call 'calm' and 'sociable',

This brings Hendriks to consider a dilemma for the counsellors, who are confronted by two wrongs (an out-of-reach ideal of the linguistic community and the meagre alternative of a clockwise way of ordering). But there are other positions from which to view the world other than from inside the head of a counsellor, who might see Peter on a bench as 'bored', or Robert endlessly arranging a rug as 'dawdling'. Although never intended to take this part, Peter and the bench 'take possession of each other' in ways that not only allow counsellors to spend their time elsewhere, but are self-similar to the 'compulsive' way in which one of the counsellors wants to have 'everything in the cupboard' in line. Indeed, Hendriks goes further and wonders whether counsellors get 'enthralled' by *breaking* repetitive behaviour, just as much as Peter and Robert seem fascinated by their performance of it. Hendriks' point is that the unobtrusive object that successfully *mediated* between rivalling positions, is retrospectively turned into an *intermediary*. Although the active part of the resident is easily underestimated here, this is a transition in which knowledge—inscribed in the material form of an egg-timer or bench rather than words—turns into power and becomes a 'means' in the hands of the successful counsellor. And it is in this instrumental form that the counsellor finds he misses the egg-timer when it leaves with Peter.

Drawing first on the everyday example of a knock on the door, Latimer's analysis also emphasizes the extent to which identity work in encounters depends, not on people alone, but on their close engagement with materials. Thus, what is usually dismissed as a mere act of courtesy, the knock, is shown to act as an intermediary that holds stable 'intricate and potentially different' sets of interests. In that the knock acts as a 'stop' on potentially disastrous circumstances unfolding, the knock can of course be considered equivalent to Hendriks' egg-timer.

Latimer contrasts two social spaces as 'networks', bedside care and the medical gaze. Opening her chapter with a short excerpt from her field work, we see first a nurse engaged at the bedside and then experience her 'cutting' the network as she moves away to associate with the doctors on the ward round. However, in her close reading of another encounter, Latimer shows how the bedside—the site of care—is no longer a complement to the operating table—the medical gaze. Or even supplement, for it seems to have been turned entirely into one of its 'sights' of operation. Through magnifying a series of displacements, Latimer shows how the patient—one of the group of 'older persons' who are the focus of the study—is instructed into his place in the network. In learning how to *be* patient, he finds out how to wait and gathers who needs to give permission for his wants.

However, against a Latourian focus on materials as 'durable', Latimer's emphasis brings out the availability of language *as* material. Once language is in play as a *technology*, it offers discursive stabilities that can, when needed, have a machine-like effect. These 'devices' not only have the force of moving about people's identities, or of blocking people's requests, they also—in Latimer's analysis—have the systematic effect of removing 'affirmation' from social processes. Yet the great difference between discursive stabilities and other intermediaries is in the relative fluidity with which stabilities in language can be made and withdrawn. In this way, Latimer brings out an incipient argument in some of the earlier papers: a division of labour is only stable when it is fluid; and its fluidity is made possible by a labour of division in which stabilities, by being brought near or made far, become motile to identity work.

After sociology's long alert over 'committing categories' on people, it is tempting to see Hendriks' 'autistic youths' and Latimer's 'older persons' as having been reduced to supplementary categories, residents and patients. Like women, they could be imagined to be part of a process that has only antipathy for the notion of complementarity—at least as Strathern has described it. But, in so far as autistics are perceived to be automata, or older people are treated as near to being death, it is more likely that they lack even a role of supplementarity. At least in Latimer's analysis, the older people seem shunned, without even a *degree* of what nurses seem to be adding to their identities. In terms of their ability to labour divisions, older people seem little better off than the chairs in Höpfl's analysis. If the autistic are for the most part made 'calm' by egg-timers, or older people are kept 'quiet' by medical form-filling, they are also sometimes full of a sound and fury that to their carers must signify little but a need for more egg-timers and more form-filling.

The melancholy of the Black Widow

Heather Höpfl

The baroque signifier proliferates beyond everything signified, placing language in excess of corporality. At the risk of appearing still more paradoxical, we might say that baroque reason brings into play the *infinite materiality* (original italics) of images and bodies. (Buci-Glucksmann, 1994:139)

To express the void by means of language, gesture, acting and props. To express absence. To express regret and remorse. The unreality of the real. Original chaos. (Notes on ideas for *The Chairs*, Ionesco, 1964)

Profound banality

The story of Ionesco's first play, *The Bald Prima Donna* (in America, *The Bald Soprano*) is well known. Ionesco had grown up with a child's fascination with the theatre but as an adult theatre had 'embarrassed' him. He disliked seeing actors making 'spectacles of themselves' (Ionesco, 1959), disliked their dehumanization. In 1948 he decided to learn English and enrolled on a course, *L'Anglais sans Peine*. This was to be a turning point in his career. The course began, as many language courses do, with assertions about the number of days in the week, definitions of 'up' and 'down', truths which Ionesco later described in *La tragedie du langage*, as 'as stupefying as they were indisputably true'. As the course progressed, the characters of Mr and Mrs Smith were introduced and Ionesco was astounded by the staggering commonplaces with which they concern themselves. That Mrs Smith should inform her husband that they had several children, that they lived near London, that their name was Smith, that Mr Smith was a clerk and so on, struck Ionesco as a profound banality. He became intrigued by the relentless and methodical quest for truth which prompted such insistent assertions of 'fact' and with the way in which the establishment of mundane truths created the opportunity for the examination of increasingly complex notions of truth, for example, 'The country is quieter than the big city . . . ' (Ionesco, 1958b). Of course, it might be said that the conversational forms of language text books is removed from the language of everyday life. After all, it serves a different function. It is there to guide sentence construction and to give practice in everyday vocabulary. However, the language of everyday experience, certainly the language of everyday middle-class experience, is full of banalities and reassurances which give shape and solidity to an otherwise indeterminate world. 'Isn't it lovely today?' 'It may rain later'. 'Stephen is coming home this weekend'. 'I once lived in Bristol'. 'Bristol is nearer to London than Lancaster'. Such banalities construct and maintain identities, sustain the notion of connectivity and commonality, and give direction in the face of separation, division and meaningless isolation.

Ionesco described his encounter with such proliferating banality as an experience of dizziness, of nausea (Ionesco, 1958b) and explained that he had had to lie down from time to time during the writing of the play so overwhelmed had he become with accumulating vacuity. Exposed to such exaggerated clichés, language itself became distended, distorted, disfigured. He experienced vertigo in the face of the monumental elevation of the commonplace. There was a further revelation in store for Ionesco. His experience of writing the play had been one of anguish, nausea and *blackness*. His play had been written as a serious work concerned with the tragedy of language and its disintegration under pressure and from overuse. Yet when he read it to his friends they congratulated him on what they saw as a very funny play. In 1949, Nicholas Bataille, director of the Theatre de Poche, encouraged Ionesco to let him stage the play and it was first produced in Paris in May 1950. During the rehearsal period the director first tried to present the play as parody, to point up the ludicrousness of the dialogue, but this did not work. Consequently, he concluded that the only way to realize the power of the work was to perform the text and to treat the platitudinous script with complete seriousness. Even so, Ionesco found himself confronted with a striking ambivalence of interpretation. The work which to him represented a human tragedy was received by audiences as comedy. It was this realization which took him to a desire to 'push everything to paroxysm, to the point where the sources of the tragic lie. To create a theatre of violence—

violently comic, violently dramatic' (Ionesco, 1959). His concern was to overthrow habitual modes of thought, to confront the *unbearable* determinacy of *worn-out* language and insufferable experience.

Swelling precedes rupture

In terms of the *labour* of division, the central concern of this chapter is with the gathering or swelling which precedes division and separation. Whether in the natural world—as in sexual and asexual reproduction, swelling and emission, swelling and rupture; or in the realm of social relations, gathering and separation, or of ideas, gathering and rupture, there is a pattern of movements which deserve some consideration: swelling/distension, distortion/disfigurement, pressure/pain, rupture/tearing, separation/differentiation, competition/conflict, elaboration/proliferation, enormity/subjection. A progression which is carried/moved by a *bearing* towards differentiation and opposition but where opposition itself submits to the overwhelming power of diversity. The site of production where the labour of division is performed is the site at which proliferation occurs and the paralysis of dependency is experienced.

The chapter explores these ideas through the work of the playwright Ionesco who in his *Le point du départ* (Ionesco, 1958a) expresses the view that 'matter fills everything, takes up all space, annihilates all liberty under its weight' (Esslin, 1968:155). His plays carry a common theme of the fear of proliferation, of overwhelming growth, of overpowering size and oppressive intervals of time, of compulsive production and re-production. The pattern of action in 'Ionesco's plays is one of intensification, acceleration, accumulation, proliferation to the point of paroxysm, when psychological tension reaches the unbearable—the pattern of orgasm' (Esslin, 1955:187). In the spirit of the notion of the labour of division, the ways in which Esslin describes Ionesco's work conveys the idea of the pressure towards rupture, the swelling to bursting as described above.

Le point du départ (as a labour, *oeuvre*, division, departure) for this paper is the Latin origin of the word *division*, from *dividere*, to share/distribute/separate. In its relationship to the Latin word, *vidua*, widow (from the Sanskrit word *vidhava*, meaning bereft of a husband), it is used here to signify separation and differentiation. The title is a verbal excess which tra*jects* these two definitions. It is intended to suggest blackness, loss, separation and, at the same time, to carry its own poetic subversion in its various connotations of consumption. There is an attempt to achieve a correspondence between form and content and to convey something of the experience of the labour to produce division. Every division effects a multiplication. The loss occasioned by separation is explored in relation to absence, darkness and weight. In the construction of the argument, an attempt has been made to force meaning towards the swelling which precedes rupture. This makes an extremely ponderous construction.

When Martin Parker, the discussant at the Labour of Division Conference (Keele, November 1995), gave his response, he said that he had read this chapter with increasing anger. It was written to evoke precisely this sense of powerlessness, frustration and, indeed, anger in the face of proliferation. The verbal conceit of the title introduces proliferation, gathering and separation, the condition of being apart, the evocations of *apartness* implicit in the notion of being *a part* of. It insinuates the shadow of separation in such a way as to precede its introduction in the figure and figurative representation of the Black Widow. It seeks to insert, locate and place loss insistently in the structure of the sentence; to inter*ject* blackness before the encounter with its ad*ject*ival counter*part*; to throw out, emit/e*ject*, precarious recursions in the ambivalence of textual insufficiency and textual excess. The blind-ing of melancholia (Gk *melas*, black, and *khole*, bile); the separation from the lost object which occasions melancholia; the attributive black which adorns the widow, widow's weeds, the garments which are worn by a widow (O.E. *waed*); widow as a word implying some preceding separation or loss; the intrusive, resonating notion of the *black widow* spider, the female of which devours her mate, whose loss is produced by consumption: these possible meanings distend and distort the apparent meaning of the title which is simultaneously absurd and banal. There is a disfiguration and a weight of association which becomes increasingly insufferable. Melancholy and loss, separation and loss, ingestion and loss, are presented within a persistent overabundance of imputed meanings, of absence made present by repetition and insistent definition: apparently lucid meanings supporting a relentless meaninglessness.

Meanings and structures are paradoxical and some to carry the opposite meaning to that to which they lay claim: where, for example, a surfeit of meaning masks an absence of meaning or other polysemic meanings. In what follows, Ionesco's work is drawn on to discuss the overabundance of meanings which attach to the nature of organization at the end of the twentieth century: intensification, acceleration, accumulation, proliferation, paroxysm and convulsive release.

The Chairs was Ionesco's third play to be staged. It is considered to be one of his most significant works. Not only does it take forward the theme of oppressive banality, it gives considerable emphasis to the notion of proliferation and to the experience of being overwhelmed. The instructions to the director of *The Chairs* indicate that 'The theme of the play is nothingness . . . the invisible elements must be more and more clearly present, more and more real (to give unreality to reality one must give reality to the unreal), until the point is reached—inadmissible, unacceptable to the reasoning mind—when the unreal elements speak and move . . . the nothingness can be heard, is made concrete . . . ' (Towarnicki, 1958).

The Chairs was first produced in Paris in 1952, directed by Sylvain Dhomme, at the Theatre Lancry. It is basically a two-hander with a third member of cast playing the role of the Orator who appears at the end of the play to deliver an important message. The two main characters are an old man of ninety-five and an old woman of ninety-four. The basic story of the play is that the old couple invite a series of distinguished guests to attend a reception to mark the life of the old man who has an important message for his distinguished visitors. The message is so important that he has engaged the services of a professional orator to deliver it. The guests arrive but are neither seen nor heard although the stage instructions call for the sounds of a room filling up with people. The sense of their presence is created by the actors who behave as though they are surrounded by an increasingly large crowd of guests, overwhelmed by their many guests. The image is thus complex and ambiguous, absurd and relentless as the old couple become frenetic in their attempts to accommodate their many (invited) guests.

The script and its staging are a poetic subversion. The old people are engulfed by absence: the significance of the proliferation which occupies the site is that first, it is solicited by the central characters themselves and second, that it is characterized by its absence. Poetic presence visually subverts the apparent absence. The effect is vertiginous. The audience is overwhelmed by multiple and ambivalent interpretations which deny a convenient stability and, moreover, which become increasingly dizzying in the face of relentless and insistent normality, the apparent security of the familiar which begins to distend, distort, disfigure and disintegrate as the ludic transfigures into the ludicrous. In other words, following his experiences of *The Bald Prima Donna*, Ionesco seeks to fracture the reassurances of the commonplace: relentless normality, relentless incursion.

Multiple interpretations

There are a great many interpretations of *The Chairs* and much discussion of the stylistic devices of the script. In the argument presented here, the intention is simpler. It is to examine the relationship between proliferation and absence: between excess and nothingness. The stage set, for example, is designed as an amphitheatre with circular walls and a recess at the back of the stage. The stage is bare. There are doors and windows, each clearly marked in the stage directions and windows along the curved walls on either side of the rear door. Stage left, there is a blackboard and a platform. Down stage there are two chairs side by side.

As the play progresses, The Old Woman fills the stage with chairs to accommodate the guests. The chairs are placed in neat rows with their backs to the (theatre) audience. The invited audience thus extends to incorporate the theatre audience. Eventually, the guest of honour, The Emperor, arrives to the sound of a fanfare of trumpets from the wings . . . the door at the back of the stage opens wide with a great crash and a strong light fills the stags. However, it is interesting that Ionesco indicates in the stage directions that the light should be 'a cold, empty light' (Ionesco, 1958:72). The figure of the Emperor is for Ionesco not a temporal ruler but 'the King of Kings' (Lamont, 1993:76). For the old couple the entrance of the Emperor is a moment of illumination and rapture. It confirms the being of the old couple. They have been graced by the appearance of the great man. Yet even this apparent consummation is a conceit. The light is cold.

Shortly afterwards, towards the end of the play, the Orator arrives. According to the stage directions he is to be 'a typical painter or poet of the last century; a wide-brimmed black felt hat, a loosely tied cravat, artist's jacket, moustache and a goatee beard, rather a smug, pretentious look about him. If the invisible characters should appear as real as possible, the Orator should look unreal' (Ionesco, 1958a:79). The Old Man goes forward to give his farewell address. 'Majesty, my wife and myself have nothing more to ask of life. Our existence has found its final consummation . . . I can now leave to you, dear friend and Orator the task of dazzling posterity with the enlightenment I bring . . . so make my philosophy known to the Universe' (Ionesco, 1958a: 81). After long moments of final recollections and remarks, the couple jump through their respective windows crying 'Long Live the Emperor!' After some further moments, the Orator gets up and faces the empty chairs and 'indicates to the invisible crowd that he is deaf and dumb; he uses sign-language: he makes desperate efforts to make himself understood' (Ionesco, 1958a:83, 84); then he produces strange moans and groans, the sort of guttural sounds made by deaf mutes.

He, Mme, mm, mm.
Ju, gou, hou, hou.
Heu, heu, gu, gou, gueu.

Helpless his arms drop to his sides; suddenly his face lights up, he has an idea: he turns to the blackboard, takes a piece of chalk from his pocket, and writes in large capitals:

ANGELBREAD

then:

NNAA NNM NWNWNW V

He turns again to his invisible public, the public on the stage, and points to what he has written on the blackboard.

Orator: Mmm, Mmm, Gueu, Gou, Gu, Mmm, Mmm, Mmm, Mmm.

Then, dissatisfied, he rubs out the chalk marks with a series of sharp movements, and puts others in their place: among them the following can be discerned, in large capitals:

^ADIEU ^DIEU ^P^

Again the orator turns to the audience and smiles questioningly, as if he hopes that he has been understood, has really said something. (Ionesco, 1958a:83, 84)

The Orator glowers in disappointment and leaves the stage. The stage directions leave the director free to interpret the appropriate moment for the final curtain in order to not let the audience off the hook too easily, to permit too simple an explanation of meaning.

The play is written as a 'metaphysical farce' (Lamont, 1993:65–87), tragic-comic, which ends in pervasive emptiness, disappointment. It offers an image of silence in the face of too much presence. In this sense, its violence is a poetic one which ruptures meanings which are strained beyond their capacity.

Proliferation and infinite materiality

In the way in which *The Chairs* is used in this argument, the structure and substance of the play are brought together in the construction of something akin to a baroque edifice, albeit a conceptual one. The play presents an overabundance of elaboration, intricacy, caprice, whimsy, stylization, indulgence, exaggeration. It swells out like the arm of a plaster cherub from a Baroque painting as, for example, in the splendid baroque churches of Weingarten and Zwiefalten in South Germany. This is similar to an argument put forward by Munro (1997) that 'discourse' is filling up our lives, like so many empty chairs to which we give presence.

Buci-Gluckmann in her analysis of baroque reason (1994) has argued that in the works of Benjamin, Baudelaire, Lacan and Barthes there is a 'baroque paradigm' which establishes itself within modernity. However, this same paradigm is prevalent in contemporary constructions, as this chapter seeks to demonstrate. According to Buci-Gluckmann, this baroque paradigm employs a common range of tropes and stylistic devices: allegory, oxymoron, open totality and discordant detail; *relations of insistence*, permanent excess which eroticizes the real by staging phantasm *founds meaning on matter and not on concept . . . imperialism of seeing*, a delight in detail as the promise of happiness (Buci-Gluckmann, 1994:140–1, after Barthes, 1977). These characteristics of the 17th-century Baroque are recognizably those of the regulatory mechanisms of neo-capitalism, the seduction of consumption, the oppression by a charade of heterogeneity, a compulsive pursuit of and delight in detail and bewildering and overwhelming massification. Buci-Gluckmann (1994:140) suggests Barthes 'saw in the baroque and the pansemic nature of the image, the site of excess meaning, *obtuse* (original italics) meaning, a signifier without a signified, which governs aesthetic pleasure' so that 'meaning is destroyed beneath the symbol'.

By intention, Ionesco's play leaves no space unoccupied as it extrudes, extending itself more and more until the audience itself is incorporated into the play, where 'matter fills everything, takes up all space, annihilates all liberty under its weight . . . speech crumbles' (Ionesco, 1958b). This is the experience of overwhelming presence and, indeed, it is the experience of awe one might have in the face of a physical edifice of great elaboration, lavish detail, meticulous and impressive intricacy. The splendour of the Baroque period is silencing and, in this first notion of silence, disempowering. There is no space left for any other response than awe. Matter fills everything. In *The Chairs*, Ionesco is able to achieve the extraordinary effect of holding the audience at the precarious point of ambivalence, between presence and absence, before language breaks down under the weight of contradiction. What overwhelms is absence in the guise of considerable presence: absence which is so visibly and, via interaction, verbally present that its presence is palpable.

Addressing the absurdity of production (both in the sense of proliferation and as performance), *The Chairs* confronts the consumption of the site of production. It assembles overwhelming and invisible forces which are absent but vividly present. Indeed, Ionesco presents the site of production of performance *qua* the site of the production of being, as the point at which 'nothingness enters the world' (Sartre, 1943:60). This equates with the notion of the site of 'theatrical' production as the hierophantic site through which spirits from the *illud tempus* enter the world. Anterior authority, the primal father, the author, the director, God or corporate capitalism: it is order and regulation which enters the site and not disorder. The site of production, in this case the site of the performance (with all common connotations still in play), is the site at which nothingness appears, pervades, proliferates, overwhelms.

The site of production (of material and abstract desires) and the site of theatrical production turn on the same axis. The site of the production of performance is the site of mortification. The sites of production of material and abstract desires are also sites of performance and, in this sense, are also sites where annihilation occurs.

Proliferation overwhelms and silences

As the end of the 20th century approaches, there is an increasing preoccupation with the elaborate production, apparently to serve the interests of consumption, and proliferation of excess, of a promised liberating heterogeneity of choice and experience, of the construction and pursuit of sublime objects of desire. The construction of sublime artefacts, objects of desire, personalities, 'life-styles', styles of interaction, ways of acting, ways of constructing identity and so on becomes an oppressive drudgery masquerading as ever-extending choice. Matter fills up all space. Choice is a bewildering illusion.

As in *The Chairs*, nothingness waits beyond the door (the rear doors of the stage) and like a gaping mouth will consume the site once obsessive pre-occupation is no longer sustainable. The door at the back of the stage is also a sexual orifice where one might fall into nothingness on entry: the abyss of the other. The play, and its parallel in human experience, induces vertigo. Too much meaning is invested in the construction of the sublime object. Fall is inevitable: collapse certain. Frenetic activity protects against the inescapable melancholia occasioned by absence. The physical presence of the chairs contrasts with the absence of the guests. Matter presides over the site of the performance, proliferates, colonises, conquers and, ultimately, silences the performers. No speech is possible in the face of overabundant, excessive, intricate construction.

As one reviewer of this chapter commented, the argument presented is subject to the same fate, so that 'the chapter too is overcome'. Quite so. However, there is another way of looking at the possibilities for resistance in the performance space even the banalities of the quotidien. There is potential for resistance in the very banality of the everyday which apparent profundity, *via* authority and authorship (*via* what enters through the rear door of the stage) seeks to repress. Division is clearly one way of achieving this repression and one which signals the political dangers of postmodern ideas. These political issues are given further attention elsewhere (Höpfl, 1997). According to Ionesco, the final defence against proliferating meanings and colonizing materiality is defiant silence (Ionesco, 1967:95). Defiant silence can be seen as an inversion of the silencing power of proliferation: an absence turned into a presence, a voice restored. Whereas the argument presented does not go as far as Baudrillard in suggesting silence as a 'positive counter-strategy' (1983b:11) by which the masses refuse to participate, the aim has been to achieve some conciliation between Ionesco's defiant silence and Baudrillard's appeal to the power of silence, where both exhort us to refuse to engage in futile discourse and wasteful, extravagant hyperbole.

Excess and political silence

Harvey's contribution to the understanding of the construction of postmodern space is instructive here and extends the conceptualization of the role of silence. He is emphatic that whereas 'post modernist philosophers tell us not only to accept but to revel in the fragmentations and the cacophony of voices through which the dilemmas of the world are understood' (Harvey, 1990:116) postmodernism is actually 'celebrating the activity of masking and cover-up, all the fetishisms of locality, place or social grouping, while denying that kind of meta-theory which can grasp the political-economic processes . . . that are becoming ever more universalizing in their depth, intensity, reach and power over daily life' (Harvey, 1990:117). Indeed, he is even more specific when he argues that postmodernism 'disempowers' and that . . . 'the rhetoric of postmodernism is dangerous for it avoids confronting the realities of political economy and the circumstances of global power' (Harvey, 1990:117). He argues that postmodernism for some—he cites Derrida as an example—has led to a retreat into 'political silence' (Harvey, 1990:117) and he notes the revival of interest in geopolitical theory and, in particular, concern for the 'aesthetics of place' as symptomatic of the compression of time and space (Harvey, 1990:284).

It has already been noted that Buci-Gluckmann (1994) has described a baroque paradigm within modernity. In this respect, perhaps it is worth extending this argument to conceptualize a baroque paradigm within postmodernity. Indeed, Owens (1980) draws on Benjamin's conception of allegory as a baroque construction to make the persuasive assertion that postmodern art, although by analogy this could be applied to postmodern production of all types, thrives on 'appropriation, site, specificity, impermanence, accumulation, discursivity, hybridization' (Owens, 1980:75; quoted in Bertens, 1995:90). If allegory is seen as a simulacrum inhabited by 'loss' and characterized by melancholy, then discursive proliferation is likewise melancholic, the widow of experience.

The problem of locating, differentiating and, moreover, dividing ideas into categories is part of the problem. Hence, whether there is a baroque paradigm within modernity or postmodernity in terms of the construction of categories is merely an accomplishment of intellectual labour. Resistance to such constructions and their defining power is an altogether different matter.

In the baroque and, indeed, in the postmodern, 'loss' is cancelled by a vociferous presence. This pandemonium is a poor substitute for the lost power of absence, for silence. The idea that the polysemic voice is always radical (Bakhtin, 1979) is plainly absurd and the idea is bought at the cost of the powerful reversal of commonality and, perhaps, defiant silence. As Cohen (1982) suggests, the relationship between political and aesthetic—here understood to be experiential rather than transcendent—forms is ambivalent. As Cohen indicates, the political is always contingent.

This process of proliferation and heterogeneity has significant implications for the notion of identity, for the occupation and definition of sites, for the understanding of weight/oppression, for the collapse of such edifices and edifications in the face of an excess of presence: '*too much* links up with *not enough* and objects are the materialization (concretization) of solitude, of the victory of the anti-spiritual forces, of everything we are struggling against' (Ionesco, 1958b:viii).

Ionesco *throws* (L. *jacere*) his audience into black comedy in order to confront them with the preposterousness of the banal; to demonstrate the insufferable weight of the commonplace; to invoke the blackness of absence and of absence parading as presence. There are considerable parallels to be drawn with organizational life and the proliferation of vacuity, of stupefying banality parading as profound truth. A straightforward example might be found in construction and testing of management 'competence'; most basic text books on approaches to management can be easily identified as inherently banal; sadly, many academic journals and academic conferences produce a vast proliferation of papers where scholars 'searching for validity and rigorous proof, prefer to deal with problems which are insignificant but which can be proved, rather than problems which are significant but which cannot be proved so rigorously . . . ' (Fromm, 1966). What is apparent is that there is more and more material being produced, proliferating, extending, distending. If Ionesco's work is in any sense prophetic, paroxysm approaches. Certainly, the distortions which precede it are all too obvious.

References

Bakhtin, M., (1979) *Die Aesthetik des Wortes*, Frankfurt a.M.: Suhrkamp.
Barthes, R., (1977) *Sade, Fourier, Loyola*, London: Jonathan Cape.

Baudrillard, J., (1988) *Selected Writings*, M. Poster (ed.), Stanford: Stanford University Press.
Baudrillard, J., (1983b) *In the Shadow of the Silent Majorities: or, the End of the Social and Other Essays*, New York: Semiotext(e).
Baudrillard, J., (1970) *La Société de consommation*, Paris: Gallimard.
Baudrillard, J., (1993) *Symbolic Interaction and Death*, London: Sage.
Baudrillard, J., (1975) *The Mirror of Production*, St Louis: Telos Press.
Baudrillard, J., (1987) *Forget Foucault*, New York: Semiotext(e).
Baudrillard, J., (1983a) *Simulations*, New York: Semiotext(e).
Baudrillard, J., (1976) *L'Exchange symbolique et la mort*, Paris: Gallimard (in translation 1993, London: Sage, below).
Benjamin, W., (1977) *The Origin of German Tragic Drama*, London: NLB.
Bertens, H., (1995) *The idea of the postmodern, a history*, London: Routledge.
Brissett, D. and Edgley, C., (eds) (1975) *Life as Theater*, Chicago: Aldine.
Brook, P., (1968) *The Empty Space*, Harmondsworth: Penguin.
Buci-Gluckmann, (1994) *Baroque Reason*, London: Sage.
Bürger, P., (1984) *Theory of the Avant-Garde*, Manchester: Manchester University Press.
Burton, R., (1979) *The Anatomy of Melancholy 1621* (abridged and edited by J. K. Peters), New York: Ungar.
Calhoun, C., (1992) 'Culture, history and the problem of specificity' cited in H. Bertens (1995) *The idea of the postmodern, a history*, London: Routledge.
Canetti, E., (1987) *Crowds and Power*, London: Penguin.
Caudwell, C., (1946) *Illusion and Reality, A Study of the Sources of Poetry*, London: Lawrence and Wishart.
Cohen, A., (1982) 'A polyethnic London carnival as a contested cultural performance', *Ethnic and Racial Studies*, 5, 23–42 cited in C. Tilley, 'Discourse and power: the genre of the Cambridge Inaugural Lecture' in D. Miller, M. Rowlands and C. Tilley (eds) (1989) *Domination and Resistance*, London: Unwin Hyman Ltd.
Cole, D., (1975) *The Theatrical Event*, Middletown, Connecticut: Wesleyan University Press.
Cooper, R., (1990) 'Canetti's Sting', *SCOS Notework*, 9, 2/3:45–53.
Cooper, R., (1983) 'The Other: A Model of Human Structuring' in G. Morgan (ed.) *Beyond Method, Strategies for Social Research*, Beverley Hills: Sage, 202–18.
Crimp, D., (1980) 'On the museum's ruins', *October*, 13:41–59.
Crimp, D., (1980a) 'The photographic activity of postmodernism', *October*, 15:91–101.
Daudi, P., (1983) 'The Discourse of Power or the Power of Discourse', *Alternatives*, IX (1983), 317–25.
de Certeau, M., (1986) *Heterologies, Discourse on the Other*, Manchester: Manchester University Press.
de Man, P., (1986) *The Resistance to Theory*, Manchester: Manchester University Press.
Derrida, J., (1981) *Dissemination*, London: The Athlone Press.
Derrida, J., (1978) *Writing and Difference*, Chicago: University of Chicago Press.
Derrida, J., (1987) *The Truth in Painting*, trans. G. Bennington and I. McLeod, Chicago: University of Chicago Press.
Esslin, M., (1968) *The Theatre of the Absurd*, Harmondsworth: Penguin in association with Eyre and Spottiswoode.

Featherstone, M., (1991) *Consumer Culture and Postmodernism*, London: Sage.

Featherstone, M., 91995) *Undoing Culture*, London: Sage.

Foster, H., (1983) *The Anti-Aesthetic: Essays in Postmodern Culture.*

Fromm, E., (1966) *Dialogue with Eric Fromm*, R.E. Evans (ed.), New York: Harper Row.

Genette, G., (1992) *The Architext*, Berkeley: University of California Press.

Harvey, D., (1990) *The Condition of Postmodernity*, Oxford: Blackwell Publishers.

Hassan, I., (1967) 'The Literature of Silence: from Henry Miller to Beckett & Burroughts', *Encounter*, 21, I:74–82.

Heidegger, M., (1959) *An Introduction to Metaphysics*, Clinton, Mass.: Yale University Press.

Holt, D., (1989) 'Complex Ontology and Our Stake in the Theatre' in J. Shotter and K. Gergen (eds) (1989) *Texts of Identity*, London: Sage.

Höpfl, H., (1997) 'The Aesthetics of Reticence: collections and recollections' in S.L. Linstead and H. Höpfl (eds) (1997) *The Aesthetics of Organisation*, London: Sage.

Ionesco, E., (1955) '*Le point du départ*', Paris: *Cahiers des Quatre Saisons*, no. 1, August 1955, trans. L.C. Pronko, New York: Theatre Arts, June 1957; by Donald Watson in *Plays*, vol. I, London: Calder (see below).

Ionesco, E., (1958a) *Plays, Volume I: The Lesson, The Chairs, The Bald Prima Donna, Jacques or Obedience*, trans. Donald Watson, London: John Calder.

Ionesco, E., (1958b) '*La tragedie du langage*', Paris: *Spectacles*, no. 2, July 1958, trans. J. Undank, The tragedy of language, *Tulane Drama Review*, Spring 1960 cited in Esslin (above).

Ionesco, E., (1959) '*Experience du theatre*', Paris: *Nouvelle Revue Française*, February 1958, trans. by L.C. Pronko, 'Discovering the theatre', *Tulane Drama Review*, September 1959 cited in Esslin (above).

Ionesco, E., (1964) *Notes and Counter Notes: Writings on the Theatre*, trans. Donald Watson, New York: Grove Press.

Ionesco, E., (1967) *Exit the King*, trans. Donald Watson, New York: Grove Press.

Jaynes, J., (1976) *The Origin of Consciousness in the Breakdown of the Bicameral Mind*, London: Allen Lane.

Krauss, R., (1979) 'John Mason and post-modernist sculpture: new experiences, new words', *Art in America*, 67, 3: 12-7, cited in H. Bertens (1995) *The idea of the postmodern, a history*, London: Routledge.

Lamont, R.C. (1993) *Ionesco's Imperatives: The Politics of Culture*, Ann Arbor: The University of Michigan Press.

Lash, S., (1990) *Sociology of Postmodernism*, London: Routledge.

Law, J., 91994) *Organizing Modernity*, Oxford: Blackwell Publishers.

Lefebvre, H., (1974) *La Production de L'espace*, Paris: Anthropos.

Linstead, S.L. (1994) 'The Sting of Organization: Command, Reciprocity and Change Management', *Journal of Organizational Change Management*, 7, 5: 4–19.

Messinger, L., Sampson, H. and Towne, R.D., (1968) 'Life as Theatre: Some notes on the Dramaturgic approach to Social Reality' in M. Truzzi (ed.) *Sociology and Everyday Life*, Englewood Cliffs: Prentice-Hall, 7–20.

Metcalfe, P. and Huntingdon, R., (1991) *Celebrations of Death, The Anthropology of Mortuary Ritual*, Cambridge: Cambridge University Press.

Miller, D., (1989) 'The Limits of Dominance' in C. Tilley, 'Discourse and power: the genre of the Cambridge Inaugural Lecture' in D. Miller, M. Rowlands and C. Tilley (eds) (1989) *Domination and Resistance*, London: Unwin Hyman Ltd.

Munro, R., (1997) *Belonging on the Move, market rhetoric and the future as obligatory passage.*

Napier, A.D., (1986) *Masks, Transformation, and Paradox*, Berkeley: University of California Press.

Norris, C., (1990) *What's Wrong with Postmodernism: Critical Theory and the Ends of Philosophy*, London and New York: Harvester Wheatsheaf.

Owens, C., (1980) 'The allegorical impulse: toward a theory of postmodernism', Part I *October*, 12:67–86 and Part II *October*, 13:59–80.

Phelan, P., (1993) *Unmarked, The Politics of Performance*, London: Routledge.

Poster, M., (1989) *Critical Theory and Poststructuralism: In Search of a Context*, Ithaca and London: Cornell University Press.

Sampson, E.E., (1989) 'The Deconstruction of the Self' in J. Shotter and K. Gergen (eds) (1989) *Texts of Identity*, London: Sage.

Selden, R., (1989) *A Reader's Guide to Contemporary Literary Theory*, Hemel Hempstead: Harvester Wheatsheaf.

Sievers, B., (1993) *Work. Death and Life Itself: Essays on Management and Organization*, Berlin: Walter de Gruyter.

Soja, E., (1989) *Postmodern Geographics: The Reassertion of Space in Critical Theory*, London: Verso.

Towarnicki, '*Des Chaises vides . . . a Broadway*', *Spectacles*, Paris, no. 2, July 1958, Letter from Ionesco to Sylvain Dhomme, in Esslin (above).

Turner, V., (1982) *From Ritual to Theatre: The Human Seriousness of Play*. New York: Performing Arts Journal Publishers.

Turner, V., (1974) *Dramas, Fields and Metaphors: Symbolic Action in Human Society*, Ithaca: Cornell University Press.

Wallis, B., (ed.) (1984) *Art After Modernism: Rethinking Representation*, Boston: David R. Godine/New York: Museum of Contemporary Art.

Wertsch, J.V., (1991) *Voices of the Mind, A Sociocultural Approach to Mediated Action*, London: Harvester Wheatsheaf.

Zizek, S., (1991) *Looking Awry, An Introduction to Jacques Lacan through Popular Culture*, Cambridge, Mass.: The MIT Press.

On words and clocks: temporal ordering in a ward for autistic youths

Ruud Hendriks

If you would help me, don't try to change me to fit your world.
Don't try to confine me to some tiny part of the world that you
can change to fit me. Grant me the dignity of meeting me on my
own terms—recognize that we are equally alien to each other,
that my ways of being are not merely damaged versions of yours.
Question your assumptions. Define your terms. Work with me to
build more bridges between us.[1]

To imagine that we can assimilate the Other in any of its forms is
hubris. Instead, it seems to me that these Others will ignore us for
most of the time. Instead, they will continue, as they always have,
to perform their specific forms of agency to one another. And all
that we can do is to say that these performances go on. And then
to create appropriately monstrous ways of re-presenting them on
those rare occasions when our paths happen to cross and we find,
for a moment, that we need to interact with them.[2]

Introduction

In social interaction with autistic persons, regular means of attuning to each other's behaviours and expectations appear to be
blocked. That much can be deduced from situations in which the
paths of autistic and non-autistic people cross—a circumstance
which occurs on a daily basis in a ward for mentally handicapped
autistic youths. None of the youths living in this ward can tell us,
for instance, what time it is. Symbolic concepts of time appear to be
incomprehensible to them. They do not seem to know what 'waiting', what 'presently' or 'tomorrow' mean. Yet, time does not pass
by daily life in this ward. In this chapter, I will study matters of

time in a residential ward for mentally handicapped autistic youths.[3] Thus, I intend to contribute to the repertoire of words and images which may be used to reflect upon the design of this practice.

In getting on with autistic youths it cannot be taken for granted that the progress and order of events and phenomena are understood in a common language. Beside or instead of words, material objects seem to play a crucial role in the temporal ordering of life in the ward. Autistic youths are better supported in surroundings where 'auti-watches'[4] rather than people tell them what time it is. An example of such a watch is a lightbar which shortens with the passage of time. Besides the counsellors and the residents, things are continuously put forward in the local establishment of temporal order.[5] However, the specific role of each of these constituents of temporal order—of counsellors, residents, and material objects—appears to be a radically different one in the different descriptions I will give of daily life in the ward.

An approved method in interpretative sociology is to become familiar with the way people interpret their world by participating in the form of life of one's object of study.[6] An appropriate way for a researcher to do justice to the way people account for the world around them, is to listen to what they have to say. Autism, however, is characterized by an innate ability to interpret the world in a way which makes sense to non-autistic people[7] and autistic people are notoriously impaired in communicative ability,[8] so it must be held highly problematic to engage in conversation with an autistic person. It therefore seems obvious to describe the way matters of time are handled—as well as the implicated roles for residents, counsellors, and material objects in the establishment of social order—on the basis of stories and interpretations of non-autistic members of the community under study, such as the counsellor's.

It is shown by such an interpretative approach that what seems natural for non-autistic participants of social life in the ward precisely seems *not* to be so natural for the youths living there. This requires specific adjustments not only in those who are working there (as will be described in the next section) but also, possibly, in the *vocabulary* to be used to describe phenomena in the field under study. It seems inevitable that common-sense notions of non-autistic existence (specifically on the distribution of agency in the construction of the social) will affect, to a certain degree, descriptions of the shared form of life in the ward. But in order to prevent that such taken-for-granted interpretations in a non-reflected upon way will be considered the only conceivable measure, it seems advisable to *distance* oneself not only in practice but also in theory (ie on a level of descriptive language), from familiar, non-autistic frames of reference. My third section explores a vocabulary which intends to detach readers of their usual way of reflecting on the unusual phenomena in the ward. Finally, I will try to indicate what can be learned from this second approach in contrast with the first one. To do this, I will concentrate on the various roles counsellors, residents and things are supposed to play in the design of their shared form of life.

The need to switch over

Monday 20 June, late shift

> Sitting at the table at five o'clock in the evening. It is fairly silent, with only some short remarks every now and then. An eggtimer rings. Peter, a big guy, 17 years of age, covers his sandwich with chocolate flakes and starts to eat. As soon as the sandwich is finished he picks up the eggtimer standing before him, and hands it over to the counsellor. She sets the clock at ten minutes. Peter waits. He waits for the signal to ring in perfect patience. As soon as the eggtimer rings, Peter continues his meal. When the last bit of the next sandwich is swallowed, he hands over the eggtimer again and whole ritual is repeated. Until four sandwiches have been eaten, three quarters of an hour have passed, and the time has come to clear the table. While the others are leaving the table, Peter compulsively shoves his chair over the floor. Then he leaves as well.[9]

Meaningful relations

Regular means of attuning to one another's behaviours and expectations, appear to be blocked during this meal. Peter, for instance, does not seem to know what 'waiting' means. For Peter is 'really' autistic, I am told. And autistic people are, among other things, notoriously impaired in knowing how to deal with matters of time.

> Peter doesn't know what 'waiting' is. Because what's waiting? How long does it take? You can try to explain it to him a hundred times . . . We know that, waiting for a train, yes, it will come. That can be surveyed. In all kind of situations we have an

idea of waiting. But I think that in autism there's a completely different concept, that they do know something about waiting, but . . . [10]

One evening, when Peter was allowed to help packing for the group's holiday later that week, he demanded to go on vacation *immediately*. It was only with difficulty that the counsellor succeeded in getting him to bed. Unprecise concepts such as 'tomorrow' or 'later' appear extremely difficult to grasp for autistic people. They seem to be lacking an overview. If one of the youths is told at noon that his parents will come visit him in the evening, he may wait in the hall for hours.

If spare time isn't filled up, this may be disastrous for autistic persons: they wouldn't know what can be done with it. We may assume that an autistic person continuously struggles with three big questions: what do they expect me to do now? How long will it take? And what to do next, when the current activity is over? [11]

Peter's awkwardness at the table is exemplary for the typically autistic inability to discern order and coherence beyond the level of what is concretely and explicitly given. In the introductory file, which specifies details of the residents on this ward, it is explained what is the matter with these people.

Autistic people do not seem to understand the world. They are incapable of ordering affairs spontaneously, of putting them in a certain order, especially when they are a little bit abstract. They do not seem to pick out the meaning of things and events (. . .). [12]

This characterization of autism, an impairment on the level of sense-making, explains why it is so hard to discuss the duration of a meal with Peter—something that seems to go without saying; an issue which demands quite some skill in communicating symbolic meanings, however, when given a second thought. Even the simplest of messages may not be understood by Peter.

Talking is very difficult for autistic people for all kinds of reasons. Most of the time you won't succeed in making them speak more. And the other way around, when we speak to them . . . For them, language is a maze of words and sounds. Most of it they don't understand at all or not very well.

Psychological explanations for autistic behaviour (as found in the introductory file) are not readily given by counsellors. Insofar as they are looking for explanations, it is on an individualized level. Lack of a shared (linguistic) frame of reference, however, makes it extremely hard for counsellors to position themselves in the experienced world of the autistic other. When it comes to interpreting the behaviour of someone like Peter, counsellors are often groping in the dark.

> The most difficult thing is that [they're] so difficult to understand. Why does [someone] suddenly have a backslide? You really want to talk that over with him but you can't get through. Everybody has this, you're eager to talk: 'Please, tell me, what's up?' It's really hard, their world is so different from ours, that I can't empathize with it at all.

In everyday life in the ward, however, one cannot escape the fact that events do have a certain duration, the need to all have supper on time, or the unavoidability of waiting one's turn every once in a while. In spite of their handicap, residents are thus continuously asked, so to speak, 'to keep an eye on the clock'. To make everyday life in the ward tick, expectations and behaviours just *have* to be attuned in one way or the other. When counsellors tell about the problems they encounter in practice, the question how to *solve* these affairs therefore is of primary interest to them. That it is pointless to bombard Peter with 'significant' gazes and to overwhelm him with complex messages like 'Please wait a moment Peter, it's not very *gezellig*[13] if you finish your meal in a rush', proves itself day after day. Those who are faced with the task of bringing mealtime to a happy conclusion, therefore, cannot but adapt.

> At first, that was what I found the hardest thing to do, to make yourself clear, to communicate a message to the resident. Because you're inclined to make sentences too long. But they don't understand these, so you'll just have to switch over.'

Concrete links

Peter does not seem to understand ordinary language. Therefore, counsellors just have to switch over. No matter how hard it is to place oneself in the position of someone like Peter, experience teaches that there are other ways than talking to make clear to him what 'waiting' is. The use of the eggtimer can be considered an example *par excellence* of such an alternative option. It shows how counsellors try to deal with the autistic inability to cope with matters of time by introducing an unadorned, non-linguistic way of ordering. In practical terms: Peter would finish his sandwiches in a rush and a turbulent evening-meal would be guaranteed if there was no eggtimer providing comfort for him.

I don't know how this works, but you can solve [these problems with waiting] by saying: if the eggtimer rings then the waiting is done, or: if all the sand has gone through the hour-glass then it's done. So that you make this [waiting] very concrete.

Residents in the ward, one more than the other, all need a lot of 'clarity', counsellors say. To organize temporal order in the ward, however, linguistic cues such as 'wait a moment' appear to be useless. Words are therefore replaced and bypassed by unambiguous physical prompts. Instead of overwhelming Peter with abstract information which presumes a high level of competence in sharing symbolic meanings, an eggtimer is put at ten minutes.

Yes, the trick is that you must . . . well, to externalize might be too easy an expression, but it's almost like materializing the kind of connections that we, in our brains so easily [make] . . . physical yes.

By moulding implicit relations into concrete (visible, tangible) links and externalizing covert meanings, for people with autism the black box of temporal order may finally become a little bit more transparent. So they might experience, sometimes for the first time in their life, as counsellors hold, that their world is not dominated by chance. Thus it can be understood why everyday life in the ward is strictly guided by a definite recurring order to mealtimes, bathroom visits, time for recreation, drinking lemonade, etc., why it is that counsellors themselves practise a predictable style of working, and why sudden changes are avoided to a large extent.

Structure is one of the key-words in treating autistic people. The concept of structure is related to what we would like to call the essence of autism: not seeing the relations, the meaning, the sense of things. Structuring then refers to all activities that are meant to clarify those connections, for instance by making them simple and explicit, by making them visible using means which sometimes look ridiculously naive to us.[14]

In Peter's case a structured approach seems to have a beneficial effect. Partly because there is an eggtimer standing on the table and partly because counsellors restrict themselves in their repertoire of actions by providing residents with concrete, eggtimer-like structures, everyone knows what he or she is expected to do. Thus, mealtimes go by in what counsellors call a 'calm' or 'sociable' atmosphere.

Living in tension

When we follow counsellors in their interpretations we may learn that the youngsters they take care of need a lot of structure. This does not mean, however, that life in the ward needs to be programmed from beginning to end. On the contrary, working on this group is far more complex than that. Sometimes well-defined patterns are deliberately *departed* from. Take, for instance, the other day when Peter got an extra round at dinner because it tasted so good. It makes good sense to break routines occasionally, a counsellor told me when I asked for clarification. Structure, then, is not a goal in itself. It is a means to an end. It is a steady basis for more flexibility, 'not because they should be more like us, but simply because they can enjoy life better because of this flexibility.'[15]

Experience teaches, however, that the degrees of freedom one can afford oneself in the care of these youths is limited. 'This may end in tears . . . ' Irene (the counsellor) weighs the risk of her sympathetic but unpredictable gesture. Thus, again and again, counsellors see themselves obliged to *distance* themselves from taken-for-granted behaviour and to restrict themselves to unambiguous actions instead. In other words, they see themselves faced with the challenge to develop a *reductionist* attitude as a stable background for the youths in their care.

> He knows what he's up to with me, and I with him, which also gives a certain amount of rest and provides a possibility to develop a nicer contact. I've a feeling that this 'consequential' approach adds to a better relationship between us.

The presupposed needs of the residents and those of the counsellors do not necessarily overlap, however. To let go of the familiar rules of social intercourse turns out to be a very hard job. Thus it can often be observed how counsellors forget about the differences between residents and themselves, and start to treat autistic people as competent members of the linguistic community instead.

> In people working with autistic people one is often confronted with ideas like: 'He doesn't want this' or 'He's putting pressure

on us'. Those are presumptions I think *we* might very well have, and an autistic person might have something like it too, but in the latter case there's no doubt that these will be radically different from ours. We are continuously attributing *our* concepts to people with autism; thinking that it will be the way we think it is.

The effort it takes to restrict oneself, according to counsellors' accounts, may have something to do with the moral mortgage resting on a reductionist approach. Those who accommodate themselves to the autistic need for a concrete hold, for instance by only speaking in very short sentences, or even more, by only 'steering' physically, often get criticised for it.

> Outsiders, who do not know about the real difficulties of autistic children, perceive such physical manipulations as a robot-like control, as a mechanistic approach, as a kind of animal training. While in fact it is a direct accommodation to the difficulties of the child himself.[16]

But not only outsiders think so. Counsellors themselves also have problems in living up the restrictions posed by working with autistic persons. I watched counsellors work in a more passionate way, rather than providing rational structures. I saw them make fun, talk and laugh. Teasing and joking appear to be a normal part of social life in the ward. More than that, I heard a lot of criticism of the purely mechanistic approach. I heard a call for love and care, and for treating these youngsters as fellow-humans.[17] Which is not only a question of pedagogy, morality or human nature.[18] The fact that it is particularly hard to treat an autistic person after the model of an eggtimer, as a radical stranger to our life-world, is also a matter of gut-feelings.

> Initially, I was horrified by the whole programme. So much structure, so many rules, that isn't workable. Everything and everyone needed to be prestructured: fixed mealtimes, a separation between dining- and living-room, etc. It went so far even that a resident would go in the shower exactly one quarter of an hour before her parents came, so that she would be finished and clothed at the very moment that they would ring the doorbell. So empty and cold, we were really dreading it. I thought that I wouldn't make it long working here. In the end, it didn't turn out so strict.

In counsellors' accounts a dilemma occurs. Kids like Peter seem to feel more at home in the mute, mechanistic world of the eggtimer than in the linguistic, meaningful world of people among themselves. This makes an extreme appeal to the coping abilities of the people around them. In everyday life in the ward, doubt on how to proceed may pop up at any time. The idea, however, that these youngsters might possibly *not* belong to human society and might be mere automatons, simply does not occur.[19] Which is also why people emphasize the importance of ongoing *conversation*: 'the form is a different one, but the ideal of communication remains'.[20]

Thus, counsellors find themselves living in tension, seeking to navigate between the perceived needs of the residents and their own needs and ideas about what meaningful human life amounts to; between the double bearings of materiality and meaning; between mute, concrete structures on the one hand and the ideal communicative situation on the other.[21] Confronted with two wrongs (the out-of-reach ideal of the linguistic community and the—from an ordinary human point of view—meagre alternative in the form of a strict, clockwise way of ordering), they prefer the second option. That is why, despite its limitations, an eggtimer is used.

Material objects as temporal nodes

Magnifying

What makes life tick on a ward for autistic youths? In order to answer this question, until now I have relied solely on the counsellors' accounts. People with autism, it can be gathered from these stories, in certain ways are offered *more* by material objects than by people. Unlike in the counsellor's life—where linguistic ordering comes first and the eggtimer is nothing more than a suitable *means* to communicate temporal messages—objective structures often provide the only hold in the life of autistic residents. Thus this interpretative approach reveals that to really be involved with autistic youths one has to *distance* oneself from familiar presuppositions about good care. But how much distance is enough? Does the vocabulary I have used until now allow us to detach ourselves sufficiently from the taken-for-granted perspective of non-autistic existence? Of course it is precisely by depending on such a familiar, interpretative background that (autistic) deviations from the norm are made visible in the first place; but the same vocabulary also takes sides in what it is supposed to study: the interpretative vocabulary shows a bias in favour of the linguistic, the speakable, the meaningful, and thus remains close to the terms in which only *some* of the participants of social life in the ward—the counsellors—understand these phenomena.[22]

In order not to reify interpretations as they are taken-for-granted in ordinary life, notably on the distribution of agency in the process of social ordering, I will here try to distance myself on a descriptive level as well. In order to do this, however, let us take one more look at the counsellors' accounts. We have seen how they started from an ordinary, linguistic frame of reference. In practice this posed so many problems that they made concessions, for instance by setting an eggtimer. However, as soon as they started to *reflect* on their work, they framed these objects in good old-fashioned linguistic terms—by referring to the instrumental role played by these objects in the care of autistic youths, for instance, or by justifying their use of mechanistic means by adhering to their own communicative intentions. Underneath these worries about and interpretations of what they are actually doing lies a dualist worldview, which divides the world along the lines of the subject/object scheme in meaningful and mechanistic halves.

What I want to do now is to draw the line a little *further*. At those places where counsellors meet their (linguistic, social, moral) limits, I will try to pursue the story-line. Where they put an eggtimer but then couch it in familiar terms, I think it interesting to go on. I will therefore shift down the level of analysis a bit by *magnifying* the practice in which objects play such a crucial role and by putting between brackets all the communicative concerns in which these objects are usually embedded.[23]

More concretely this amounts to a description of processes of temporal ordering in the ward, in a way which does not focus on the stories or the intentions of the counsellors but puts material objects at the beginning of analyses (rather than as a balancing item). Thus, I imagine material objects no longer as passive means in the hands of the counsellor, as a neutral service-hatch for meanings to be passed through,[24] but as *nodes* around which other elements (counsellors and residents, words, gestures, organizations, things, bodies) are temporally centred. Temporal order, then, is seen no longer as an elusive concept, to be found solely in the heads of the counsellors or in the linguistic community, but as a *result* of the ways in which heterogeneous elements in their mutual interaction perform agency in temporal affairs. As a derivative of the (partly) material labour of ordering.[25]

This approach is no longer validated by asking ourselves if—autistic or non-autistic—members of the community under study would recognize themselves in this analysis, nor by measuring the degree of correspondence between their experienced world and my description of events.[26] I will ignore the epistemological status of the claims of the counsellors and others who speak on behalf of the residents (as a more or less faithful representation of the autistic other) and will take their claims *literally* instead, magnify them, and use that as an analytical frame to describe all the events in the ward.[27] This may allow us to learn something about temporal ordering in this ward for autistic youths, without automatically having to take a non-autistic perspective and paint this on a practice which is partially constituted by non-linguistic elements.[28] Instead readers are offered a chance to let themselves be surprised by an *exaggeration* of their own (non-autistic) interpretations of an autistic world. After all, there are so many other points of view, so many other places in the world than the head of the counsellor.[29] As far as the ward is concerned, let us begin downstairs.

Downstairs/noon

Spatial characteristics provide a steady background for temporal order in everyday life in the ward. For instance, during daytime all activities (mealtimes, recreation, drinking lemonade) are centred on the ground-floor. The youths only find themselves upstairs when taking a bath or when it is time to go to sleep, early in the morning and at night. Activities which come in a certain temporal sequence are marked out in the design of the ward and in the spatial organization of its interior. For residents who do not comply with the material separation of day and night, for instance, a small gate has been installed at the stairs, so that the way up can be blocked. For a first short history, when entering the ward we ignore the blocked stairs on our left and walk straight ahead into the living-room: it is getting on for noon.

Downstairs in the sittingroom some apparently unobtrusive and silent objects can be found which affect everyday life in the ward to a large extent. The bench, for instance, performs a significant role in how Peter's day is organized. This bench seems good for lying on. Better than the table, for instance, possibly because of its form and material outfit. Moreover, counsellors agree with the bench being used for such purposes. Peter can often be found lying on the bench. After he has come home from school, for instance, before lemonade is drunk. Or during the summer holiday, when there is no school. He is called a 'specialist in lying down'.

Wednesday 20 July, early shift

'I bet they begin to feel bored stiff', one of the staff members con-
cludes after glossing over the ward during a short visit. It's a
sweltering day. Outside in the garden Robert is on the swing.
Peter has installed himself on the bench. From this position he
looks around a bit, watching what happens in the garden or elsewhere inside his range of view. But most of the time he just looks
straight ahead and simply lies there. 'Well, as long as Peter can
lie down he's pretty comfortable', Irene, who's preparing a meal
in the kitchen, reacts to the visitor's words.

Here we have time. *Not* an abstract concept of time which is
hidden in the head of the visitor and projected on Peter's behaviour. Nor an intrinsic quality of events as they unfold themselves
on the bench, I will argue, but an *effect* of (partially silent) interactions which develop around the bench and involve a wide
range of elements such as: Peter's lying on the thing, the summer's holiday, the warm weather, Robert's swinging in the garden, the counsellor in the kitchen and the visitor's look and
words. For a moment these few elements constitute the loosely
knit fabric in which temporal structure is bred; the fabric from
which a coherent plot can be read[30]—a brief history which
describes the phenomenon of boredom as an empirically observ-
able practice. Part of the information I have used here reaches
us (reader and researcher) via the words of the visitor, but these
same words risk to obscure other, non-linguistic parts of the
phenomenon under study: actors which do not reside in the
counsellor's head or the linguistic community, and risk to get
underestimated because of their silence. However, it is precisely
these 'minor' details and the unobtrusive part *they* play which
are of interest to us in exploring the micro-physics of temporal
performances. Together these elements form a small, mundane
and local network, in which, loosely at first, a coherent order of
time is constituted; a network from which the product only
appears to come loose easily once it has been given a name.
'Boredom' is a linguistic translation of the specific way temporal
order is performed in this case.

It might be no coincidence that it is a relative outsider who finds
himself translating the shared performance of Peter-and-the-bench
in terms of its possible meaning 'boredom'. Maybe the visitor is not
that much embedded in the material structure of the ward and its
characteristic, tangible logic. On those who are more familiar with

everyday life in the ward, the joint venture of Peter-and-the-bench has a completely different effect. The bench—conceived as a node in the organization of the shared form of life in the ward—after first having enrolled Peter in his role of a specialist in lying down, now allows *counsellors* to spend their time elsewhere in the ward. In the kitchen, for instance, without having to worry about Peter. For Peter is lying on the bench. Thus we witness how a slightly different configuration may result in a radically different form of time; an effect which translates into a certain *praxis* rather than interpretations or words.

How would the lying-on-the-bench finally translate for Peter? For, although it was never put there to play this part, Peter and the bench take possession of each other completely. This results in a lying-down act, to be sure. Maybe also in being left in peace. The bench with Peter on it, which organized the counsellors' consent by allowing them to spend their (precious) time somewhere else, forges a sufficiently stable link to affect life at other places as well. The whole constellation allows Peter to be on his own for a while. But again, this already comes down to translating lying on a bench into a familiar *meaning*. In practice one just has to learn to live with the fact that Peter is lying down all the time. And maybe there is not so much more to say.

> Some things you can . . . like Peter. This guy was lying down all of the time, and you reckoned with that, that's Peter. But some things you just cannot understand, why they do such things. That's what makes them autistic.

Upstairs/evening

Although autistic residents seem to have trouble understanding symbolic concepts of time, and counsellors often grope in the dark when it comes to communicating with the residents, time does not pass by everyday life in the ward. Temporal regularities may be seen to revolve around seemingly insignificant objects like a bench. If such a material node succeeds in creating sufficiently strong links between a sufficient amount of other elements circulating in the ward, fragile temporal structures may hold for a while. Which is how time is concretely realized in the ward. Which also sounds more peaceful than it is. Let us move upstairs to highlight another phenomenon which may be observed in everyday life in the ward: the occurrence of clashes in time.

Friday 19 August, late shift

> On his way to the bathroom Robert comes to a sudden halt right
> in front of the bathroom-door. He positions his feet neatly on the
> floor along an imaginary line. With one of his feet he lifts up, a
> little, the small rug which is lying there on the floor. He almost
> goes inside the bathroom, but then comes out again. This is
> repeated a few times. Meanwhile he looks over his shoulder with
> a strange tension in his body. He shakes his body from time to
> time, with his arms folded up over his breast, as if he's hugging
> himself. Then he pushes the open door of the bathroom firmly
> against the door-post around the corner. Watching how it fits?
> Once again. His feet again, the rug again. Finally he enters the
> bathroom.

Particular geometric characteristics of the door-posts in the corner
between the bathroom and one of the sleeping-rooms, and a small
rug, seem to attract Robert's attention. We might say that the fur-
nishing of the bathroom prepossesses Robert in its favour by invit-
ing him to develop a special *fascination* for its localized material
logic. Robert has—or should we say *is*?[31]—a weakness for angles,
straight lines, material resistances and strained bodily movements.
This should not be seen as an intrinsic quality of Robert, nor of
autistic people in general, but rather as an inclination which is
partly produced by the circumstances Robert finds himself in. An
unusual inclination maybe, but not as long as we only have to do
with the small constellation as sketched above.

The particularities as they are performed in the privacy of the
bathroom[32] figure in a completely different plot when counsellors
arrive on the scene. Because of the institutional context counsellors
are connected with—a context in which schoolhours, the end of the
shift, and the necessity to all have breakfast at one and the same
time, play an important role—they develop a very different fascination with the possibilities of the bathroom than Robert. A bathroom visit better not take hours in the temporal logic of
institutionalized life. Thus, opaque performances as they take place
in the bathroom may translate into what counsellors call Robert's
'dawdling all the time'.

A situation like this, in which different fascinations (stemming
from different network configurations) perform diverging temporal
orders, often occurs in practice. Sometimes as a form of peaceful
coexistence. In other circumstances, however, such a case easily
leads to conflicts. Especially in situations in which counsellors and

residents move around in a space where shared temporal coordinates (carried by objects, words, sounds, gestures, etc.) are missing, while they still do have to manage things together.

To make life tick, it may turn out to be necessary to reconcile such radically diverging fascinations as they are sketched above. Which is not always feasible. If a compromise or otherwise satisfying solution is not found, there is always the possibility that an armed peace may be established. Which does not necessarily mean that institutional frames settle the matter.[33] For instance, counsellors too may find themselves compelled by the temporal coordinates which are performed in the joint venture of the door-post, the rug and Robert. After the first (rug and door-post) succeeded to enroll the latter (by allowing Robert to elaborate 'his' interest in angles, straight lines, and bodily movements) it appears quite hard not to comply to the course of time as it is organized by these, often underrated, non-linguistic constituents of social order in the ward. The specific form temporal order takes when counsellors are enrolled as such is called—in the counsellor's vocabulary—'waiting'. Patiently waiting until Robert's temporal routine, temporally, falls apart when he enters the room. A forced performance of 'patience', which may eventually lead counsellors to 'hurry', whether they want to or not.

Downstairs/afternoon

Friday 8 July, late shift

> While I am clearing the table, Peter returns to the dining-rom. He takes up his chair and puts it on two of its four legs. Thus making it easier for him to check the underside of the other two. With the palm of his hand he sweeps off some dust and crumbs from the underside. Then he checks the other two. When he is finished he puts down the chair with a firm gesture. Again and again. Then he shoves the thing towards the table's edge. Moving it centimetres to and fro. He is keeping his hand at a short distance as if keeping the chair's balance. He seems to prepare to go away, then turns back again, and finally seems to succeed in pushing the chair in the right position. Then he runs away.

Just like Robert in the bathroom, Peter is completely enthralled by the material logic of the furniture in the dining-room. Peter's behaviour testifies to a fascination with flat surfaces, an absence of crumbs and dust, and neat positioning. A weird fascination, maybe, but not so strange that counsellors do not recognize it as something they might share.

> Sometimes we make fun of it, like: you work with autistic people and so you become a bit like them. But I think everybody has this. For instance, I want to have everything in the cupboard, mugs, etc., this must all be in line. And Robert's dish has to be on top; it's smaller than the others. It's simply compulsive.

Counsellors make fun of their own ritualistic clinging to a certain arrangement of dishes in the cupboard. Nevertheless, they often try to keep Peter from performing *his* ritual which revolves around the chair. In the configuration as it unfolds when therapeutic concerns come on—concerns which are constituted by a network in which specialized expertise rather than the furniture, the residents, or the counsellors who learned to live with such 'tics' form the centre of organizational activities—it seems only reasonable to breach Peter's 'rigid behaviour'.

> Because if you don't, you will get autistic people who suffer from the structures they invent themselves, or with the counsellors whom they compel to go along in a structure, and from which there is no way of getting them out. That's why we think it's important to teach them that things may go different every now and then.

In the configuration as it evolves right now, there is not so much room for making fun. In this set-up Peter appears as an 'autistic patient' *par excellence*. He is cast without a sense of time, which explains why he is fleeing in what, henceforth, is defined as 'compulsive' and 'stereotypical' behaviour. From now on, Peter's fascination is turned into a minor, or at least a pathological one. Counsellors, on the other hand, are cast in an opposite role, as competent members of the interpretative community. Because they have interpretative abilities at their disposal, for them the heterogeneous performance of Peter-and-the-chair translates into what only *they* are supposed to recognize as a (meaningful) *sign* of Peter's actual condition: his lack of temporal grip, which may have led him to flee in (what counsellors call) 'endless repetition'. A pattern in which he seems to be entirely locked-up, as only the counsellors can survey.

> Yes, they do the same things almost every day. That is, the same movements, etc. You wouldn't find that so much on another

ward (. . .). I think that if you would observe them during one week and write down precisely where a resident goes, what he does, etc., then the material he uses may very well be different, but according to me he would do the same basic things every day in exactly the same way.

Counsellors may speak in terms of 'reasons' to justify their breaching of Peter's routine. However, in practice they often become as much 'enthralled' by breaking repetitive behaviour, as residents like Peter or Robert become fascinated with the performance of it.

Just like Robert with this foot over there—a barren footstep in the lawn—he always needs to step on that spot when he passes it by. Only if you say 'Go on! and don't keep standing there!' he won't. But I think that if you would give him the opportunity, he would go back and do it anyway.

Downstairs/morning

To realize unity in the course of time it may be necessary to translate diverging, clashing fascinations into one co-ordinated action. Which is not always easy in a residential setting for autistic youths. Sometimes, however, an actor may be cast in a position to *mediate* between counsellors and autistic youths and to reconcile their apparently incompatible interests. Such a responsible task may be delegated to a human but also to a non-human actor. Sometimes even better to an object, especially when words are not enough. A small device, the eggtimer, for instance, succeeded in aligning all the clashing elements at the breakfast table and in translating their unruly forces into one co-ordinated performance of time. The eggtimer tempered Peter's pace, thus satisfying the counsellor's fascination with an orchestrated participation in the meal. At the same time it made clear what 'waiting' is and what is 'enough', thus enrolling Peter in his compliant role.

The eggtimer thus became a central actor in the heterogeneous organization of the mealtime—a material node around which other actors, counsellors and residents, could be temporally gathered. The translation underlying this result consists of transforming the colliding interests and diverging roles into a well-attuned participation of all to the meal. Such a change, however, could only be realized by making the newly enrolled actors believe or experience that, although they are *all* enrolled in a new part (thus feeding each other's fascinations), they can still (or even better) pursue their own inclination. A successful translation makes it seem as if nothing changed at all except the *other's* compliance to the new rule (from the counsellor's perspective: the compliance of the resident). Thus, the unobtrusive object that successfully *mediated* between different rivalling positions, is retrospectively turned into an *intermediary*, and considered a passive *means* in the hands of the successful counsellor.

Accountability for success or failure, however, is not as easily settled among the network constituents as such an account would have us believe. What this retrospective account overlooks is the fact that for temporal structures to be realized, *all* entities which make up the eggtimer-routine in one way or another need to co-operate in practising mealtime. Without the seamless co-operation between the counsellor who has to set the clock and the resident who draws the counsellor's attention by pointing to the thing when she risks to forget her part, the mealtime breaks down immediately.[34] Time is a locally produced effect; temporal routines will not last a minute longer than the fragile networks they are made of.

'Right of speech' in matters of time is decentred over the ward and cannot be easily assigned to one responsible actor. What carries 'weight' is spread out all along the line. Moreover, a new configuration of temporal order in the ward leaves none of its constituent elements untouched. *All* are translated along the way. In exchange with its new context, the eggtimer starts to translate its surroundings according to its own requirements as soon as it is introduced. Little remains the same, when counsellors and youths begin to attune their mealtime to the clock, learn to pass it over, to reach out for it, to ignore it sometimes, and to react to its signal. Temporal order as it unfolds itself in the ward has its own, irreducible logic. And thus is may happen that one of the counsellors finds himself missing the eggtimer, one of these early mornings at the breakfast table. He had gotten so used to its availability that, willingly or not, he is quite inconvenienced now that Peter has moved to another unit, and the eggtimer with him.

> I missed it already! I really missed the eggtimer! I sat there the other morning, and I always used to do this with Jason, that I made him a sandwich, as soon as the eggtimer rang for Peter. Now my first thought was: when should I make this sandwich for Jason? At breakfast that was. It was so weird. I thought, shit, the eggtimer!

Conclusion: between words and clocks

By studying social interactions on a ward for autistic youths, first from an interpretative point of view and, subsequently, by employing an estranging vocabulary, some of the specific difficulties confronting autistic and non-autistic people in their mutual interaction could be signalled. On a ward for autistic youths it cannot be taken for granted that the progress and order of events and phenomena are understood in a common language. In interactions with autistic people, one of Wittgenstein's remarks on the tricky nature of language and the need for safe passways gains extra significance. To people with autism, abstract communicational means like words often have no meaning at all. The same, however, goes for the counsellors: in everyday life in the ward *any* further step along alphabet street might as well lead one into the wrong direction.

> Language sets everyone the same traps; it is an immense network of easily accessible wrong turnings. And so we watch one man after another walking down the same paths and we know in advance where he will branch off, where walk straight on without noticing the side turning, etc. etc. What I have to do then is erect signposts at all the junctions where there are wrong turnings so as to help people past the danger points.[35]

For autistic *and* non-autistic people to find security in uncertain times, unambiguous signposts are needed everywhere: for both parties, as the contrast I developed in this chapter reveals. Before ending, however, let us return one more time to the presumptions of the *counsellors* with regard to the events in the ward.

In the eyes of counsellors the needs of the *residents* are their main concern. That is why, according to counsellors, mutual efforts should be made in order to provide residents with temporal grip. Rather than demand only them to adapt, we should try to make room in society at large for an autistic form of life. But people who are brought up within the scope of the linguistic community can hardly be expected to give up all of their certainties at once. Thus it comes as no surprise that the choice of how to provide temporal grip is caught between two familiar extremes: while a strict, clockwise ordering of autistic lives may not be ideal (because, in human terms, restricted), it is still preferable to (what seems to be) the only sensible alternative, namely, forcing autistic people to function without any structure, thus ruling out the possibility for them to participate in human society at all.

Possibly an approach which is modelled after the nature of things *is* our best option in this particular case, as a kind of meagre alternative ('meagre' from a non-autistic point of view) for a blocked communicative situation. When counsellors speak on behalf of the residents we cannot escape the conclusion that people with autism are offered more grip, sometimes even literally so, by so-called careless, mute objects (such as an eggtimer) than by people themselves: predictable behaviour and iron regularity; the thing-like traits counsellors, in order to communicate with residents, can only try very hard to simulate.[36] Which is, from a familiar, non-autistic point of view, a counter-commonsensical and extra-ordinary thing to do already. An interpretative approach thus provides important directives for care and an argument against prejudice with respect to the moral standard of working-procedures in the ward.

Still, local opportunities may present themselves to question some of our beliefs a little bit further. In this chapter I have tried to create a space in which some of the hidden flaws of an interpretative perspective could be discerned. From an interpretative angle it appeared difficult to escape the tendency to couch in general and familiar terms the specific ways in which counsellors, eggtimers and residents relate to each other. For instance by attributing events as they unfolded in the ward entirely to the intentions, the efforts and mistakes on the counsellor's side. On the other hand, the active part of residents in the process of temporal ordering, as well as the transformative power of other non-linguistic constituents of social life in the ward, are easily underestimated. As we have seen, the latter only appear as *instruments* to meet the underdetermined character of signs of the time in a world without words. The fact that counsellors themselves need (and may become as enticed by) concrete structures in their interactions with autistic residents, as well as the fact that counsellors also get trapped by the language, tends to be easily overlooked. As far as matters of time are concerned, interactions in the ward are too easily viewed as a *planned and restricted derivative* of the way expectations and behaviours are attuned in ordinary life.

How to write a common history of counsellors, residents and eggtimers without sticking to the counsellor's perspective in advance? How to acknowledge that what matters on the work-floor does *not* leave participants of everyday life in the ward untouched? As it necessarily cannot leave *theory* untouched, seeking to describe these events? When counsellors start to speak for the youths, the idea can be heard that in the care of autistic people one must *dis-*

tance oneself from what counts as being 'involved' in ordinary life. With the object of contributing to the repertoire of words and images which may be employed to reflect upon the shared form of life of autistic and non-autistic people, this conclusion is extended in its consequences in the final part of my chapter.[37] Conceptions of what is important in autistic lives are consistently given a second thought and, because of their heuristic value, used as a framework to describe the whole process of temporal ordering in the ward.[38]

Despite its principal limitations,[39] the reconstruction of events in the ward by using a vocabulary which seeks to detach itself from non-autistic presuppositions seems to create room for non-linguistic elements involved in the constitution of temporal order in the ward. By taking spatial structures as a point of entrance, instead of seeing them as passive means in the hands of the counsellors, it is described how temporal order is partly an *effect* of performances and trials of force taking place in a network of heterogeneous actants. Rather than treating them as ready-made concepts, residing in the heads of the counsellors and in the realm of the linguistic community, temporal structures (such as boredom, waiting, impatience, and even abstract conceptions of time), are all described as the local, mostly unplanned, and concrete result of network building.

Not only do small mobile objects such as eggtimers perform a temporal logic; the material structure of the furniture, its position in the ward, as well as the specific spatial layout of the first and second floor, also draw upon and recreate their own temporal context.[40] Where matters of time are at stake, they perform agency as well, despite their inability to share a language with the ones who are often *believed* to be in charge.[41] The temporal organization of life in the ward is decentred over its practice. Moreover, the construction of temporal order leaves none of its constituents untouched: all capacities and roles are redefined along the way. The specific, partially non-linguistic way in which temporal order is realized, therefore is not only a product of the counsellors, but as much an achievement of the residents and the furniture. In order to account for the way counsellors, eggtimers and autistic youths mix, more than 'interpretation' is needed.

A final remark on the possibility of discussing the moral issues which have come up in an interpretative description, now that competent members of the language community are dislodged of their pivotal role.[42] Maybe this: a familiar image is that those who advocate a non-linguistic approach to autistic people as the next best, or the least harmful, alternative are inclined to serve this approach with a humanist sauce. As soon as the care of autistic youths is discussed the metaphor of 'conversation' appears.[43] That counsellors have learned to distance themselves from familiar notions of meaningfulness and care on the level of *working-procedures* is hardly taken into account on the level of the (self)*descriptions* of these procedures. A way of doing which seems to reside on the (dehumanizing) side of the objects, is presented and justified to the outside world with an appeal to good 'communicative intentions'.

Maybe we cannot understand inter-human affairs in another way than in terms of 'conversation'. No matter how sympathetic these accounts may be, insofar as they can be considered an effort to reconcile the unbearable tension between an ideal communicative situation on the one hand and a mute, thing-like condition on the other, the difference (and thus the tension) between them returns by the backdoor. My account takes a radically different stance from familiar, humanist pleas for understanding and recognition of what matters in autistic lives. Which does not imply that I do not sympathize with such calls. Indeed, I think autistic people also have their right of speech. Where matters of time are concerned all actors have their right of speech. But in order to recognize to what extent and in what specific form they exercise it already, we may have to question our assumptions more radically than we thought.[44] For our paths have crossed already, 'equally alien to each other'.[45]

> While the others are leaving the table, Peter places his chair with neat precision along a seam in the carpet. Then he leaves as well.

Acknowledgements

I am most grateful to the personnel at W. who kindly welcomed me into their midst, and to the residents, for having made it possible for me to witness the processes of social ordering they are both engaged in. Although the youths could not have a voice allowing me into their everyday life, it is my sincere hope I did succeed in allowing them into mine. For their support and commentaries on earlier drafts I would like to thank Ruth Benschop, Stuart Blume, Steve Brown, Maarten Derksen, Emilie Gomart, Hans Harbers, Annemarie Mol and Gerard de Vries.

Notes

1 Sinclair, 1992:302.
2 Callon & Law, 1995:504.
3 The material discussed in this chapter was gathered between June and September 1994 in W., a residential institution for mentally handicapped people in the Netherlands. Participant observation took place in a ward where seven women and men were involved in the care of six mentally-handicapped autistic youths, aged between eleven and twenty.
4 Peeters, 1994.
5 Of course, objects such as a watch, the electronic signalling-system indicating the time until the arrival of a tram, etc., also play an important regulatory part in non-autistic people's lives. For the moment, focussing on the role of material objects therefore does not indicate any principal distinction, but only refers to a relative difference between autistic and non-autistic people's needs.
6 In science and technology studies Harry M. Collins is a prominent defender of this approach: 'What one is trying to do as a sociologist is (among other things) to discover the range of ways of experiencing the world that are generally available to actors in particular cultural locations in particular societies. The best way of doing this is to come to share the form of life of the actors, and to find out at first hand if this is how actors might reasonably see things' (Collins, 1994a:316).
7 See, for instance: Frith, 1993; Peeters, 1994.
8 Schopler & Mesibov, 1985. The autistic disorder is a subgroup of the *Pervasive Developmental Disorders* under the chapter of *Disorders usually first evident in infancy, childhood, or adolescence* or DSM-IV (American Psychiatric Association 1994). Autism is a pervasive developmental disorder, which means that it is a disorder on a central level with widespread effects on the development of the child. Following the DSM-IV definition, people with autism suffer a qualitative impairment in social interaction, in communication, and display restricted repetitive and stereotyped patterns of behaviour, interests and activities; they show delays or abnormal functioning in at least one of the following areas: social interaction, language as used in social communication or symbolic or imaginative play, with onset during infancy or childhood (before 36 months of age); and their disturbance is not better accounted for by Rett's disorder or Childhood Disintegrative Disorder. People with autism often have an additional more or less severe mental handicap. Frith (1993) reports that about 15 per cent of the autistic population reaches an IQ in the normal or supranormal range. About 70 per cent of people with autism have an IQ of below 70.
9 Observation made in W. For reasons of privacy, all residents and counsellors have been given fictional names.
10 All quotes, unless mentioned otherwise, originate from (partly informal) interviews I had with the counsellors and members of the (advisory) autism-team, and from fieldnotes. These and other quotes that stem from Dutch sources are translated into English by me.
11 Notice that this quote rests heavily on non-autistic categorizations of time which are projected on the autistic person's experience.
12 De Jaegher, 1989:2. In this chapter, I will primarily follow the counsellors in their everyday practice, which means that I will not deal with explanations of autistic behaviour in any detail. Still, to mention one of them: according to the

theory of mind hypothesis (eg Baron-Cohen, Leslie and Frith, 1985; Frith, 1993), social and other problems with meaning as they are seen in autism, can be explained by a cognitive defect. These authors hypothesize an impairment in the mechanism which normally allows people to make meta-representations, that is, not only to represent the world but also to think or reason *about* these representations. A so-called 'theory of mind' enables one to think about other people's mental states, to deduce their thoughts from ambiguous external signs, to anticipate the other person's actions and thus to engage in social intercourse. In autistic minds this mechanism appears to be damaged.

13 *'Gezellig'* is the Dutch expression for a sociable atmosphere, with associations as broad as cosy closed curtains, an open fire, flowers on the table, drinking coffee with the entire family, talking about the weather, and avoiding improper subjects like the infamous black sheep of the family. The broadness of the category does not imply there is no order in *gezelligheid*. On the contrary, in order to behave 'sociably' it is extremely important to be *tactful*. Georg Simmel considers the sociable situation to be the ideal playground for necessarily tactful and self-restrained social intercourse, which would explain why people with autism cannot see the point of remarks referring to it: 'Von den soziologische Kategorien her betrachtend, bezeichne ich also die Gesellikeit als die *Spielform der Vergesellschaftung* und als—mutatis mutantis—zu deren inhaltsbestimmter Konkretheit sich verhaltend wie das Kunstwerk zur realität'. See for this interpretation of the concept of *Geselligkeit*: Simmel, 1984 (1917):53.

14 De Jaegher, 1989:3.

15 Peeters, 1995.

16 Peeters, 1984:33–4.

17 This may appear to be a personal argument against the conditioning of autistic youths in favour of a more humanistic approach towards them. However, that is not the position I want to argue here. The argument is that it is counsellors *themselves* who mention humanistic qualities as an indispensable and normal part of their job, and who perform such a humanistic approach in practice. Such humanist or moral concerns play an ambiguous role, however, as will be shown further on.

18 A psychological theory explaining difficulties in this respect presupposes a cognitive mechanism which makes people look for hidden meanings, intentions, etc., no matter what the exact nature of events one is confronted with. 'This is understandable if we assume that the attribution of states of mind is pervasive and compulsive' (Frith, 1993:46). Also see Sherry Turkles' (1986) book on this point, in which she describes how children attribute anthropomorphic characteristics to their computer, like for instance the ability to cheat.

19 Cf. Wittgenstein, 1994 (1953):126e/par. 420: 'But can't I imagine that the people around me are automata, lack consciousness, even though they behave in the same way as usual?—If I imagine it now—alone in my room—I see people with fixed looks (as in a trance) going about their business—the idea is perhaps a little uncanny. But just try to keep hold of this idea in the midst of your ordinary intercourse with others, in the street, say! Say to yourself, for example: "The children over there are mere automata; all their liveliness is mere automatism". And you will either find these words becoming quite meaningless; or you will produce in yourself some kind of uncanny feeling, or something of the sort. Seeing a living human being as an automaton is analogous to seeing one figure as a limiting case or variant of another; the cross-pieces of a window as a swastika, for example'.

20 Peeters, 1995.
21 For a more detailed analysis of the tension between humanistic and mechanistic extremes, as well as an evaluation of the moral costs and benefits of such a dualistic conceptualization, see Hendriks, submitted.
22 In its logocentrism such a point of view mirrors the deeply-rooted presumption that language speakers, members of the interpretative community, are primarily responsible for the way social order is accomplished. For a critique on the logocentric bias in mainstream social theory see Callon & Law, 1995.
23 Distance with respect to the interpretations of non-autistic members of the community under study is not as easily realized by a researcher who is, to a certain extent, familiar with the language and skills of the counsellors. Researcher and counsellors suffer the same handicap: both of them are (at least in this respect) 'too common'. If this is already true for members of the interpretative community at large (Peeters, 1994), it is even more of a problem for someone who used to work as a counsellor with autistic youths, as I did between 1984 and 1987. During the time I did my fieldwork I was continuously inclined to anticipate and take things for granted. When it comes to distancing oneself from a familiar perspective on events in the ward, it is not so much ordinary language speakers but autistic people who are, thanks to their impairment, in a relatively privileged position. Although their epistemological status is not unproblematic, autobiographical accounts by autistic people may contain a wealth of information about an autistic worldview. To mention only one of these: Grandin & Scariano, 1986. In an interview with Oliver Sacks, some years later, the (high-functioning) autistic Temple Grandin discusses her experiences in a non-autistic society: 'Most of the time', she says, 'I feel like an anthropologist on Mars', (Sacks, 1993:112). In this chapter I have chosen another method of distancing from familiar frames of reference, namely by magnifying the role of material objects.
24 As is illustrated, for instance, in the following quote: 'What you can see here is that the youths know already what's going to happen by sitting in a specific chair. Thus, sitting in the chair has a communicative meaning, much more than all the talking going around here'.
25 Actor-network theory provides some excellent examples of stylistic experiments with a naturalized use of, among others, the vocabulary of nature ('Forces'), which is meant to describe heterogeneous processes of ordering in a less logocentric, thus more symmetrical way. For actor-network accounts which have inspired me in giving a voice to the non-linguistic ways of ordering I have explored here, see, among others: Akrich & Latour, 1992; Callon & Law, 1995; and Latour, 1988a & 1988b.
26 On the other hand there is no need to exclude the possibility of correspondence either. To avoid confusion on this point, I have not made any use of autobiographical sources. One of these, however, I do not want to deny the reader, because it is particularly revealing in showing how an autistic person struggles with mechanical terms—trials of force and fragile connections—to get a hold on the nature of social relationships: 'I decided that getting along with people was like a sliding door. The door has to be approached slowly; it cannot be forced, otherwise, it will break. Relationships with people are the same way. If they are forced, the relationship doesn't work. One little shove can shatter everything' (Grandin & Scariano, 1986:124).
27 Stefan Hirschauer (1991, 1994) explores a comparable style in his analysis of a cultural practice like surgery. Stories of surgeons could be used to gain access to

the surgical form of life. Hirschauer takes a different stance. Instead of considering (self-)representations of surgeons as a representation of what they believe and intend to be revealed by sociology, he takes them literally: '[R]ealizing that there were no people in surgeons' descriptions of an operation, I took them at their words. The consequence of this hyper-realist reading was that I described an operation as an encounter of two bodies, consistently applying the surgeons' perspective to themselves. While surgeons look in the body for the anatomic images which have been made of it, I was looking in surgical practice for the descriptions surgeons made of it' (Hirschauer, 1994:342). A literal reading of texts on autism is possible a good candidate for simulating an 'autistic world', not only because of the *content* of these accounts. 'Autism' may also resonate in a *method* of 'taking literally'. Literal understanding is considered typical for the autistic syndrome (Van Berckelaer-Onnes, 1992).

28 For the relative methodological license of the stranger, see, for instance, Georg Simmel's (1908) 'Excurs über den Fremden': 'Die Einheit von Nähe und Entferntheit, die jegliches Verhältnis zwischen Menschen enthält, ist hier zu einer, am kürzesten so zu formulierenden Konstellation gelangt: die Distanz innerhalb des Verhältnisses bedeutet, dass der Nahe fern ist, das Fremdsein aber, dass der Ferne nah ist' (Simmel, 1908:509).

29 To paraphrase Annemarie Mol, 1993.

30 By the observer who is familiar with the ordinary concept of 'boredom' as well as with the estranging vocabulary in which it is conceptualized here. Also see Mol & Law (1994) for this point with regard to topological ordering. Mol and Law note that a description of spatial arrangements as a network-effect presupposes a regional topology: displacement in space is only *displacement* if it is seen from a regional point of view (p. 649). In the same way, an analysis of the production of temporal order as a network-effect presupposes familiarity with symbolic conceptions of time, if only having some bearings in order to recognize changes and stability in the progress and order of events. These strange forms of time are distortions of familiar concepts.

31 I hesitate to employ the verb 'has' here, because it suggests a gap between the subject (Robert) and his properties (a certain weakness) on the one hand, and the outside world (with straight angles, etc.) on the other. The vocabulary I am looking for here precisely tried to avoid such subject/object schemes familiar to non-autistic thought. In the same spirit, terms like 'fascination', 'inclination' or 'interest' should not be seen only as (subjective) psychological processes. For a very interesting study of these matters in the case of methadone, see the work of Gomart, 1997.

32 For a historical analysis of the way private and public are entangled in the development of the bathroom, and thus cannot be used as unproblematic analytic point of departure, see Benschop, 1992.

33 Power differences are here considered as network-effects. I will not treat these chapters extensively here, although they do get a short mention in the last section of the chapter. This surely does not do justice to this complicated matter, and may paint a rosy picture of the distribution of right of speech in matters of time. However, because of the point of this chapter—to question familiar (logocentric, interactionist) conceptualizations of ordering-power—I consider this imbalance to be justified.

34 The strength of the links between all the different parts is continuously tested. For instance when counsellors 'forget' to set the eggtimer. Normally Peter will

protest against this and the link between him and the eggtimer proves strong enough to get the counsellor back in line. This suggests that it is not in spite of a radical gap between linguistic and non-linguistic elements but because of the continuously tested and empirically established specificities and differences, that autistic youths, counsellors, eggtimers and others manage to attune to one another's performances and to accomplish a coherent temporal order.

35 Wittgenstein, 1980:18e.

36 Which is also the lesson which can be drawn from applying Collins' theory of morphicity (Collins, 1990; Collins & Kusch, forthcoming) on the residential care of autistic youths (Hendriks, submitted). However, because Collins' approach reifies the dualistic order of a human, socialized order (constituted by so-called polymorphic action) on the one hand, and a machine-like order (simulated by so-called mimeomorphic action) on the other, his theory seems to fit a logocentric dimension perfectly. As a consequence it is also prone to the shortcomings of concentrating exclusively on linguistic ways of ordering.

37 A risk of this approach is that it focuses on the bizarre, the pathological side of autistic persons to such an extent, that it will only enlarge the distance between us and them. On the other hand the whole point of this exercise (to confront the reader with an exaggeration of his/her own interpretation of an autistic world) is to make the (non-autistic) reader sensitive to the *shared* characteristics of autistic and non-autistic lives—an interface which risks to get overlooked by an unreflected focus on language and meaning.

38 Such a hyper-realistic magnification of 'what a handicap means' may possibly be used as a heuristic device to think about (coping with) handicapped lives in general. Such an exaggeration of an 'autistic world' need not be restricted to texts. In a faculty building of the University of Groningen (Netherlands) there is an elevator which contains a mechanism for wheelchair-users, which makes sure that the door remains open for about 15 seconds after opening it. The non-wheelchair-user entering the elevator is emerged by surprise in a *material magnification* of the 'handicapped' situation.

39 For language sets everyone the same traps, autistic people as well as social theorists. 'Which is why, though we cannot, to be sure, *say* very much about it, we do not wish to link a notion of agency to linguistic re-presentation. For signification—or so we have suggested—is more general than talk. It comes in all kinds of forms. And some, though only some, we can imagine. Others, no doubt, we will never know' (Callon & Law, 1995:503).

40 The concept of the script as it is developed by Akrich and Latour (1992) for technical devices and settings, may be a useful concept in this respect, which acknowledges the agency of non-human, non-socialized entities in the reconstruction of their context. The prescription of an artifact for instance, is defined as: 'What a device allows or forbids from the actors—humans and non-human—that it anticipates; it is the morality of a setting both negative (what it prescribes) and positive (what it permits)' (Akrich & Latour, 1992:261).

41 Notice that writing 'despite' is already to fall prey to a linguistic bias. It is precisely *because* of the pragmatically defined differences between eggtimers, counsellors and youths, that the fragile networks of temporal order may occasionally hold.

42 Also see Mol & Mesman, 1996.

43 Such a logo-centric legitimation in pleas for an adjusted, nonverbal, reductionist approach of handicapped persons, in which 'conversation' and 'communication'

Ruud Hendriks

remain the model for a meaningful way of sharing a form of life, is found in literature on handicaps in general. See, for instance: Goode, 1990 (esp. p. 30) and
Widdershoven, 1995 (esp. p. 29).
44 '[T]here are many other ways to delegate action than by speaking. And an ideal
community does not need to be a linguistic community. Delegates are there in
many forms and colours: angels, instruments, written pieces, machines, affec-
tions, goods, fictions' (Latour, 1995:33–4) (my translation).
45 Here I refer to the first and second motto of this chapter. Sinclair is a high functioning person with autism, asking us to question our assumptions. Callon &
Law make a plea for monstrous forms of re-presentation in case our and the
other's paths happen to cross.

References

Akrich, M. and Latour, B., (1992) 'A summary of a convenient vocabulary for the
semiotics of human and non-human assemblies' in E. Bijker and J. Law (eds)
Shaping technology/Building society; studies in socio-technical change, Cambridge,
Mass.: MIT Press, 259–64.
American Psychiatric Association, (1994) *Diagnostic and Statistical Manual of
Mental Disorders, Fourth Edition*, Washington, DC: APS.
Baron-Cohen, S., Leslie, A.M. and Frith, U., (1985) 'Does the autistic child have a
"theory of mind"?', *Cognition*, 21:37–46.
Benschop, R., (1992) *A room of his own; a history of the bathroom*, Leiden: Scriptie
RU.
Callon, M. and Law, J., (1989) 'On the construction of sociotechnical networks;
content and context revisited', *Knowledge and Society: Studies in the Sociology of
Science Past and present*, 8:57–83.
Callon, M. and Law, J., (1995) 'Agency and the hybrid *collectif*', *South Atlantic
Quarterly*, 94:481–507.
Collins, H., (1990) *Artificial Experts; social knowledge and intelligent machines*,
Boston, Mass.: MIT Press.
Collins, H., (1994a) 'Dissecting surgery: forms of life depersonalized', *Social Studies
of Science*, 24:311–33.
Collins, H., (1994b) 'Scene from afar (Reply)', *Social Studies of Science*, 24: 369–89.
Collins, H. and Kusch, M., (forthcoming) *Homo Artificiosus: how humans and
machines mix*.
de Jaegher, L., (1989) *Structuur en zichtbaar maken van verbanden bij de behandeling
van autistische personen*. Report.
de Vries, G., (1996) 'Should we send Collins and Latour to Dayton, Ohio?', *EASST
Review*, 14: 3–10.
de Vries, G., (1992) 'Consequences of Wittgenstein's farewell to epistemology' in
Dominique Pestre (ed.) *L'étude sociale des sciences—Bilan des années 1970 et 1980
et consequences pour le travail historique*, Paris: Centre de Recherche en Histoire
des Sciences et des Techniques, Cité des Sciences et de l'Industrie, 15–33.
Frith, U., (1993) (1989) *Autism; explaining the enigma*, Oxford: Blackwell Publishers.
Gomart, E., (1997) *Surprised by methadone*, paper presented at the WTMC
Winterschool, Leusden, February 1997.
Goode, D., (1990) 'On understanding without words: communication between a
deaf-blind child and her parents', *Human Studies*, 13:1–37.

Grandin, T. and Scariano, M.M., (1986) *Emergence; labelled autistic*, Novato: Arena Press.

Hendriks, R., (1994) 'Autisme: een mengeling van vreemd en vertrouwd', *Kennis en Methode*, XVIII:12–39.

Hendriks, R., (submitted) 'Eggtimers, human values and the care of autistic youths', submitted to *Science, Technology, and Human Values*.

Hirschauer, S., (1991) 'The manufacture of bodies in surgery', *Social Studies of Science*, 21: 279–319.

Hirschauer, S., (1994) 'Towards a methodology of investigations into the strangeness of one's own culture: a response to Collins', *Social Studies of Science*, 24:335–46.

Latour, B., (1988a) *Science in action; how to follow scientists and engineers through society*, Milton Keynes: Open University Press.

Latour, B., (1988b) *Irreductions*, published with *The Pasteurization of France*, Cambridge, Mass.: Harvard University Press.

Latour, B., (1995) 'De antropologisering van het wereldbeeld—een persoonlijk verslag', *Krisis*, 15:29–37.

Meire, M., (1994) 'Autisme; een muur van onbegrip', *Weekend/Knack*, 18, 4 May: 38–42.

Mesibov, G.B., (1986) 'A cognitive program for teaching social behaviors to verbal autistic adolescents and adults' in E. Schopler and G.B. Mesibov (eds) *Social behavior in autism*, New York and London: Plenum Press, 265–83.

Mesibov, G.B., (1992) 'Treatment issues with high-functioning adolescents and adults with autism' in E. Schopler and G.B. Mesibov (eds) *High-functioning individuals with autism*, New York and London: Plenum Press, 143–55.

Mol, A., (1993) 'Decisions no one decides about; anemia in practice', paper presented at *Ethics in the Clinic. An international conference on normative and sociological aspects of clinical decision making*, Universiteit Maastricht.

Mol, A. and Law, J., (1994) 'Regions, networks and fluids: anaemia and social topology', *Social Studies of Science*, 24: 641–71.

Mol, A., and Mesman, J., (1996) 'Neonatal food and the politics of theory: some questions of method', *Science, Technology, and Human Values*, 26: 419–44.

Nowotny, H., (1989) 'Social theory, time and human agency', paper prepared for the volume *Social Theory and Human Agency*, SCASS, 29 September–1 October 1989.

Peeters, T., (1984) *Uit zichzelf gekeerd; leerprocessen in de hulpverlening aan kinderen met autisme en verwante kommunikatiestoornissen*, Nijmegen: Dekker & Van de Vegt.

Peeters, T., (1994) *Autisme; van begrijpen tot begeleiden*, Antwerpen/Bussum: Hadewijch.

Peeters, T., (1995) Interview, Antwerp, 23 June, Antwerp: Opleidingscentrum Autisme.

Sacks, O., (1993) 'An anthropologist on Mars', *The New Yorker*, December 27:106–25. Also published in Sacks, O., (1995) *An anthropologist on Mars; seven paradoxical tales*, London: Picador, 233–82.

Schopler, E. and Mesibov, G.B., (eds) (1985) *Communication problems in autism*, New York and London: Plenum Press.

Simmel, G., (1984) (1917) *Grundfragen der Soziologie (Individuum und Gesellschaft)*, Berlin/New York: Walter de Gruyter.

Simmel, G., (1908) 'Excurs über den Fremden', *Soziologie; untersuchungen über die Formen der Vergesellschaftung*, Berlijn: Duncker & Humblot, 509–12.

Sinclair, J., (1992) 'Bridging the gaps: an inside-out view of autism (or, do you know what I don't know?)' in E. Schopler and G.B. Mesibov (eds) *High-functioning individuals with autism*, New York and London: Plenum Press, 294–302.

Turkle, S., (1986) *Het tweede ik: computers en de menselijke geest*, Groningen: Wolters-Noordhoff.

Widdershoven, G., (1995) *Principe of Praktijk; een hermeneutische visie op gezondheid en zorg*, inaugural lecture, Universiteit Maastricht, 14 November.

Wittgenstein, L., (1994) (1953) *Philosophical Investigations*, Oxford: Basil Blackwell.

Wittgenstein, L., (1980) *Culture and Value* , edited by G.H. Von Wright in collaboration with Heikki Nyman, translated by Peter Winch, Chicago: Chicago University Press.

Older people in hospital: the labour of division, affirmation and the stop

Joanna E. Latimer

Sister [moves over to patient's bedside and leans down] How are you feeling? Is your shoulder sore?
Mrs Weston . . . ? my leg.
Sister You got a bad knock yesterday—can you remember what happened?
Mrs Weston I was at the island and crossing the road when the car came and hit me . . . [inaudible] . . . I am usually so careful. I didn't see him.
Sister Ach, well, don't worry. [takes patient's hand].
Mrs Weston [goes on speaking I cannot quite hear. The doctors arrive at the bed].
Sister [turns away from the patient as the doctors arrive at the bed; the patient goes on speaking, turning to me]
Mrs Weston . . . and a policeman came over on the other ward but I—[Sister and the Doctors walk off to join the ward round].

Introduction

In what follows, division is not to be understood simply as the manufacture of hierarchies of difference which produce some hated, inferior and separate Other. Systems of distinction, as is increasingly acknowledged, keep in play and also help constitute, ideas of difference. But systems of distinction also keep in play the possibility *of* difference, in ways that may be overlooked, particularly where systems of distinction are deployed to institute *hierarchies* of difference. In this chapter, as in an earlier piece on the continuous 'constituting' of classes (Latimer, 1997a), I will argue that it is this possibility of keeping difference in play which affords the motility through which the maintenance of multiple identities is possible.

© The Editorial Board of The Sociological Review 1997. Published by Blackwell Publishers, 108 Cowley Road, Oxford OX4 1JF, UK and 350 Main Street, Malden MA 02148, USA.

In hospital work there is a more or less tacit division of labour in which nurses are 'supposed' to be friendlier and closer to patients than other hospital staff. Especially more junior nurses. Sisters and charge nurses may become hard-boiled and distant, and senior nurses (the Matrons of yesteryear) even more so. But, not so long ago, patients could have a laugh with nurses, make them a cup of tea, share a sandwich on the night shift. These are not just my memories of nursing, we see these alignments in popular and documentary representations of nurses, like the *Singing Detective*, *The English Patient* and the *National Health*.

Over an eight-month period my observations of conduct in an acute medical unit (Latimer, 1994), never included nurses and patients in such alignments. Rather than alignment, I found division. The division, constantly and incessantly being manufactured, managed and reproduced, was not between doctors and nurses, nor between staff and managers; at least not that I can find in my field notes. Instead, it lay between nurses and patients. This seems an anomaly because nurses are usually constituted—and constitute themselves—as the mediators or moderators between two social spaces which rely on an old division: the bedside, which entails an engagement with patients as sentient and experiencing embodied persons, and the distant work of the medical, exemplified by the ward round, through which the operation of the medical gaze anatomizes and heals the sick body. Nurses are usually seen as moving between these two networks, from the bedside to the ward round, like in the extract at the beginning of the paper, as at the same time they help hold them apart.

In the current setting, nurses do not hold these spaces apart, rather nurses hold older people at the threshold of both spaces. They do not just help keep the older person from participating in any authoritative way in the social space which is medicine, which is after all perhaps fairly standard in an acute medical setting, but, remarkably, they also do not even affirm the older patient as a person in the social space of the bedside. These observations contrast with more recent nursing discourse, which, drawing on notions of patient advocacy, figures nurses as helping to translate features of one network into the discourses of the other, and back again.

One explanation for this contrast may lie partly in the focus of the study. The focus of the study was people over the age of seventy-five: a category of patient made problematic through many interrelated and heterogeneous effects. This category is constituted through the literature in geriatric medicine, nursing and health service management as a special group: they are figured as the *very old*. As the very old they are figured as not only close to death, but as *slow* to recover from illness, or as likely not to recover *fully* at all and, thereby, to have residual and, critically, costly continuing needs. For the acute sector of the health services, with its increasing emphasis on throughput, very old people constitute a target to be managed: either they are to be kept out of the service altogether, with arguments such as that treatment and care would be futile, or, as once in, they are to be processed quickly, so that they do not block up the flow through the system (see Latimer, 1977a, b, in press and forthcoming).

My theme here develops from the idea that identity is constituted through processes of attachment and detachment, what others have referred to as 'extension' (Fernandez, 1986; Munro, 1996a; Strathern, 1991). These processes of extension are, however, also processes of inclusion and exclusion, through which categorizing and classifying are accomplished (Douglas, 1966; Douglas and Isherwood, 1980). Identity, as categories or classes of person or thing, is made up by being 'bodied forth' (Strathern, 1995), in such materials as a play of tropes in language (Fernandez, 1986) or a headdress composed of materials of exchange (Strathern, 1994). Older people, extended through notions of futility and closeness to death, can be excluded as inappropriate to a medical domain.

What I want to suggest, in the light of these ideas of extension, is that figuring older people as close to death but as possibly slow to die, brings to the surface a complicity between the division of labour on the one hand, including nurses' relative positions to other hospital workers, and the labour of division, as the continuous identity-work which nurses do, on the other. Patients and the labour of division around them and their care, emerge as both materials for production, aspects of which are divided amongst doctors, patients and nurses, as well as the materials of extension, through which both perform their participation as having multiple identities. And, critically, through these as multiple, motile and heterogeneous processes, many things remain the same, for example, the hierarchy of difference between divisions such as being old and being young, being a nurse and being a doctor.

Thus, an important aspect for the current study is the relationship between the nature of participation on the one hand, as a *labour* of division, the work of joining and rendering, dividing and distinguishing; and the affirmation of place or position on the other hand, conferred both through participation in the division of labour *and* through labouring division. However, in indexing one of the great social debates, I want to move beyond an exclusive focus on people. The processes to which I am drawing attention certainly entail encounters between people. But they also sustain and are sustained by encounters, between people and things (including language, bureaucratic proforma and other materials). This relationship between extension and the labour of division is explicated further in the next section through detailed discussion of a simple convention, knocking on the door.

Knocking on the door: redistributing the labour to affirm position

Raffel (1991), in discussing issues of justice, reworks Lyotard's example of the possibility of a (new) response to coming upon a closed door. Raffel sees Lyotard as suggesting that there could be a new convention: upon finding a closed door which a person wants to enter, s/he should say 'Open the door'. This, after all, is certainly an option and, perhaps, a better one than simply barging in on whoever has closed the door. But Raffel raises the traditional response of knocking on the door as a preferable alternative (not in each and every circumstance), to anyone interested in matters of justice. Rather than merely review Raffel's complex discussion, what I want to do here is to draw on his example of knocking on the door as a convention which, on analysis, is concerned with more than courtesy. It is concerned with encounters between people and how materials play a part in those encounters, to keep in play an undecideability over authority and the precise distribution of divisions.

The closed door can be considered as a division, constructed through an alignment between the person within, the intermediary (or door), and the person who wants the door open. The work done to accomplish the maintenance of, or change in, the door's status can be considered as 'labour'. The difficulty is over interpretation of the door's status, as either a barrier or an entrance. Simply entering treats the door as a barrier. The door is in the way and the person wishing to enter the room just removes it. On the other hand, calling out to open the door also treats the door as a barrier but commands the other person to open the door, through calling attention to the desires of the person wanting to enter the room.

The knock, as a convention, mediates in a number of different ways. Thus, the knock acts to minimize the intrusion. While the knock makes audible the possible wishes of the knocker, that they may want access to the room, to something in the room, or to the person in the room, it also constitutes a deferral in two senses. The knock defers entry (however momentarily), as well as deferring to the person on the other side of the door: by giving the person inside a chance to refuse to answer or the opportunity to open the door (they may be busy and ignore the knock, the knock gives them a moment to collect themselves, etc.). The knock, then, affirms the priority of the existing position, in this case that the person inside is assumed to have closed the door, and expects it to remain closed, unless *they* say something, or do something, which changes the status of the door. In this way, the intermediary (the closed door) and the convention for entry (the knock) conjoin together, to suggest the possibility that the person knocking cannot *know* for certain the situation of the person inside. This conjunction allows for ambiguity and ambivalence. Of course, there are different types of knocks: a peremptory rap on the door at three in the morning may announce to an armed robber the arrival of the police! But even so, it is interesting how the police do (apparently) knock before they break the door down.

Second, the knock affirms that both participants have *position*. As Raffel (p. 77) points out, Lyotard's alternative, the statement 'Open the door', simply realigns who has authority, where authority is constituted as the person who is allowed 'to determine what is expected'. If the convention of the knock is adhered to, then the person on the inside of a closed door is momentarily deferred to: they are figured as having some (temporary, provisional and partial) authority. I would like to suggest that what is attractive about the convention of knocking is that both people are implicated in determining whether or not access should be given (the door opened), and at what point. However, there is a further condition, as Raffel puts it:

> . . . in knocking even though the person without would normally at least have some desire to get in, we would say that instead of *him* saying that the door should be open, it is always left to the person within to fulfil this role (p. 77)

The example of the knock makes a string of connections: a convention, a complicity between the labour of division (the continued maintenance of the door's status) and the division of labour (who is responsible for doing what work—shutting, knocking and opening). And, importantly, there is the question of who or what has authority/responsibility, which seems to be constituted in relation to the tacit affirmation of position.

So the convention does more than keep the labour of division and the division of labour in play. It also intrudes a stop. To emphasize this point I shall go over the ground again. If the door stages a division, both parties, through a convention, are in play over its maintenance. While the situation is specific and local, there is also something larger going on, something to do with the way in which people relate to each other. Thus barging in, or even demanding that the door be opened, can seem offensive (not in all circumstances, of course). Not just because they may offend the sensibilities of the person who has closed the door, but because their option seems to stem from a desire to shift to another mode of authority, in which the person 'inside' becomes the agent of the person outside. But the difficulty here is that the person outside does not necessarily have the person inside, and their position, in mind (see also Strathern, 1988). These options therefore seem to position the person on the outside as singular and so sure of him/herself,to put him/herself at the centre of relations. Neither of these alternatives really allow for the possibility of uncertainty or ambivalence (over, for example, why the door has been closed in the first place). Only knocking gives to the other person, the person inside, the stop, and the door acts as the intermediary, the hinge upon which there is possibility for both to act with the other in mind. In this way the knock has something to do with affirmation. On the one hand the knock affirms the right of the door to be closed, it affirms that the person inside has position, over determining what is to be expected, and, therefore the knock can be ignored, or answered with a reply, such as 'I'm busy'.[1] But on the other hand it also affirms the position of the person on the outside, as it allows him/her to request entry, but tentatively and with regard.

In the following sections I present material to discuss the question of affirmation. In order to show how older people are placed in the social space of an acute medical setting, I analyse closely an example of one older person's attempt to participate in the labour of division. Through a series of conventions which parallel the different ways of attempting entry when coming upon a closed door, the patient attempts to participate in the labour of division, to contribute to the determination of what is expected, but through both mundane and subtle forms of displacement, involving not a door but bureaucratic forms and linguistic strategies as her extensions, the nurse sustains her alignment with authorities which lie outside her relation with the patient. The exchange can be considered 'a language game' (Lyotard, 1984), except that there are other materials providing the extensions through which each participant makes their moves. The effect is to position the patient in ways which lead to his remaining at the threshold, able only to confirm authorities which are coming from elsewhere.

Placement/displacement

The older people I encountered in the current study were placed according to staff's categorizing of them, which in turn affected the ways in which they were positioned, both literally and figuratively. To do their categorizing of patients, nurses and doctors drew upon and aligned heterogeneous materials. But patients did not participate in determining what was to be included or excluded, they did not authorize the making or unmaking of divisions, or the making up of ideas of difference. In order to keep patients in their place in this way, staff quite clearly also displaced them. Patients were moved about, both literally (for example, as they got better they were moved up the wards, away from the nurses' station and the 'centre') and figuratively. In a sense it was as if the older people were constantly kept at the threshold, outside the door; and at the threshold, in the 'in-between', it was easier for an exercise of power to take effect (Munro, 1996b).

One effect of staff's moves was to enlist the complicity of some older people in their displacement as full persons, to enrol them in the work of being made visible as medical objects. Where the older person was unable to respond and diminish themselves as a socially differentiated individual, that is, where they were unable to 'do' patient, their insistence on their socially differentiating extensions acted against them. Their insistence was read as a lack of control and co-operation, and, as such, could be read as signs that they were, indeed, too old to have a medical future. To have a future as a medical patient they also had to have a 'prospect ahead of them'; of a life, that is, not as too much of a burden on family and health and social services. Once assignable to the class of the decrepit, confused or demented, these older people were always at risk of having made available to staff the very materials that would accomplish their own disposal. So that staff, vigilantly surveying patients' conduct for signs (of any sort), could deploy these materials to shift explanations for an older person's troubles, and thereby alter their identity. These shifts were from medical grounds onto other grounds, which suggested, for example, that a patient's illness effects were psychosomatic in origin, or simply due to their extreme old age. Patients who persisted on performing their difference as persons, rather than diminishing their difference as individuals to be medically categorized, could be refigured as social, so that both they, and staff's responsibilities for them, were (partially) disposed of (Latimer, in press).

Critical to understanding how participants manage a labour of division is an examination of the precise and specific nature of how both placement and displacement affect movement, in objects as well as subjects. Some of the ways in which such movement was accomplished is presented in the excerpts that follow. In reading these excerpts, it is important to keep in mind that something had happened to each of the older people in the study fairly suddenly; that they were shocked and ill, sometimes very ill. And when they are ill, older people may be reminded of how close they are to death. But they were displaced in other ways. Not only were they being instructed as to how to conduct themselves, I want to suggest that they were being positioned in ways that gave them no 'stop' on the processes of identity-making, and no opportunity for affirmation.

Displacement

The following extracts are drawn from an encounter between an eighty-year-old gentleman, who had just been admitted to the ward from the Accident and Emergency Department (A&E), and a student nurse. According to the information sent from A&E the doctors think the patient probably has a urinary tract infection. He has had high fevers with shaking. I am calling him 'Major' because he was a professional services man of some rank and because he referred to himself by his title, it was one of his extensions. The nurse, on the other hand, did not introduce herself.

[Major Stevenson is in bed, lying fairly flat. Student Nurse goes to the side of the Patient with forms. She leans on the bedside locker to write, and turns to the patient when she speaks to him—she is standing above him—not close.]
Major Stevenson If you could—I am not sure if I have any money—but if you could phone my wife?

Student Nurse Right, what is the number?
Major Stevenson What?
Student Nurse What is the phone number?
Major Stevenson Oh, yes. It's [says phone number]. Tell her they've made a decision to keep me in, this hospital, ward 10.
Student Nurse Right—can I ask you a few questions first?
Major Stevenson Yes—certainly.
[Patient's mouth is terribly dry—he looks quite sallow and unwell]
Student Nurse What's your address, please? [**and so on, for demographic details.**]

The materiality of the nursing assessment form gives the nurse access to Major Stevenson. But the nurse and the patient are communicating in a very particular way. The patient, used to giving orders and being in authority, as he told me later, asserts himself at the beginning of the encounter, but in a way which is hesitant and has the nurse's agenda in mind: he knocks on the door—'If you could—I am not sure if I have any money—but if you could phone my wife?' The nurse acknowledges his request but *defers* it until later, and makes a move which asserts her work of asking questions is to come first. The precise move positions the patient: it puts Major Stevenson outside the labour of division, the authority for framing the situation is coming from elsewhere.

This deferral is critical and constitutes the first displacement. Major Stevenson's response—'Yes, certainly'—is not an affirmation, it is merely a confirmation, of the nurse extended through the forms, as aligned with bureaucratic authority.

Student Nurse Right, do you know why you were admitted?
Major Stevenson I'm not quite sure—I had these pains, and shaking yesterday, I thought [. . . ? his speech peters out].
Student Nurse . . . Do you take any medicines at all?
Major Stevenson They're all in there [points to plastic shopping bag on bed table. Student Nurse fetches bag and gives it to him. He takes out the tablets and reads off the labels to her].
[**This takes several minutes**]
Student Nurse That's OK—we can get the others later. How are you on your feet—any problems?
Major Stevenson Not really—OK—I get around.
Student Nurse Do you use a stick at all?
Major Stevenson Oh, yes.
Student Nurse How tall are you?

Major Stevenson About five foot five and half.
Student Nurse And what weight are you?
Major Stevenson About 9 stone.
Student Nurse Do you have any problems with your bladder?
Major Stevenson I'm always on the run. [smiles]
Student Nurse But that's because of your frusemide [a diuretic] isn't it [not a question]. How about your bowels?

[. . . And on until . . .]

Student Nurse Do you have any activities—what hobbies have you got?
Major Stevenson None now. I used to do a great deal of walking—up into the Moorlands and up North—can't do it now.
Student Nurse Do you have any social workers or home helps?
Major Stevenson No, we employ.
Student Nurse How often?
Major Stevenson Monday and today—she came in to do the ironing. Because my wife's like me—heart trouble.
Student Nurse [writes].

The interview can be seen as a series of moves in a language game (Lyotard, 1984), beginning with the first displacement, which holds Major Stevenson on the nurse's ground. The moves put a stop on the patient's attempt to participate in the work of instituting what has significance to imply that his meanings, his life-world and his experiences of illness are subordinate to, and can be set apart, as extraneous to the main work of the setting. For example, he says he just gets around with a stick and cannot go walking like he used to. Why this is or how this affects his life is not a ground which is explored by the nurse. Further, he and his wife have heart trouble, but how this affects him and his life is not pursued, even though they may be pertinent in an acute episode of illness. Indeed, the nurse does not pursue many of the patient's leads. His statement at one point—'I'm always on the run'—creates an aperture for an affirmation, but the nurse refuses the opening—'But that's because of your frusemide isn't it (not a question)'.

The implication is that, in some mysterious way, these 'facts' are telling her (or someone else) something about the patient. But the purpose of the nurse's questions remain hidden from Major Stevenson (and quite possibly from the nurse). This is the second displacement of interest. She does not allow him to participate in the production of significance, or in defining the grounds upon which any interpretation is made: she does not let him help translate these aspects of himself or his identity into understandings about him as a patient and his care. (And it has to be said that no-one else does at a later date.) She treats these aspects of his life and of his self as separate from each other and as matters of fact (see Raffel, 1979), and conducts the interview as if she is revealing the facts of the matter. She makes him do (a lot of) work in revealing the matters of fact, like reading off the drugs for her. The key to the significance of these matters of his self and his identity is held elsewhere: they are simply data, which the nurse is collecting, to be consumed by others.

> **Student Nurse** If we need to get in touch with your wife—I'm going to give her a ring just now—but if we needed her in the night is that the right . . . ? [pointing to the number he has already given to her]
> **Major Stevenson** Yes.
> **Student Nurse** I'll just do your blood pressure and pulse.
> **Major Stevenson** I would like a drink of some kind.
> **Student Nurse** I'm sorry?
> **Major Stevenson** I would like a drink of some kind. I'm very dry.
> **Student Nurse** Right. [Continues to write. She turns to the patient holding nameband] I need to put this band on to tell who you are, and your date of birth. And I'll check with the doctor if it's all right for you to have something to drink. [puts nameband on]
> **[puts on nameband etc.]**
> [N.B. Approximately one and a half hours later the patient is given a drink and is told by both the doctor and the Staff Nurse that he must drink as much as possible].

Towards the end of the interview Major Stevenson breaks in again, and says he would like a drink. This is more than a knock, it is a statement which attempts to realign the position, and authorize, by drawing attention to self. It is not a strong move, it is not as strong as the command, 'open the door', but it is an assertion of desire, which would normally be difficult to refuse (as refuted—desires, like feelings, cannot be checked!). But even this cannot put a stop on the nurse. In an echo of the beginning of the interview the nurse indicates she did not hear, so Major Stevenson repeats his request and this time gives an account of his request. So now there is a critical difference: at the beginning of the encounter he did not *justify* his request for his wife to be informed of his admission, but he does justify his request for a drink. The earlier deferral of his request, a

deferral to other orders than those agreed between the two participants, and the following procedure appears to have produced an
important effect: a shift over what can be taken as self-evident or
common-sense, so that an account becomes necessary. His justifica-
tion for wanting a drink, that he is very dry, indicates how he is
now ready *to explain himself*. But the account he gives, holds his
concerns on grounds which have it seems, little authority. Being dry
holds his concern on grounds which are only related to his own
senses, and to his experience of his body, not, as it emerges in the
current setting, a discourse with much authority.

Then comes the third interesting displacement worth noting. The
nurse once again defers Major Stevenson's request, first to put the
name band on, and then she, in her account, establishes a new
aspect of the order of things—Major Stevenson, like her, 'needs'
permission from the medical staff before he can have a drink. This
hierarchy and division of labour helps her to rank his wants, and to
relay how the permission which Major Stevenson requires of the
nurse also has to originate from elsewhere. The nurse in her coun-
termove draws on the notion that she is merely a conduit. This
effacement is a realignment that helps put a stop on his move to
authorize his wants and needs. Her alignment with sources of permission, which lie at a distance to the encounter, helps to align her
with a network in which there are authoritative discourses, and persons sanctioned to draw upon these. Through these processes of
extension her identity as a member is marked, as at the same time
her continued legitimate participation in the labour of division is
sustained. Major Stevenson is kept at the threshold: he is not permitted to determine or mediate the nurse's response, because he
does not have the authority to legitimate his thirst *as a need* to
which the nurse should respond: a drink requires authorization
from someone else, someone with *authority*. In this way discretion
is transmitted, to someone/thing outside the space of the interaction.

What I want to draw attention to is how this displacement helps
accomplish the exclusion of Major Stevenson as a member: he is
positioned through displacement to confirm the particular forms of
division, but he is not invited to participate in the labour which, in
deploying systems of distinction, produces and reproduces divisions, in this case the divisions between patients and staff, experts
and lay people, medical and social needs. Through fracturing
Major Stevenson into aspects of himself, his life-world is surveyed
and rendered. As an individual, he is reduced to a set of traits and

284

parts, and the composition of his identity is to be determined in terms of drugs, diet, mobility, allergies etc. And, as an individual, an experiencing subject, he has no other authority to contribute to this labour of division, except as a witness. As a witness, he is called upon merely to attest. He can only confirm the grounds upon which his identity as a patient is being rendered.

The nurse's conduct helps as well as many other features of the setting (see Latimer, forthcoming) relay to Major Stevenson his position, and hers. She is aligned with other authorities, not with him. She is a conduit through which the network flows to the bedside. There is no even momentary let up, no moment in which they come together to refigure the bedside as alternative or complementary, and affirm their mutual belonging. His understanding of her moves, accomplishes the institution of a particular form of relationship between him and staff. He is self-disciplined and trusting enough to take the instruction and 'do' (Garfinkel, 1967) patient, to be patient.

In summary, what I have covered here are some of the important aspects of one version of the labour of division: there are people who make moves to claim the authority to make things significant, or figure themselves as the conduits through which authority flows. Their authority in the present case is not as individuals, but is deeply involved in matters of discourse, where discourse helps provide the grounds upon which significances can be constituted. And why not? This is a hospital, after all, and the purpose here is to identify the cause and cure of ill-health. Let's not get romantic ideas about consensus, or letting patients collaborate in care planning. The reader should not make the mistake here of expecting staff to treat patients as centres of discretion (Munro, 1997). The implicit assumption is that staff would be there all day, having to persuade. But what is important is to emphasize the position that older people were put in, as only able to confirm others' renderings of them.

Confirming/affirming: an idea of difference

What emerges from the extract analysed above, is an example of how the older people in the study were positioned so that they did not authorize the grounds upon which their identity or their needs were constituted. The precise method may vary, but the effects were systematic and relentless. Instead of alignments which were affirming, older people were involved in confirming or ratifying their continued identification as belonging to a category. So they were put (and they were, as we have seen with Major Stevenson, implicated in the putting) in a weak position. As Isaacs (1976), a very highly regarded British geriatrician suggested, older people are positioned to 'take what they can get'.

There is, then, a difference to which I want to point: a difference between affirming a patient as a member (of the hospital, etc.) who can participate as an authority in the labour of division, to affect and determine what is to be expected, and affirming them as, at least, sentient, as beings. In the present study older people, as patients, do not enter into the labour of division at all. Or rather they enter in a peculiar and mediated way. They are left to confirm or ratify the grounds upon which others make their moves to divide up and reorder the world. Perhaps, this is hardly surprising given earlier attention to such well-accepted theories as 'disengagement'.[2] But it is surprising in the context of nursing.

It is already a truism demonstrated in the endless sociological analyses of medical encounters that patients are not there really to participate in the labour of division in the narrow sense of diagnosis and treatment. But what is remarkable in the current context is that they were excluded from other forms of sociality, which I have been referring to as the social space represented in the narrative of 'bedside care'. Instead, what emerges is the extraordinary language games patients are forced to engage in, even at the point of being very ill.[3]

I would like to suggest that affirmative encounters are akin to some conventions, like the knock on the door, they affirm position and minimize intrusion, and affirm relative positions of authority. Indeed, at best, both participants are affirmed as members *even* as they labour divisions. Questions arise then over the matter of the stop: the intermediaries which help to affirm and realign authority (a door, a convention, or other materials, desires and devices) which help halt a displacement, and hence 'cut the network' (Strathern, n.d.).

Cutting the network

The hospital I studied was not a complete desert. During their interviews with me, two of the Staff Nurses talked about a patient that the medical staff had decided 'not to treat'. The nurses had been consulted for their 'opinion' as to how this patient should be managed. There appears to have been some division amongst the nurses and between some of the nurses and the doctors. This was the only occasion in the study that such a division became explicit.

Both these nurses were against the decision not to treat this patient because they felt that the medical staff had made their decision based upon their assessment of the patient's 'quality of life', when the medical staff, they felt, were not in a position to judge this. They said that they were in a better position to judge a patient's quality of life. Here, one of the Staff Nurses is talking about this patient, Mona:

> **Staff Nurse** . . . I can appreciate that it is a very difficult decision [not to treat the patient with anti-biotics] but, em. I don't feel that—the medical staff were saying that she had no quality of life etc., but I feel that I don't think it's up to them to decide, in her case, and I think that em, I feel that she should have been treated.
>
> **Researcher** When you say quality of life with Mona, you think she's go . . . , her quality of life warrants her to continue to be treated. How do you know that?
>
> **Staff Nurse** Well, for a start I think she was happy enough. She, I think she was quite content, maybe you or I or one of the doctors wouldn't be happy sitting in a chair in a ward all day and probably having to go into some sort of an institution for the rest of your life but I don't think, em, in her case, I don't think she would have minded that. And I feel that, I just feel that she should have been treated, I don't think the medical staff ever saw her as we did either, like, em, one of them said yesterday, she was shouting out quite distressed yesterday and I sort of went in, and asked for her to written up for opiates, and he said, 'Oh yes, that's the first time I've heard her even speak, she's just sat there mute for six months.' And I said, 'That's rubbish, she has not.' He says, 'Oh, she just used to sit there and stare into space the whole time.' I says 'Well, you don't know her very well then'.

From Staff Nurse's talk here she is associating 'quality of life' with how a person feels about their life—'happy enough', 'content'—and with what *their experience* is of their situation—'maybe you or I or one of the doctors wouldn't be happy . . . but I don't think she would have minded that'. The question arises is how did Staff Nurse know how Mona felt, or how did she think she knew? Staff Nurse draws on the idea that she experienced the person 'Mona', that by being with and seeing her in a certain way, Staff Nurse has constructed her identity in relation to something other than medical or nursing discourse.

Staff Nurse goes on to mention how the doctors have allowed their understanding that Mona's family could not take her home, to influence their decision:

> **Staff Nurse** . . . and I think what annoyed me more than anything else, was the fact that they said they were going to stop them [the anti-biotics] because she had poor home circumstances and her family couldn't take her home, and I don't think you should base your criteria on whether to treat somebody or not on what sort of home circumstances they have. The way they were saying was almost as if she had had a caring family that were willing to take her home then they would have carried on the anti-biotic treatment.

What emerges in Staff Nurse's talk here is that there is a complicit medical and managerial social space in which the patient becomes disposable. On this occasion at least, it is not one she is prepared to collude in. She is aligning herself with Mona, not just as a patient, but as a person with feelings.

The second Staff Nurse also talked about Mona. She also says that the decision had partly been made because Mona had nowhere to go:

> **Staff Nurse** Yes, because her quality of life was actually quite good. I mean I'm not one for treating people whose quality of life is poor, you know, but I, em, I thought her quality of life was really. Maybe, what, six weeks ago she was very, she seemed happy within herself and although she was a blocked bed, which is what they're probably thinking about, her quality of life was good, and I don't think we had the right to turn round and say you know 'tough, you've got a chest infection, tough . . . we're going to let you linger and linger and linger'.

This Staff Nurse is also stating that she knew what Mona felt like 'within herself', that she was 'happy'. This is her criterion for judging that Mona's 'quality of life was actually quite good'. Staff Nurse also brings into play the notion that she believes or suspects that the medical staff are allowing the fact that Mona is going to be difficult to move on to inform their decision about Mona: 'she is a blocked bed'. Staff Nurse is not as annoyed at this aspect as the first Staff Nurse, her own use of metonymy here indicates that she can understand how this would be taken into account: Mona is reducible to the status of her bed-state. But what this Staff Nurse sees as the problem is one of communication with the doctors—that they did not *know* Mona as well as the nurses did, they had not experienced Mona the 'person', and yet they did not take into account the view of people who did know, the nurses:

Staff Nurse Because we know Mona better. The way that they can assess quality of life from the end of the bed is different from the way that we can assess quality of life, when we see her at half ten at night sitting down in the day room having a really good chat and a joke, she's a very, very witty lady, you can enjoy her company.

Both nurses feel able to judge someone's quality of life because they feel that they know the patient as a person and that this is somehow important. The difference arises through their accounts of their proximity to the patient. Proximity seems to have two senses for them: first, a literal one ('at the end of the bed' etc.); and second, a discursive one, in the way that categories frame the person as an object for the medical gaze (*or*, left as merely a person, 'you' are seen as a potential 'bed-blocker'). The nurses are arguing that doctors are attempting to assess quality of life 'from the end of the bed', while the nurses are closer to the patient, they experience her in the everyday life-world of the ward. They are putting forward notions of a different social space to that sustained through the medical gaze: the one of bedside care. This is affirming in a different way to that of being included in medical categories through the operations of the ward round.

Nurses in the current study do not usually count their feelings about patients as persons in any way relevant to their assessment of patients. In stark contrast to the episode with Major Stevenson, Mona's difference, and her worth, is being constituted through figuring her as a feeling subject, to whom the nurses respond. Mona has come to matter in her relationships as *someone*, who makes others laugh, and with whom one can have a chat. A critical aspect of their talk here is that neither Staff Nurse mentions what, if anything Mona had said about her situation—there is a sense in which she has not participated as an authority, her difference they are saying is being marked through their experience of her. Mona is not being included as an authority in any obvious sense, she is not a participant in the labour of division constituted as the work of determining what is to be expected. But she is being affirmed, as

289

participant in other ways, in what would commonly be called the 'social life' of the ward, or community. It is her humanity which they are stressing, and which they say the doctors could not see because they were 'too far'.

The Staff Nurses are both expressing how they attempted to cut the network, a complicit medical and managerial alignment, which was attempting to dispose of Mona, by putting into play notions of Mona as a person in relation to a community. They align them-selves with her to do this. But it didn't work, Mona was not treated and she died, quite slowly. After all, these were only staff nurses, even they do not have much authority in the current setting, and the discourses which they are drawing upon to review Mona's iden-tity had little weight, in a similar way to the ways in which Major Stevenson cannot authorize his needs through reference to how he feels (thirsty). At least, however, the nurses here appear to be affirming Mona's identity as a participant in community, and as a being with whom they relate in particular ways. They are still engaged in the heroic narrative of saving a life, but they are draw-ing on different materials of extension to do this. But, Mona was only fifty-four, she was not old. Against the group of patients I focused on in the study, she was comparatively young. It is signifi-cant that in their interviews with me, these nurses, to perform their distinct identity as different from doctors, draw upon a case of a younger person for their materials of extension. This I take to be just one of the ways in which being old is consistently and relent-lessly degraded as a category of person in nurses' labour of division.

The heroic and the mundane

Universities and hospitals are currently being imagined as orga-nized around delivery to groups. This is one aspect of the division of labour which is linked to the labour of division: as Goffman (1961) points out, through these groupings, persons being delivered to are reduced to 'blocks', a mass of similar attributes which can be delivered to en masse. Delivery is accomplished through routines, except in relation to specific *individual* differences (digoxin rather than an anti-biotic, a special diet rather than the trolley meal, a help wash rather than a bed bath). Individuality is ascertained as variations on a theme. Nor, within such a labour of division, is there a need for the participation of those being delivered to. As we have seen in the case of Major Stevenson, divisions are instituted through 'gaze', and other orders and organizational devices, so that patients in the division of labour, and the labour of division become materials for extension.

As much as such processes may tread on someone's sensibility, they presumably suffer them for all sorts of reasons. But people also work hard to find moments to reaffirm their sense of identity as, if not invested with authority, as at the very least human, or sentient, or belonging in some diffuse way. Relatives bring in favourite drinks, photos of loved ones are placed on lockers, nurses and patients come together in moments of exchange, humour and empathy ('What a pretty nightie, is it from Marks?'; 'Yes, my daughter brought it for me'). It may be in these incredibly mundane moments that these other, less heroic (perhaps) forms of affirmation consist.

As Featherstone (1992) and others suggest, it is not just through the narratives of the heroic life that meaning gets constituted. Meaning is also constituted through the little discontinuous acts of the everyday. And, as I said at the beginning of the chapter, it is traditionally nurses who provide some of this labour, but not as emotional labour (Hochschild, 1984). Rather (momentary and temporary), alignments with patients were the extensions which provided some of the marks of nurses' own, distinctive identity. The difficulty in the present context, stated at the beginning of the chapter, is the absence of such moments between nurses and the older patients in the study.

Let's revisit Major Stevenson and the student nurse and try to rewrite their scripts in a way that seems less incarcerating and illustrates the sort of thing that I mean:

Major Stevenson If you could—I am not sure if I have any money—But if you could phone my wife?
Student Nurse Of course, let me write down the 'phone number.
Major Stevenson Oh, yes. It's [says phone number]. Tell her they've [we've?] made a decision to keep me in, this hospital, ward 10.
Student Nurse Right—she must be worrying about you, I'll just get the trolley phone and you can speak to her yourself. Then I'll ask you a few questions.
Major Stevenson No, you ring, then you can tell her what's going on—I haven't a clue and I'm exhausted.

This conversation is unimaginable in the setting. I am not sure if I can get over to the reader just how impossible it would have been for a nurse and one of the subjects of the study to have had such an *exchange*. I would like to call this exchange affirmatory: both actors *for a moment* belong in ways to make a mutual centre, a space, however contrived and temporary, in which they are momentarily undivided. They are not knocking on the door because the door is not closed. But they are feeling the way. Neither is taking a line of authority over the other. Neither knows for sure. But both have position, and regard, for the other: there is trust and tact, so that both can intrude stops and starts, both can mark and mediate division and difference.

The extent to which this, or any sort of mundane celebration of belonging was systematically absent from relations between the older people and nurses was astonishing. Nurses either blocked access or, where there appeared to be such moments, on closer analysis they turn out to be reproducing the disciplined space operated by nurses, but in which some patients are also to some extent complicit. For example, at first glance in the extract at the beginning of the chapter Sister seems to be being solicitous, but on analysis it appears that Sister is checking up on the patient. Her questions are all directed by some purpose: is the shoulder sore—Sister is assessing the amount and type of analgesia Mrs Weston needs; can she remember what happened—Sister is assessing her mental state. Sister is bringing to the bedside the medical gaze extended through managerial concerns about throughput to include the surveillance of the patient and their life for signs of potential blockage to her disposal and the flow. At the bedside, in her interrogation of the patient she extends the network, and her alignment with the doctors, there is no cut. This is emphasized as she walks off with the doctor to join the ward round, leaving Mrs Weston droning on about what had happened and how she feels: Sister does not bother to mark the break, the division, as she leaves one space to re-enter another, because there is none.

The able older people in the study, like Major Stevenson, were partly reacting to moves: they participated in the authoring of categories, but only in a partial and prefigured way. Rather than repositioning others or affirming the grounds upon which their identities were constituted, they were left to *prove* themselves 'response-able' (Minkler, 1995). They were not able to call others to account or even affirm the accounts of others: they were the ones who were doing the background accounting work to justify the grounds others positioned them on. The able older people drew on cultural notions of responsibility and self-determination, resignation and

attributions of rationality (McHugh, 1970) to distinguish themselves as response-able. These were just some of their extensions.
This was no small matter. It was the older person's very ability to
respond to staff's moves, and diminish themselves, through which
they were able to demonstrate that they were response-able, that
they were still not in-human, even if they were less than full persons. Through these extensions, older people were read by staff as
still not quite geriatric, as still (partially and precariously, at least)
not quite fully disposable. So that staff's interpretations of the 'illness' effects the older person displayed could be held on legitimate,
medical grounds, rather than other (eg 'social', or 'psychological')
grounds.

In analysing older people's own discourses, it emerged that for
them it was in their interest to keep face through being constituted
as legitimately ill. Illness and disablement legitimated by the medical excuses and justifies, it is quite simply respectable, and it will
help 'in' hospital. But it doesn't necessarily carry with it any position: as stressed earlier, being constituted as medical does not give
membership, and the authority to participate in the labour of division.

Discussion

There are several matters to discuss as to why nurses in the current
study are dealing with older people in the ways that they are. I have
already discussed how older people are a marked category in health
service work, because they can block the flow through the beds. But
there are further complex divisions being laboured in the present
setting which are critical to the reproduction of the social spaces
with which we are concerned, the space at the bedside, representing
care, and the space on the ward round at the end of the bed, representing the heroic project of the medical gaze.

Nurses work both in and between these two divided spaces, but
the legitimation for the care a nurse gives at the bedside flows out
of the labour of division on the ward round. At the bedside the
patient is her supplement, and her work is complementary to the
doctor's work, while on the ward round she is the doctor's supplement. However, this situation relies on the patient providing the
appropriate materials for her extension, as both the doctor's supplement and in her own relation to the patient as his complement:
in the current setting there is something about the older patients

and something about the nurses which makes the encounter of one by the other an occasion for a division.

I think this is partly to do with the failing status of age in contemporary societies, but it is also to do with how older people are figured as having illness which is chronic and possibly incurable, but which is not necessarily fatal. This means that all sorts of non-medical aspects of older people have to be brought into the purified medical space of the ward round (such as Major Stevenson's wife's health, or Mrs Weston's capability in respect of crossing the road, to name but a few). It is not just that staff have not got time for these matters, rather it is that they are, in the division with which we are concerned, simply polluting. The older person's proximity to death (but without the dignity of their actually being in the process of dying) drags the mundane work of the functional and social aspects of patients' lives into the foreground, over-shadowing the potentially heroic work of nurses. So that older people are not interesting as a treatment space, an object of cure, and in the current setting, it is only as such an object that they can really be legitimated for nurses as subjects worth caring about.

Conclusions

In the current study it appears that patients and staff are together engaged in authoring identity but that there are particular conditions of possibility under which participants are authoring self: following Foucault, authorship is itself both a reiteration and a response. There are methods which do not need to coerce, for they already prescribe.

The older patients in the present study do not affirm, they merely show themselves to be response-able to others' moves. However, throwing light on what constitutes these conditions is a lot easier than changing them. While Lyotard's (1984) work indicates the possibility of moving others through changing the grounds upon which matters are being constituted, he also demonstrates that this is easier said than done. In a language game reacting is not enough—there is only confirmation of the other's grounds. The older people, prefigured as they are, are not in a position to be key players in the labour of division. Rather, they are configured as material to be worked on.

In this particular hospital setting, nurses themselves seem to be complicit in keeping older people at the threshold. There is a strange perversion of an old division of labour: nurses' observations of patients as persons are deployed, sure enough, but not to affirm the older person as belonging to the world of the human; instead, they are used to help keep in play possibilities for the older person's identity to be shifted, from inclusion in categories appropriate to an acute medical ward, to inclusion in categories such as geriatric or social. Ironically it is frequently the machines, the so-called non-human, which, temporarily, are able to confirm the older person as medical, and as an appropriate patient, and in this limited sense of inclusion, as human.

The explanation for the desert is complex and relates perhaps to how nurses are busy doing other identity-work, concerned with marking themselves, not just as the conduits of authority but as having their own authority as professionals. Keeping older people at the margins of the centre may help them centre themselves. Aligning themselves with patients as persons is a risky business, and is very different from observing patients for signs of being persons to help accomplish their disposal as non-medical. These divisions are the stuff of everyday life in hospitals, they help keep the flow moving as well as help mark the identity of those working in them as experts with special sight. Nurses may have been participating in and accomplishing these divisions as a show of their own connections and to help affirm their own identity. And maybe it is also to do with wider societal relations, in which older people are figured quite simply as at the threshold, and as in-between, work and dependency, life and death.

I have raised the question of the stop and of cutting the network, to show that, in the case of older people, putting a stop on their exclusion involves more than inclusion in decision-making, as it is commonly flagged up. It requires a mutual sense of belonging in a much wider sense. This, however, is deeply problematic in the current context and depends upon the nature of the network. The difficulty is that even the various conventions cannot cut the network. Conventions, like the knock on the door, emerge not as immutable but as translatable. In their deployment and translations there may be further material for reaffirming or, more likely, there will be material for extension for those in a position to position others, and act as if there is no stop.

Joanna E. Latimer

Notes

1 It should be noted at this point that for deaf older people, a system could be fitted by the door, involving a button, an electric circuit and strategically placed bulbs, so that, to take the place of a knock, when the button is pressed red bulbs light up. My point here is that there may be different intermediaries required to assist people with particular disabilities to help give them the authority to participate in the labour of division. Ruud Hendriks in his chapter (this volume) exemplifies this very well.

2 Hazan (1994) describes disengagement theory, which has dominated gerontology, as follows: disengagement theory 'defied the conventional notion that the apparently universal marginality of the aged is a result of pressures on them and contrary to their desires by proposing successful ageing as contingent upon the mutual disengagement of the aged and their social environment. According to the theory, disengagement takes place at three levels: on the general societal level, the presence of the aged is redundant and disturbing. The social system is impeded in its operation by the presence of elements whose sudden and final departure from it might cause dramatic disruption. In these circumstances, social forces preempt the rupture by expelling elderly people from the social world. . . . On the second, behavioural level, disengagement strikes the desired balance between expectations and ability. As the aged's control of society diminishes, expectations of them must be adjusted. Mutual disengagement allows for the reorganization of resources to meet personal needs and social imperatives. On the third level, disengagement allows the aged to prepare for death . . . and the smooth path towards their inevitable demise. Detachment proceeds from the outer circles of social involvement, such as family, and the force that motivates and regulates it is inherent to the individual' (pp. 45–6). Neat isn't it: what about raging against the dying of the light?

3 The extent of and ridiculousness of this work resonates well with a moment in *The English Patient*, when the hero emerges from a three day walk in the desert, having left his injured lover in a dark cave, desperately seeking some form of transport to rescue her, only to come across members of the British army filling in forms.

References

Douglas, M., (1966) *Purity and Danger. An analysis of the concepts of pollution and taboo*, New York: Ark Paperbacks.
Douglas and Isherwood, (1980) *The world of goods: Towards an anthropology of consumption*, Harmondsworth: Penguin.
Featherstone, M. and Hepworth, M., (1991) 'The mask of ageing and the postmodern lifecourse' in M. Featherstone, M. Hepworth and B.S. Turner, *The Body. Social Process and Cultural Theory*, London: Sage.
Featherstone, M., (1992) 'The Heroic Life and Everyday Life', *Theory, Culture and Society*, 9(1):159–82.
Fernandez, J.W., (1986) *Persuasions and Performances. The Play of Tropes in Culture*, Bloomington: Indiana University Press.
Garfinkel, H., (1967) *Studies in Ethnomethodology*, Englewood Cliffs, NJ: Prentice-Hall Inc.

Goffman, E., (1961) 'On the Characteristics of Total Institutions' in P. Worsley (ed.) (1978) *Modern Sociology*, Harmondsworth: Penguin.

Hazan, H., (1994) *Old Age. Constructions and Deconstructions*, Cambridge: Cambridge University Press.

Hochschild, A.R., (1983). *The Managed Heart. Commercialisation of Human Feeling.* Berkley: University of California Press.

Isaacs, B., (1976) 'We make moulds and pour old people into them', *Occupational Therapy*, July, p. 171.

Latimer, J., (1994) *Writing Patients, Writing Nursing: The Social Construction of Nursing Assessment of Elderly Patients in an Acute Medical Unit*, PhD Thesis: University of Edinburgh.

Latimer, J., (1997a) 'Giving Patients a Future: the constituting of classes in an acute medical unit', *Sociology of Health and Illness*, 19(2):160–85.

Latimer, J., (1997b) 'Figuring Identities: older people, medicine and time' in A. Jamieson and C. Victor (eds) *Critical approaches to ageing and later life*, Milton Keynes: Open University Press.

Latimer, J., (in press) 'The Dark at the Bottom of the Stair: participation and performance of older people in hospital', *Medical Anthropology Quarterly*.

Latimer, J., (forthcoming) 'Organizing context: Nurses' assessments of older people in an acute medical unit', *Nursing Inquiry*.

McHugh, P., (1970) 'Commonsense conceptions of deviance', in H.P. Dreitzel (ed.) *Recent Sociology*, No. 2, New York.

Minkler, M., (1995) *Critical Perspectives on Ageing: New Challenges for Gerontology*, Opening Plenary, British Society of Gerontology Annual Conference, Keele University.

Munro, R., (1996a) 'The Consumption View of Self: extension, exchange and identity, pp. 248–73, in S. Edgell, K. Hetherington and A. Warde (eds) *Consumption Matters, The Productivity and Experience of Consumption* The Sociological Review Monograph, Oxford: Blackwell.

Munro, R., (1996b) *Complexity and post-structuralism: a tale of two monsters*, Presentation at the Workshop, *Complexity*, Centre for Social Theory and Technology, Keele University.

Munro, R., (1997) *Power, Conduct and Accountability: re-distributing discretion and the technologies of managing*, Proceedings, 5th Interdisciplinary Perspectives On Accounting Conference, Manchester: Manchester University.

Lyotard, J.F., (1984) *The Post-modern Condition: A report on knowledge*, Manchester: Manchester University Press.

Raffel, S., (1979) *Matters Of Fact*, London: Routledge and Kegan Paul.

Raffel, S., (1991) *Habermas, Lyotard and the Concept of Justice*, Basingstoke, Macmillan.

Strathern, M., (1988) *The Gender of the Gift*, Berkeley: University of California Press.

Strathern, M., (1991) *Partial Connections*, Maryland, USA: Rowman and Littlefield Publishers Inc.

Strathern, M., (1994) 'Pre-figured features: A view from the Papua New Guinea Highlands' in J. Woodall (ed.) *The Visual Construction of Identity*, Manchester: Manchester University Press.

Strathern, M., (1995) *The Relation. Issues in Complexity and Scale*, Cambridge: Prickly Pear Press.

Strathern, M., (n.d.) Cutting the network.

Notes on contributors

Ruth Benschop is doing her PhD at the Theory and History of Psychology Department, University of Groningen in the Netherlands. Her research can be summed up at an historical exploration of instruments in experimental psychology. She is particularly interested in the scattered ways in which instruments function. In relation to this she is also interested in the various roles mundane materials perform in experimental psychology.

Steven D. Brown is a lecturer in social and organizational psychology at Keele University and a member of the Centre for Social Theory and Technology. He has published articles on critical social psychology, STS and organization studies. His research interests include the role of carrying out work (around Groupware and the mediation of memory) as part of the ESRC's Virtual Society programme.

Robert Cooper is Professor of Social Theory and Organization and Director of the Centre for Social Theory and Technology at Keele University. His current research is in cultural cybernetics, knowledge and imagination, and modern art as a form of social commentary.

Karen Dale works in the Industrial Relations and Organizational Behaviour Group at Warwick University and has previously worked in the NHS and local government. She has published on gender and equal opportunities and is currently writing a book on the body and organization theory.

Ruud Hendriks is at the University of Maastricht where he is finishing his PhD. He was trained as a counsellor in a residential institution for mentally handicapped and autistic young people and has studied health sciences. He is an editor of *Kennis en*

Method (Knowledge and Method: Journal for Empirical Philosophy).

Kevin Hetherington is a Lecturer in Sociology at Brunel University. He has written on spatiality, identity, museums and material culture. Recent books include *Consumption Matters* (co-edited with Stephen Edgell and Alan Warde, Blackwell, 1996), *The Badlands of Modernity* (Routledge, 1997). Forthcoming books include: *Expressions of Identity: Space and the Politics of Identity* (Sage, 1998), and *New Age Travellers* (Cassell, 1998).

Steve Hinchliffe is a Lecturer in Geography at the Open University. His work has focussed to date on nature, place and space and on the politics and spatialities of representation. He has recently published in *Society and Space, Transactions of the Institute of British Geographers* and *Environment and Planning A*.

Heather Höpfl is Professor of Organisational Psychology at Bolton Business School. She is currently Chair of Standing Conference on Organisational Symbolism. Her research interests are in dramaturgical approaches to organisational behaviour and in etymology.

Joanna Latimer read English Literature at Queen Mary College, London before going on to train as a nurse at University College Hospital. As a medical Ward Sister she won a research fellowship, and completed her PhD at Edinburgh, on the medical care of older people. Developing her own form of textual analysis, she focussed on medicine and nursing as spaces through which Euro-American culture is accomplished. Publications include papers in *Medical Anthropology Quarterly, Sociology of Health and Illness, Journal of Advanced Nursing* and *Nursing Inquiry*, as well as her book, *The Conduct of Care*, in which she retheorizes the knowledge practices of nurses.

John Law is Professor of Sociology at Keele University. He has written widely on technology, organization and spatiality. He is now working on dis/ability, materiality, corporeality and identity, and also on the normative, political and ontological implications of heterogeneity. His recent publications include *Organizing Modernity* (Blackwell, 1994), and edited collections with Brita Brenna and Ingunn Moser on *Machines, Agency and Desire* (University of Oslo, 1998) and Annemarie Mol on *Complexities in Science, Technology and Medicine* (Duke University Press, 1998).

Rolland Munro is Reader in Accountability at Keele University. He is the author if many articles and book chapters on knowledge, membership, power, time and self. Recent articles, which include 'Belonging on the Move', 'The Cultural Performance of Control' and 'Connection/Disconnection', draw together traditional sociological themes with material from his extended field studies on the use of ambiguity and distance in large organizations. He is the editor, with Jan Mouritsen, of *Accountability: Power, Ethos and the Technologies of Managing*.

Martin Parker is a Lecturer in Social and Organizational Theory and a member of the Centre for Social Theory and Technology at Keele University. He holds degrees from the Universities of Sussex, London and Staffordshire and, until 1995, taught Sociology at Staffordshire University. His writing and research covers organizations, culture and social theory. He has edited or co-edited four books: *Postmodernism and Organizations* (1993), *Towards a New Theory of Organizations* (1994), *The Dilemmas of Mass Higher Education* (1997), *Ethics and Organization* (1997) and has written many journal articles.

Marilyn Strathern is William Wyse Professor of Social Anthropology at the University of Cambridge. Her interests are divided between Melanesian (*Women in Between*, 1972) and British (*Kinship at the Core*, 1981) ethnography. *The Gender of the Gift* (1988) is a critique of anthropological theories of society and gender relations as they have been applied to Melanesia, while *After Nature* (1992) comments on the cultural revolution at home. A monograph on comparative method is called *Partial Connections* (1991). Her most recent publications are the co-authored *Technologies of Procreation* (1993) and an edited volume *Shifting Contexts: Transformations in Anthropological Knowledge* (1995).

Tony Watson is Professor of Organization at the Nottingham Business School, Nottingham Trent University. He writes in journals and books about industrial sociology, people, work, organizations and discourse. Books currently available include his ethnographic study *In Search of Management* (1994), a textbook, *Sociology, Work and Industry* (1995). Soon to appear is a study called something like *The Emergent Manager*.

Index